RE
LO

The Ultim... ...ns

THE UNIVERSITY OF
WINCHESTER

by Anthon...

EXPLORE
AUSTRALIA

Explore Australia Publishing Pty Ltd
85 High Street
Prahran, Victoria 3181, Australia

Explore Australia Publishing Pty Ltd is a division
of Hardie Grant Publishing Pty Ltd

Published by Explore Australia Publishing Pty Ltd,
2011

Concept, maps, form and design © Explore
Australia Publishing Pty Ltd, 2011
Text © Anthony Roberts, 2011

National Library of Australia Cataloguing-in-
Publication entry

Author: Roberts, Anthony, 1981-

Title: Reel locations the ultimate
                travel guide to Aussie films /
                Anthony Roberts.

Edition: 1st ed.

ISBN: 9781741173550 (pbk.)

Subjects: Motion picture locations—
                Australia—Guidebooks.

                Motion pictures—Australia—
                Guidebooks.

                Motion pictures, Australian—
                Guidebooks.

                Australia—Guidebooks.

                Australia—Description and
                travel.

Dewey Number: 791.43750994

The maps in this publication incorporate
data copyright © Commonwealth of Australia
(Geoscience Australia), 2006. Geoscience
Australia has not evaluated the data as altered
and incorporated within this publication, and
therefore gives no warranty regarding accuracy,
completeness, currency or suitability for any
particular purpose.

ISBN-13 9781741173550

10 9 8 7 6 5 4 3 2 1

Printed and bound in China by C & C Offset
Printing Co. Ltd

Publisher's note: Every effort has been
made to ensure that the information in this
book is accurate at the time of going to press.
The publisher welcomes information and
suggestions for correction or improvement.
Email: info@exploreaustralia.net.au

Publisher's disclaimers: The publisher cannot
accept responsibility for any errors or omissions.
The representation on the maps of any road or
track is not necessarily evidence of public right of
way. The publisher cannot be held responsible for
any injury, loss or damage incurred during travel.
It is vital to research any proposed trip thoroughly
and seek the advice of relevant state and travel
organisations before you leave.

Contents

Foreword

A movie location is more than a mere backdrop for actors or action. It is an essential element of the story. It shapes how the director, cinematographer and actors will tell the tale. My first major role in a film was in *Wake in Fright*, which we shot in and around the New South Wales outback mining towns of Broken Hill and Silverton in 1969. The isolation, the shimmering heat and the seemingly endless plains, the single line of rail or road stretching straight as a gun barrel to the horizon are real 'characters' on the screen. It is these elements as much as the script and performances that help to make the film convincing.

Since *Wake in Fright*, I have worked for over forty years in this exciting film industry, collaborating with an array of immensely talented actors, directors and film crews on some extraordinary productions, in some of the most spectacular locations in this country.

Sunday Too Far Away allowed me to spend time on the sheep station 'Carriewerloo', north of Port Augusta in South Australia; *The Man from Snowy River* saw me riding with genuine Snowy River horsemen in the breathtaking High Country of Victoria; *The Sum of Us* gave me an opportunity to enjoy my hometown of Sydney – what a thrill it was to take the helm of one of Sydney Harbour's famous ferries; and for one of my most recent films, *Australia*, I had the pleasure of working with Baz Luhrmann around the extraordinarily beautiful Kununurra in Western Australia.

If you're a lover of film who wants to recall a world of Australian celluloid, or simply a traveller looking for some interesting holiday spots, I recommend you visit some of the outstanding locations in this book – these grandiose movie sets, if you will. Some of them have changed greatly over the years, while others remain completely recognisable and untouched by time. I guarantee you, though, that all of them have their own unique story to tell, as well as having been an essential part of the story that they have helped to tell on screen.

Jack Thompson AM

About the author

Anthony Roberts is a freelance writer based in Melbourne. He has written for *The Australian, Handle* magazine, Funtastic and Explore Australia Publishing, and had some success in television scriptwriting competitions in the US. His early memories of Australian film include being captivated by *Picnic at Hanging Rock* as a six year old, and wearing out his VHS copy of *Young Einstein*. You can often find him skulking around the Rivoli Cinemas in Camberwell.

Author's thank-yous

A book like this only comes to fruition with the help of numerous people – from responding to my pestering emails trying to track down locations, to the many lengthy phone conversations about the nitty gritty of this or that shoot – I am forever grateful to every single person who had a hand in helping me write this book.

I would like to thank my editor, Jo Tayler, for tweaking my words and sentences into shape. Many thanks to Senior Editor Melissa Krafchek and Publications Manager Astrid Browne at Explore Australia Publishing – without both of you this book would still be just an idea in one man's head.

My sincere gratitude goes to Russell Boyd, Rolf de Heer, Peter Lawless, Charlie Lovick, Sue Maslin, Malcolm McCulloch, Kestie Morassi, Jane Needham, Phillip Roope and Elspeth Radford for generously giving your time and agreeing to be interviewed for this book.

A special thanks for your patience to Katie Saarikko at the National Film and Sound Archive, as well as Kathryn McLeod and Amanda McCormack.

I would also like to thank the following for their help and input: Adam Bayliss, Craig Bolles, Geoff Burrowes, Matt Carroll, Michael Clarkin, Robin Dalton, Stephan Elliot, Mark Evans, Judy Fisk, Dinitee Haskard, Kevin Hatswell, Matt Hearn, Maude Heath, Lynda House, Christina Hyde, Clayton Jacobson, Merle Jochheim, Dov Kornits, Sally McLennan, Nathan Morris, Vicki Niehus, Anna Slowiak, Steve Topic, Chris Wallis-Smith, Anwyn Watkins and Cameron Wood.

A huge thanks goes to Jack Thompson for writing the foreword and just for being the incredible actor that you are, bringing to life so many characters in so many great films.

And finally, to my parents Judy and Paul, thank you for your support throughout this project – and for letting me stay up late and watch movies when I was a young lad.

Introduction

I sit on the edge of my bed at the Burra Motor Inn just waiting for a glimmer of light. Sunrise is scheduled for 7.11am, but the anticipation is too much for me. I jump into my trusty hire car and navigate the vacant streets of this former coppermining town. I park and make my way to the front of the Redruth Gaol. Goosebumps start to prickle my skin – and not from the chill in the air. To me this is hallowed ground. It looks exactly like it did in the film, just a few more chips in the paint. I make my way inside. It's an eerie sensation to follow in the footsteps of Lieutenants Harry Morant and Peter Handcock; to pass through a building that's almost 150 years old and walk where they walked, stand where they stood. To know that director Bruce Beresford yelled 'action' dozens of times as he worked with the cast and crew to make *Breaker Morant,* one of this country's greatest-ever films.

But the experience doesn't end there. Just a short journey west and I'll find the Bon Accord Mining Complex, another location for the film. Down the Bruce Highway is Cactus Farm, yet another location. If I continue further south I'll hit Adelaide, where they shot the movie *Shine*. If I travel south-east into Victoria I'll eventually reach the former goldmining town of Castlemaine, a shooting location for *Romulus, My Father*. North-east to the rolling green hills of Robertson, in New South Wales, is where they shot *Babe*. If I head due north up to the tropical Whitsundays there's Bowen, where they recreated 1940s Darwin for Baz Luhrmann's epic *Australia.*

If I travel north and west to the crocodile-infested swamps of Arnhem Land, I can see the country where they shot *Ten Canoes*. From here, via Darwin for The Adventures of *Priscilla, Queen of the Desert, Crocodile Dundee* and *Australia* locations, I'll head south-west through the red sands of the Pilbara to the places where they shot *Japanese Story*.

The aim of this book is to take readers on a fun and informative journey through the locations where some of Australia's greatest feature films were shot. Hopefully you'll yearn to travel to these remarkable spots and see them, feel them, smell them for yourselves.

In each chapter I introduce you to a film, its people and back story. We visit the main shooting locations and touch on some of the places of interest in the area. There's also info on places to stay and places to get a bite to eat. And at the end of each chapter, you'll find some interesting film trivia or an interview I conducted with someone connected to our Aussie film industry – some of them are award-winning masters in their field.

I encourage you to take a dip in the cool waters of Bondi Beach like Jimmy from *Two Hands*. Go horseback riding through the stunning mountains of the Victorian High Country like the cattlemen in *The Man from Snowy River*. Follow in the footsteps of Stewart Kane and his buddies from *Jindabyne* by going fly-fishing at Island Bend in Kosciuszko National Park.

You're probably thinking: how can you have a book about the most significant and memorable Australian films and not include *The Castle*? It sure is a true Aussie classic, but I wanted to avoid hate mail by directing readers to spend their hard earned dollars on a holiday to Essendon Airport.

Enjoy your travels and your appreciation of great Australian films!

Anthony Roberts

Just some of the Australian film locations ...

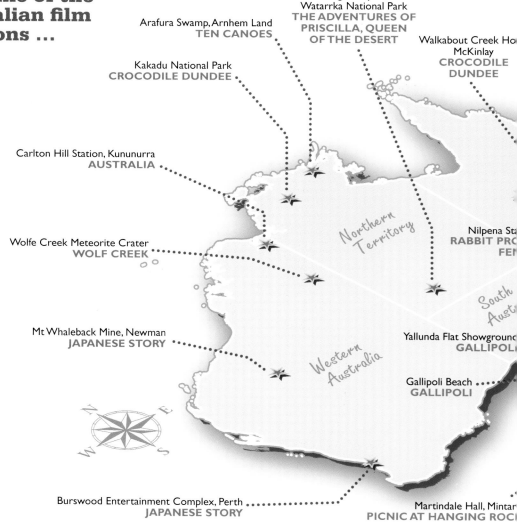

Arafura Swamp, Arnhem Land
TEN CANOES

Kings Canyon,
Watarrka National Park
**THE ADVENTURES OF
PRISCILLA, QUEEN
OF THE DESERT**

Walkabout Creek Ho
McKinlay
**CROCODILE
DUNDEE**

Kakadu National Park
CROCODILE DUNDEE

Carlton Hill Station, Kununurra
AUSTRALIA

Nilpena Sta
**RABBIT PRO
FEN**

Wolfe Creek Meteorite Crater
WOLF CREEK

Mt Whaleback Mine, Newman
JAPANESE STORY

Yallunda Flat Showgroun
GALLIPOL

Gallipoli Beach
GALLIPOLI

Burswood Entertainment Complex, Perth
JAPANESE STORY

Martindale Hall, Mintar
PICNIC AT HANGING ROC
Redruth Gaol, Burr
BREAKER MORAN

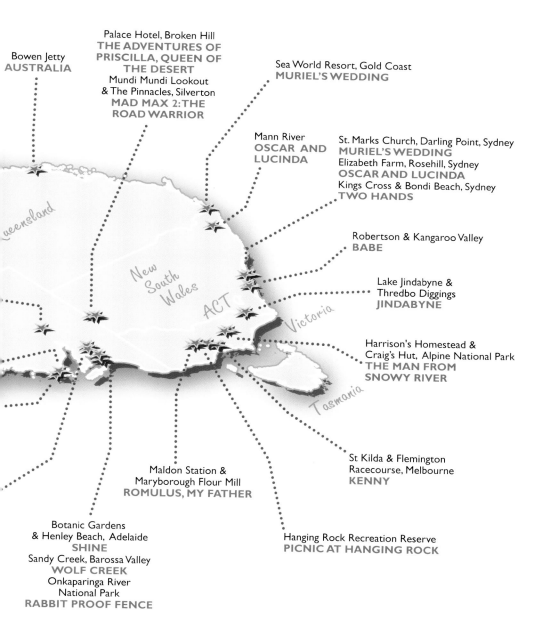

Bowen Jetty
AUSTRALIA

Palace Hotel, Broken Hill
**THE ADVENTURES OF
PRISCILLA, QUEEN OF
THE DESERT**
Mundi Mundi Lookout
& The Pinnacles, Silverton
**MAD MAX 2: THE
ROAD WARRIOR**

Sea World Resort, Gold Coast
MURIEL'S WEDDING

Mann River
**OSCAR AND
LUCINDA**

St. Marks Church, Darling Point, Sydney
MURIEL'S WEDDING
Elizabeth Farm, Rosehill, Sydney
OSCAR AND LUCINDA
Kings Cross & Bondi Beach, Sydney
TWO HANDS

Robertson & Kangaroo Valley
BABE

Lake Jindabyne &
Thredbo Diggings
JINDABYNE

Harrison's Homestead &
Craig's Hut, Alpine National Park
**THE MAN FROM
SNOWY RIVER**

St Kilda & Flemington
Racecourse, Melbourne
KENNY

Maldon Station &
Maryborough Flour Mill
ROMULUS, MY FATHER

Hanging Rock Recreation Reserve
PICNIC AT HANGING ROCK

Botanic Gardens
& Henley Beach, Adelaide
SHINE
Sandy Creek, Barossa Valley
WOLF CREEK
Onkaparinga River
National Park
RABBIT PROOF FENCE

The Adventures of Priscilla, Queen of the Desert (1994)

> I hereby christen this budget Barbie camper ... Priscilla, Queen of the Desert!
> — *Felicia*

Director: Stephan Elliott
Writer: Stephan Elliott
Producers: Al Clark, Michael Hamlyn
Cast includes: Hugo Weaving, Guy Pearce, Terence Stamp, Bill Hunter

ABOUT THE FILM

When going through the extensive list of great Australian films, there is a strong case to be made that *The Adventures of Priscilla, Queen of the Desert* is indeed our most successful. The gaudy comedy about two flamboyant cross-dressers and a transsexual flapping from Sydney to Alice Springs on a lavender-coloured bus (aptly named 'Priscilla') was a critical and box office daaaaahling when released domestically in 1994. It was later released in the United Kingdom, also to much success.

The film ignited the careers of the now internationally renowned Hugo Weaving and Guy Pearce, and spawned a successful stage musical in Australia and the UK. It even played a part in the parade for the Closing Ceremony of the 2000 Olympic Games in Sydney, for heaven's sake! Surely you remember the 2-metre-tall, silver-coloured stiletto heel atop the Priscilla bus rolling around the Olympic Stadium?

Another notch in the film's belt is its Academy Award — a rarity for Australian feature films. Costume designers Lizzy Gardiner and Tim Chappel won the Oscar for their spectacular designs, namely the infamous 'thong dress', which only cost $7 to make. Gardiner made a splash on the red carpet of Hollywood's night of nights in a frock made out of 254 gold American Express credit cards (one of her designs that didn't make it into the movie).

Pop culture references and awards aside, *Priscilla* is a kitch-filled romp driven by sharp dialogue and even sharper performances. Terence Stamp — usually cast in tough-guy roles and thus a very unusual casting choice — was a revelation as the grieving trannie Bernadette. He was nominated for a Golden Globe and a BAFTA Award for the role. Weaving and Pearce were simply fabulous, as was Australian screen legend Bill Hunter as the affable Bob.

 REEL LOCATIONS

Mitzi (Weaving), Bernadette (Stamp) and Felicia (Pearce) at the top of Kings Canyon

Broken Hill
New South Wales

The first major stop on the fabulous 'Priscilla Express' was the dusty outback town of Broken Hill, on the edge of New South Wales, right near the South Australian border. Due to its bone-dry landscape, Broken Hill was initially considered uninhabitable, but the discovery of silver in the 1880s attracted prospectors from far and wide, hoping to strike it rich.

In 1885, a syndicate of seven men snatched up the land for a bargain-basement price and quickly discovered they were sitting on the largest silver–lead–zinc lodes in the world. They formed a company and floated it, selling shares in the Broken Hill Proprietary Company (BHP). A hundred and twenty-five odd years later, BHP Billiton is the largest mining company in the world.

Today, Broken Hill is popular not only as a tourist destination, but also as a base for a number of local and international productions. *Mission Impossible II* (2002) was shot here, while local films, *Mad Max 2: The Road Warrior* (1981), *The Last Days of Chez Nous* (1992), *Reckless Kelly* (1993) and *Dirty Deeds* (2002) also used the town as a backdrop. The town even has its own multi-million-dollar desert studio. It doesn't have a broken hill anymore, though – mining saw to that being dug up and carted away.

VISITOR INFO

Broken Hill Visitor Centre

Cnr Blende and Bromide sts; (08) 8080 3560; www.visitbrokenhill.com.au

THINGS TO SEE AND DO

Argent Street

The main drag in town (pun totally intended) was the location for the scene in which the flamboyantly attired Mitzi (Weaving), Felicia (Pearce) and a reluctant Bernadette (Stamp), cross the street and the thong dress is gloriously unveiled to the world for the first time. In the background you can see the old town hall and the distinctive red brick tower of the Broken Hill Post Office. The crossing takes place near Oxide Street. No pink wigs were harmed in the shooting of this scene.

Stephens Creek Art Gallery and Owl Barn

A roadhouse opposite the former local pub, now an art gallery, was the site for the scene where the helpful mechanic Bob (Hunter) tows broken-down Priscilla to the garage. This is where Bernadette asks the gruff local the name of his dog, to which he replies, 'Herpes. If she's good, she'll heal.' The local was played by Mitch Powell, the owner of the unusual owl museum. Mitch's wife, Valerie, who has unfortunately passed, also had a role in the film. A laminated production call sheet from *Priscilla* is still taped to the front door of the gallery.

The quirky space has an interesting assortment of close to 4000 furry, ceramic and crystal owls; one fabric owl is a towering 7 feet tall.

The interior of the gallery was also used for the scene where the girls, Bob and Bob's chemically imbalanced wife Cynthia (Julia Cortez) have an awkward dinner, as well as the scene where Cynthia breaks open the kitchen cupboard and finds her secret stash of ping pong balls. The art gallery and owl barn is closed on Thursdays. *Silver City Hwy, via Broken Hill; (08) 8088 5301*

Malenrouge Hotel Motel

Formerly Mario's Hotel Motel (not to be confused with the old Mario's Palace featured in the film, which is now The Palace Hotel), this modest motel was used for some scenes set in Coober Pedy, acting as the lodging for Felicia and the girls for the night. Director Stephan Elliott recalls shooting all night in the motel and when they wrapped in the morning, hearing the announcement that Sydney had just been selected to host the 2000 Olympic Games. *172 Beryl St; (08) 8088 5944*

Silverton and the Mundi Mundi Lookout

Travel around 25 kilometres north-west of Broken Hill and you'll find one of the busiest filming locations in all of Australia. A few of the exterior scenes of Priscilla driving through the Australian outback were shot in and around Silverton and the Mundi Mundi Lookout. (See the *Mad Max 2: The Road Warrior* chapter for more information about Silverton.)

Art galleries

For a small town in the middle of nowhere, Broken Hill has an oddly exuberant art scene. There are over 20 art galleries in town, none more famous than the Pro Hart Gallery. The local-born miner-turned-artist and knockabout bloke is one of the legends of the Aussie art world (and possibly no less famous for what he's been doing to carpet on TV ads for a long time). Here you can view the largest collection of Pro Hart works in Australia. *108 Wyman St; (08) 8087 2441; www.prohart.com.au*

Railway Mineral and Train Museum

An old-time museum displaying historic railway machinery and a mineral collection, it incorporates the unique Hospital Museum and

Mitzi dances up a storm in the South Australian desert

> You've got to be kidding!
> – *Bernadette, upon entering Mario's Palace Hotel*

the Broken Hill Migrant Museum. It's well worth a visit for an interesting journey through the history of the town. *180 Blende St; (08) 8088 4660*

Royal Flying Doctor Service

Remember *The Flying Doctors* TV series? Well, (depending on your age) you should! It ran for nine seasons on Channel Seven in the '80s and early '90s and gave TV viewers an insight into this great flying ambulance. The New South Wales department of the RFDS is located out at Broken Hill Airport, where visitors can see the operations of the airborne medicos first hand, as well as peruse the Mantle of Safety Museum and pick up a few souvenirs. *Broken Hill Airport; 8080 3714; www.flyingdoctor.org.au*

Argent Street in Broken Hill –
the main drag in town

Lake Menindee

Around 90 kilometres south-east of Broken Hill is Lake Menindee, the spot where the ladies go for a playful dip in the cool waters with a gorgeous outback sunset as their backdrop. Lake Menindee is part of the stunning Menindee Lakes, which include Lake Cawndilla, Lake Wetherell and Copi Hollow. The area is great for birdwatchers. *Via Menindee Rd*

WHERE TO STAY

The Palace Hotel

Don't even think about staying anywhere else in town, you simply must stay here in this incredibly unstylish hotel featured in the film. You remember – the place where our trio gasp in horror at the passé murals covering every inch of the grand foyer. The room that housed the ladies on their overnight stay is now called the 'Priscilla Suite' and can be requested when booking. The hotel was also used to shoot the girls' first wild night at the local watering hole where Bernadette spouts her famous line to the butch-looking Broken Hillian woman, 'Now listen here, you mullet. Why don't you just light your tampon and blow your box apart? Because it's the only bang you're ever gonna get, sweetheart!' Classic! *227 Argent St; (08) 8088 1699; www.thepalacehotelbrokenhill.com.au*

All Nations Hotel

Another Priscilla location, the hotel was used for the scene where the girls 'shake their groove things' to Peaches and Herb for the locals (on advice from Bob). This is before Cynthia hijacks the room and puts on a particularly inappropriate ping pong show. The hotel has standard pub meals and modest accommodation. *331 Eyre St; (08) 8087 3541*

Royal Exchange Hotel

On Argent Street opposite the post office, this Art Deco boutique hotel has 24 modern rooms from standard to deluxe. Close to most of the town's attractions. *320 Argent St; (08) 8087 2308; www.royalexchangehotel.com*

CARAVANS AND MOTORHOMES

Broken Hill City Caravan Park

Powered, unpowered and ensuite sites, with cabin and bungalow accommodation. They also have an 'Olympic Family Cabin', which was purchased from the Olympic Village in Sydney. *Rakow St; (08) 8087 3841; www.brokenhillcaravanpark.com.au*

Lake View Broken Hill Caravan Park

Relaxed park overlooking the serene waters of Imperial Lake, with ensuite and bedroom cabins, a swimming pool and children's playground. *1 Mann St; (08) 8088 2250; www.familyparks.com.au*

The people of Broken Hill meet
Mitzi and the famous thong dress

Menindee Lakes Caravan Park

Located 5 kilometres west of Menindee, you can rent powered or unpowered caravan sites and camping spots as well as cabins. *Shore Rd, Menindee; (08) 8091 4315; www.menindeelakes. com/accommodation.htm*

WHERE TO EAT

Bells Milk Bar

Hands down the most popular milk bar on the planet. People have come from all over the world to try Bells' delicious original '50s-style malted milks and soda spiders. There's also a museum attached. Don't be too embarrassed to fill your suitcase with all the delicious Bells homemade syrups and cordials available for purchase. *160 Patton St; (08) 8087 5380; www.bellsmilkbar.com.au*

Broken Earth Restaurant

Billed as 'a little piece of heaven on earth', this rusty modern complex sits on the highest peak of a remnant dump. Enjoy a meal while watching a spectacular sunset or partake in a casual lunch after visiting the Miners Memorial on site. *Federation Way; (08) 8087 1318; www.brokenearthrestaurant.com.au*

Broken Hill Musicians Club

Not the flashiest of joints, but if you want to fill your belly and still have change from a tenner, this is the place to go. Cafe and community club with all-you-can-eat buffet and daily specials from as low as $7. Live entertainment Thursday to Sunday and two-up games late Friday and Saturday nights. *276 Crystal St; (08) 8088 1777*

CINEMA

Village Silver City Cinema

Shows latest-release films as well as special screenings. Session times can be found in the local rag, *Barrier Daily Truth*. *41 Oxide St; (08) 8087 4569*

TOURS

Silver City Tours

Half-day tours of the town take in locations such as Argent Street and The Palace Hotel. *380 Argent St; (08) 8087 6956 or 1300 723 583; www.silvercitytours.com.au*

Broken Hill City Sights Tours

Choose from half-day, full-day and sunset tours of the town and surrounding areas. *51 William St; (08) 8087 2484; www.bhoutbacktours.com.au*

During the making of the film, the producers of *Priscilla* **were troubled when they got wind of another movie in production about drag queens, called** *To Wong Foo, Thanks for Everything! Julie Newmar.*

After they read the script, however, they realised it was quite different from *Priscilla*. **The film, released in 1995 starring Wesley Snipes, John Leguizamo and the late Patrick Swayze, received sub-par reviews.**

> Now look, you blokes watch your back. This is a pretty tough little town. They get up in the morning, they go down a hole, they blow things up and they come up again. That about sums things up.
> – Bob

Coober Pedy
South Australia

From the Aboriginal phrase 'Kupa Piti', roughly translated to mean 'white man's hole in the ground', Coober Pedy is home to the biggest opal field in the world. The town is responsible for almost 80 per cent of the world's gem-quality opals. There are thousands of mines strewn across the town, so don't fall in (seriously)! Open and unprotected mine shafts are a danger, so either know the area well or stick with tours. The unbearable heat and harsh dryness of Coober Pedy have forced most of the town's inhabitants to live in underground homes.

Coober Pedy was yet another pit stop for Priscilla and the gang on their way to Alice Springs. Considering its inhospitable climate and landscape, Coober Pedy has thrived as a film hub. Local and international productions shot in town include *Mad Max: Beyond Thunderdome* (1985), *Burke and Wills* (1985), *Until the End of the World* (1991), *Pitch Black* (2000), *Red Planet* (2000), *Kangaroo Jack* (2003) and *Opal Dream* (2005).

VISITOR INFO
Coober Pedy council offices
Hutchinson St; (08) 8672 4617; www.opalcapitaloftheworld.com.au

THINGS TO SEE AND DO
Underground Video

Visit the video store that restless and cheeky Felicia wanders into looking for a good time. Much like VHS technology, the shop is no longer pertinent and ceased operating a few years back. However, though quite derelict, it still stands. *Wright Rd*

Coober Pedy Drive-in

While they might seem as relevant as fondue sets and leisure suits to city dwellers, the drive-in is still a stalwart in many country towns. The Coober Pedy Drive-in is no exception. It was a feature location in *Priscilla* in the scene where Felicia nearly gets beaten to a pulp by a band of rough Pedy locals. A derelict hotel nearby was used for the scene when Mitzi and Bernadette have dinner and they see Felicia being chased through the window.

The outback open-air cinema still operates today and shows new releases and classics. Screenings are fortnightly on Friday and Saturday nights. Contact the visitor centre for upcoming movies and session times. *131 Hutchinson St; (08) 8672 4617*

The Breakaways and Moon Plains

Around 30 kilometres north of the main township is the breathtaking scenic valley of multicoloured outcrops where Priscilla breaks down, stranding our lovable camp trio. Here Felicia paints the bus bright pink (or lavender) and the girls put on an impromptu cabaret show to Gloria Gaynor's catchy chick anthem 'I Will Survive'. Plenty of tours run to the area and entry passes are available from the visitor centre and other outlets in town.

Painted Desert

The gloriously coloured hills of this remarkable land, 80 million years in the making, were the backdrop for the scenes of Bernadette drifting around looking for help after Priscilla breaks down. Some locals have renamed this area 'Priscilla Hill'.

It's best viewed in the bright light of day when the sun strikes the mineral-rich soil and creates a cascade of yellow, red, brown, white and black. There are plenty of air and four-wheel-drive tours to get a good look at the area. *Located around 190 km north-east of Coober Pedy, off Stuart Hwy on the way to Oodnadatta*

Crocodile Harry's Underground Nest

The bizarre story of Crocodile Harry is a fascinating one. Born in Serbia, he moved to Australia after World War II and became a crocodile hunter, working his trade in and around Kakadu National Park for over a decade. He then moved to Coober Pedy to mine opals. Although he passed away a few years ago, his eclectic and downright outlandish underground home, filled with hanging bras, moulded statues and walls festooned with addresses of the many girls he seduced, is still open to visitors. This cave of the weird was featured in *Mad Max: Beyond Thunderdome* and the film *Ground Zero* (1987). *(08) 8672 5298*

Space Ship from Pitch Black

Built for the Vin Diesel movie *Pitch Black* (2000), this large prop spaceship was left behind after the production. Local lore states that over 20 litres of sunscreen was used to protect Vin Diesel's shiny dome during filming. The prop space ship is located just out front of the Opal Cave shop. *Hutchinson St*

Umoona Underground Mine and Museum

An award-winning centre built in a former opal mine, you can learn about the history of Coober Pedy, take an on-site mine tour (which includes a dug-out home) and watch the documentary in the underground cinema. *Hutchinson St; (08) 8762 5228; www.umoonaopalmine.com.au*

WHERE TO STAY

The Underground Motel

You haven't experienced Coober Pedy until you've woken up a few metres below the earth's surface. The Underground offers a number of clean, air-conditioned and – most importantly – affordable dug-out rooms. Continental breakfast included. *Catacomb Rd; (08) 8672 5324; www.theundergroundmotel.com.au*

Down to Erth Bed and Breakfast

Usually when one thinks of bed and breakfasts, images of cosy country cottages or romantic seaside bungalows come to mind. In this case, however, 'chance of seeing mole people' best describes what might be the most unique B&B experience of your life. Underground apartments with refreshing pool and continental breakfast. *Lot 1795 Wedgetail Crt; (08) 8672 5762; www.downtoerth.com.au*

Desert Cave Hotel

Another unique underground stay, this cave has 50 luxurious suites with wi-fi and free in-house movies. Cafe, restaurant and opal shop on site; tour and accommodation packages available, including a Painted Desert tour. *Hutchinson St; (08) 8672 5688; www.desertcave.com.au*

CARAVANS AND MOTORHOMES

Opal Inn Hotel Motel Caravan Park

Powered sites with barbecue and grassed camping areas; budget motel units also available. *Hutchinson St; (08) 8672 5054; www.opalinn.com.au*

WHERE TO EAT

Tom and Mary's Taverna

The most popular restaurant in town serving Greek cuisine with mouth-watering meat platters and deliciously authentic dips. Bookings advised, as it can get hectic during the dinner rush. *Shop 4, Lot 2 Hutchinson St; (08) 8672 5622*

John's Pizza Bar

Another local fave eatery, try the Coat of Arms pizza topped with our proud national emblems, emu mettwurst and smoked kangaroo with cranberry jam, spinach and camembert. *Shop 24, 1 Hutchinson St; (08) 8672 5561*

TOURS

Radeka's Desert Breakaway Tours

This half-day tour visits The Breakaways, Moon Plains and Crocodile Harry's domicile of debauchery. Operating 365 days a year without fail. Radeka's also has underground accommodation (motel, budget and dorms). *1 Oliver St; (08) 8672 5223; www.radekadownunder.com.au*

Oasis Tours

Offering sunset tours of The Breakaways and Moon Plains as well as tours of the town and mines, departing from the Oasis Tourist Park (with caravan and cabin accommodation). *Hutchison St; (08) 8672 5169 or 1800 060 541; www.oasiscooberpedy.com.au*

Dusty road near Coober Pedy

Mullock heaps from opal mining in Coober Pedy

DID YOU KNOW?

On display in the video store scene in Coober Pedy is a poster for the movie *Frauds*, a film made by *Priscilla's* director Stephan Elliott. Released in 1993, it was his directorial debut and starred Hugo Weaving and UK band Genesis front man Phil Collins.

Elliott had a small cameo in *Priscilla*, acting as one of the casino hotel employees when the bus arrives in Alice Springs.

Rugged ranges of Watarrka National Park

Farm near Alice Springs

Alice Springs
Northern Territory

Simply known as 'The Alice', this settlement on the Todd River in the MacDonnell Ranges is the second biggest town in the Northern Territory. The vibrant Red Centre town is overflowing with Aboriginal culture and heritage. Although fairly modernised, it still holds a strong link to its past. There's an abundance of natural wonders to visit, from the Alice Springs Desert Park to Olive Pink Botanic Gardens. Alice Springs was the second-to-last destination for Priscilla, and Lasseters Hotel Casino the scene of Mitzi, Felicia and Bernadette's triumphant drag show. Alice Springs has also been used as a location for other Australian films and TV series, including *Walkabout* (1971), *A Town Like Alice* (1981) and *Samson and Delilah* (2009).

VISITOR INFO
Tourism Central Australia
60 Gregory Tce; (08) 8952 5800 or 1800 645 199; www.centralaustraliantourism.com

THINGS TO SEE AND DO
Lasseters Hotel Casino
Mitzi, Felicia and Bernadette perform their drag show in the former Conellen Room in the international-class casino and hotel. The room no longer exists; it was knocked down in 2002 to make way for the Alice Springs Convention Centre. Once named the Reef Bar, a horseshoe-shaped bar now called the Casbah Lounge was used for the scene where Mitzi reunites with wife Marion (Sarah Chadwick). Other scenes were filmed on the gaming floor (near the money wheel) and in Kings Restaurant (which is now called Samphire Restaurant and is no longer recognisable from the movie). Lasseters is a popular nightspot in Alice Springs, whether for a stint at the blackjack table or a squiz at a cabaret show. *93 Barrett Dr; (08) 8950 7777 or 1800 808 975; www.lhc.com.au*

Alice Springs Cultural Precinct
This is the epicentre of cultural attractions in The Alice. Visit the Araluen Centre for Aboriginal art, the Museum of Central Australia for some natural history and the Yeperente Sculpture, which depicts a Dreamtime

That's just what this country needs: a cock in a frock on a rock.

– Bernadette

Caterpillar (from which evolved the MacDonnell Ranges according to Arrernte traditional beliefs). *Cnr Larapinta Dr and Memorial Ave; www.araluen.nt.gov.au*

Alice Springs Desert Park

You mustn't visit Alice Springs without taking time to walk around this magnificent wilderness retreat. Start with one of the easy walking trails, where you'll be able to spot hundreds of species of plants and animals. There are also guided tours, interactive displays and films. After a visit here, the acclaimed naturalist David Attenborough declared, 'There is no museum or wildlife park in the world that can match it'. *Larapinta Dr; (08) 8951 8788; www.alicespringsdesertpark.com.au*

Olive Pink Botanic Garden

Take a self-guided walk around Australia's only existing arid-zone botanic garden, named after anthropologist Olive Muriel Pink and featuring hundreds of central Australian plant species. The garden also hosts a number of events and musical performances. *Tuncks Rd; (08) 8952 2154; www.opbg.com.au*

WHERE TO STAY

Lasseters Hotel Casino

A four-and-half-star hotel with standard and deluxe rooms, as well as fancy-pants suites. All rooms have a private balcony or courtyard, many with magnificent views of the MacDonnell Ranges. Gamblers and card sharks won't want to leave. *93 Barrett Dr; (08) 8950 7777; www.hotel.lhc.com.au*

Desert Rose Inn

Budget private rooms best suited for the young and sociable, who will take advantage of the communal lounge, TV room and swimming pool. *15 Railway Tce; (08) 8952 1411; www.desertroseinn.com.au*

Ooraminna Station Homestead

Unique farmstay lodgings with authentic accommodation options in the Police Station and Gaol and Wooden Slab Hut. The Police Station and Gaol were originally built as a set for *The Drovers Boy*, a film project that was never completed. *93 Todd St;(08) 8953 0170; www.ooraminnahomestead.com.au*

CARAVANS AND MOTORHOMES

Old Ambalindum Homestead

Powered and non-powered sites with camping also available, as well as homestead and bunkhouse accommodation. *Arltunga Tourist Dr (Binns Track) via Ross Hwy; (08) 8956 9993; www.oldambalindumhomestead.com.au*

WHERE TO EAT

Overlanders Steakhouse

A stalwart on the Alice Springs dining scene, this icon serves up some of the best grub in the Red Centre. If you're brave try 'The Drover's Blowout', a set menu that includes courses of crocodile, kangaroo, camel and emu – you'll OD on Australiana. Look out for the framed original poster of *A Town Like Alice* signed by actress Virginia McKenna. *72 Hartley St; (08) 8952 2159; www.overlanders.com.au*

Camel safari near Alice Springs

Well, ever since I was a lad I've had this dream, a dream that now, finally, I have a chance to fulfil … To travel to the centre of Australia, climb King's Canyon, as a Queen, in a full-length Gaultier sequin, heels and a tiara.
— *Felicia*

DID YOU KNOW? **Many names were tossed around for the three main parts in the film, including John Cleese, Tony Curtis, Jason Donovan, Colin Firth, Tim Curry and Rupert Everett. Bill Hunter was cast on the suggestion of Terence Stamp and agreed to star in the film without having read the script. He was filming *Muriel's Wedding* at the same time and had to shuttle back and forth between the two productions.**

Bojangles Saloon and Dining Room

There isn't a local in town that won't recommend this multi-award-winning bar and eatery, which provides diners with some of the best tucker in the Territory. While the sane ones stick with the delicious camel and stout pie and their famous mixed grill, those slightly unbalanced might want to try the 'Big Bugger', a mammoth 600-gram T-bone steak. You get a certificate if you finish it! *80 Todd St; (08) 8952 2873; www.bossaloon.com.au*

Hanuman

One of the best dining experiences in The Alice, this stylish place oozes essence of Asia, from the oriental furnishings to the Thai-, Nonya- (Malay) and Indian- inspired menu, which is more suited for communal dining, although the massaman curry and camel tenderloins are so good you won't want to share. Takeaway also available. *82 Barrett Dr; (08) 8953 7188; www.hanuman.com.au*

CINEMA

Alice Springs Cinema

Located in Todd Mall, screens new releases in an intimate setting. *Todd Mall, Gregory Tce; (08) 8592 4999*

TOURS

Northern Gateway Holidays

Choose from their long list of outstanding tours, including balloon flights with breakfast, the 'hop on, hop off' Alice Springs town tour and champagne sunset flights. Extended safari and Uluṟu adventures also available. *74 McMinn St, Darwin; (08) 8941 2167 or 1800 813 288; www. alicespringstours.com*

Watarrka National Park
Northern Territory

The Luritja people have lived in this area for over 20 000 years. On the western edge of the George Gill Range, around 430 kilometres west of Alice Springs, this spectacular conservation area is home to hundreds of species of plant and animal life in its rugged ranges, gorges and rock holes. The final scenes of *Priscilla* were filmed here – when Felicia lives out her dream of climbing King's Canyon as a queen.

VISITOR INFO

Watarrka Ranger Station

(08) 8956 7460; www.nt.gov.au/parks

THINGS TO SEE AND DO

Kings Canyon

Arguably the most iconic shot in the Australian cinema canon is that of the three men dressed as women standing at the top of King's Canyon with the sun setting behind them. There was no trick photography or location illusions for this one – the three actors and production crew had to deal with sunburn, sweat, running make-up and general exhaustion as they made the arduous climb to the top of King's

In one of the final scenes Mitzi says an emotional goodbye to Bernadette outside Lasseters Casino. But the filming didn't go quite to plan. When Weaving went to hug Stamp, he accidentally burst one of Terence's fake breasts (played by a condom filled with custard). The actors successfully fought off the urge to collapse into hysterical laughter and pulled off the scene magnificently.

Canyon for this special shot. (The filmmakers initially wanted to shoot this scene on top of Uluṟu, but were rejected by the Uluṟu Board of Management who felt the shoot was a violation of Indigenous Australian spiritual beliefs and practices.)

The canyon will take your breath away, particularly at sunset, when its 100-metre sandstone walls glow gold and red and all shades between. Ancient marine fossils in the rocks have been exposed by the elements, telling a story of 300 million years of environmental change. Two main walks showcase the wonders of the Canyon; the breezy Rim Walk takes in the unique rock formation known as The Lost City as well as the aptly named Priscilla's Crack. More experienced trekkers should do the 6-kilometre Canyon Walk, while the really intrepid can do the 22-kilometre overnight Giles Track.

WHERE TO STAY

Kings Canyon Resort

This enormous resort is a perfect base for exploring the park. It offers standard and deluxe spa rooms, budget lodges and caravan and camping facilities. There's also a petrol station, general store and laundry facilities on site for road trippers looking to stock up and scrub up. *Luritja Rd; (08) 8956 7442 or 1300 233 432; www.kingscanyonresort.com.au*

CARAVANS AND MOTORHOMES

Kings Creek Station

A working cattle and camel station with caravan facilities, camping and safari cabins. Other services include camel and quad-bike safari tours and helicopter flights of Kings Canyon and surrounds. *PMB 164, Alice Springs, off Ernest Gilles Rd; (08) 8956 7474; www.kingscreekstation.com.au*

WHERE TO EAT

Carmichael's Restaurant

The perfect place for a hearty breakfast before you take on Kings Canyon or nightly buffets bearing more food than you can handle. Located at the Kings Canyon Resort; other eateries here include the Desert Oaks Bistro and the Outback BBQ and Grill. *Luritja Rd; (08) 8956 7442; www.kingscanyonresort.com.au*

TOURS

AAT Kings

One-day luxury bus tour starting at Kings Canyon and finishing in Alice Springs. *(08) 8952 1700; www.aatkings.com.au*

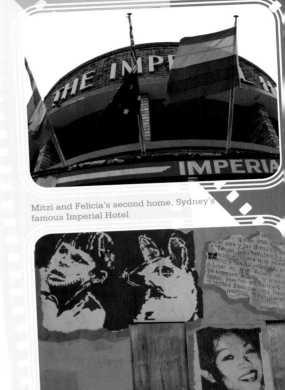

Mitzi and Felicia's second home, Sydney's famous Imperial Hotel

A decorated building on Erskineville Road not far from the Imperial

DID YOU KNOW? Back in the '90s, *The Drew Carey Show* recreated one of *Priscilla*'s musical numbers with an unforgettable dance off against 'Time Warp' from *The Rocky Horror Picture Show*. YouTube it!

Adventure Tours Australia

Offering a number of longer outback tours that take in Kings Canyon. *(08) 8132 8230 or 1800 068 886; www.adventuretours.com.au*

OTHER LOCATIONS

Imperial Hotel Sydney, New South Wales

The Imperial Hotel is high on the list of Australia's gay and lesbian venues, billing itself as 'Sydney's home of drag'. The hotel was used in the beginning of the film as the starting-out point for Priscilla, when the gang are farewelled with balloons and streamers before they hit the road. The drag show that opens the film, featuring Mitzi and Felicia, was also shot there, as was the final show.

Remarkably, both drag scenes were shot in one day, equating to a huge 12 minutes of screen time – which is generally unheard of in moviemaking. Elliott had wanted to open with the ABBA song 'One of Us', but the filmmakers were still negotiating the rights to use the music so Charlene's 'I've Never Been To Me' was used as a last-minute substitute. *35 Erskineville Rd, Erskineville; (02) 9519 9899; www.theimperialhotel.com.au*

Camperdown Cemetery Sydney, New South Wales

This historic Newtown cemetery, in Sydney's inner west, was the location for the funeral of Bernadette's partner early in the film. *St Stephens Anglican Church, 189 Church St, Newtown; (02) 9557 2043; www.ststephens.org.au*

AND ANOTHER THING ...

BOX OFFICE BULLION: THE TOP TEN HIGHEST GROSSING AUSSIE FILMS

Rank	Film title	Release date	Distributor	Australian box office takings
1	Crocodile Dundee	30/4/1986	Hoyts	$47 707 045
2	Australia	26/11/2008	Fox	$37 555 757
3	Babe	14/12/1995	UIP	$36 776 544
4	Happy Feet	26/12/2006	Roadshow	$31 786 164
5	Moulin Rouge	24/5/2001	Fox	$27 734 406
6	Crocodile Dundee 2	26/5/1988	Hoyts	$24 916 805
7	Strictly Ballroom	20/8/1992	Ronin	$21 760 400
8	The Dish	19/10/2000	Roadshow	$17 999 473
9	The Man from Snowy River	25/3/1982	Hoyts	$17 228 160
10	The Adventures of Priscilla, Queen of the Desert	8/9/1994	Roadshow	$16 459 245

Information courtesy of the Motion Picture Distributors Association of Australia, www.mpdaa.org.au

Road trippin'

Here are some other classic Aussie road trip flicks to get your motor running.

CHARLIE AND BOOTS (2009)

The second highest grossing Australian film of 2009 tells the story of the grieving Charlie (Paul Hogan), who is forced to take a road trip to the northernmost tip of Australia with his estranged son Boots (Shane Jacobson). This comedy charmer was shot along the east coast of Australia, taking in the towns of Warrnambool, Tamworth and Tenterfield up to the Cape York Peninsula.

SUMMER CITY (1977)

Set in the early 1960s, this early Australian road film is famous for being Mel Gibson's first feature. The story revolves around a group of young men who plan a trip to the beaches north of Sydney for a last surfing holiday with one of their mates who is getting married. The film was shot in and around Sydney, particularly at Catherine Hill Bay, a beach town just south of Newcastle. The film was written and produced by former surf champion Phil Avalon and also stars John Jarratt and Steve Bisley.

THE GODDESS OF 1967 (2000)

This darkly whimsical and little-known film is about a Japanese man (Rikiya Kurokawa) who travels to Australia to purchase a car – A Citroen DS, known as 'the Goddess'. Things don't quite go to plan for the foreigner when he picks up the vehicle from BG (Rose Byrne), a blind woman who ends up accompanying him on a trip across the Australian outback. Much of the film was shot in and around Lightning Ridge in New South Wales, a place known for having some of the richest black opal deposits in the world.

THUNDERSTRUCK (2004)

This road comedy, starring Sam Worthington and Stephen Curry, sees four hardcore AC/DC fanatics travel cross-country to scatter the ashes of a friend next to Bon Scott's grave. The journey takes the buddies all the way from Adelaide to Fremantle Cemetery, Bon's actual resting place. The majority of the film was shot in rural South Australia in the towns of Strathalbyn, Callington, Burra and Murray Bridge. Some scenes were shot in Sydney, Perth, Adelaide and Fremantle.

CACTUS (2007)

A taut, suspenseful thriller about a man being kidnapped from his city home and taken on an epic journey through the Australian outback with his mysterious kidnapper. The film stars Travis McMahon, David Lyons and Bryan Brown and was shot in the rural New South Wales towns of Bathurst, Broken Hill and Cobar. When the pair enters the town of Cullen in the film, which doesn't exist, they are really entering Wilcannia.

ROAD GAMES (1981)

This early '80s road thriller is basically Hitchcock's *Rear Window* on wheels. The film stars Americans Jamie Lee Curtis and Stacy Keach and centres around a serial killer who lures unsuspecting victims on a desolate Australian highway. The film was shot in Diggers Rest and Port Melbourne in Victoria, as well as Eucla, Perth, Madura and various spots along the Nullarbor Plain in Western Australia.

BONDI TSUNAMI (2004)

The film follows the adventures of a group of young Japanese surfers travelling down the east coast of Australia in their 1961 Holden station wagon. The premise is rather simple – they smoke, they drink, they surf. Along the way they take in a monumental amount of memorable Australian locations, including the Big Pineapple near the town of Woombye in Queensland, the sleepy pothead town of Nimbin and the coastal city of Coffs Harbour, both in New South Wales.

BENEATH CLOUDS (2002)

This film tells the story of two Aboriginal youths, Lena (Dannielle Hall) and Vaughn (Damian Pitt), who form an unlikely bond as they travel across north-west New South Wales. The film was shot in Lithgow, Gunnedah, Blacktown, Moree, Currabubula and Riverstone. Directed by Ivan Sven, the film slipped very much under the radar in 2002, but was nominated for six AFI Awards and won two awards at the prestigious Berlin Film Festival.

SPIDER AND ROSE (1994)

This dysfunctional road film sees the cantankerous Rose (Ruth Cracknell) coupled with the rebellious young ambulance driver Spider (Simon Bossell) as he chaperones her to Coonabarabran in New South Wales for her 70th birthday party. The film was shot in rural New South Wales, including the town of Coonabarabran, known as the Astronomy Capital of Australia.

KISS OR KILL (1997)

Lovers on the run after a botched robbery scam is the premise for this 1997 crime–romance starring Matt Day and Frances O'Connor. The cat-and-mouse pursuit takes both criminals and police across the vast South Australian outback. The film was shot in Ceduna, Port Augusta, Streaky Bay, Penong and along the Nullarbor Plain.

SIAM SUNSET (1999)

Directed by John Polson, *Siam Sunset* tells the story of an accident-prone British designer who hops on an outback tour bus filled with eccentric Aussie travellers after his wife is randomly killed by a flying refrigerator. Most of the film was shot in *Priscilla* country and two main shooting locations were at Coober Pedy and The Breakaways. The film was co-written by Andrew Knight, one of Australia's most prominent television comedy writers and producers (*The D Generation*, *Fast Forward*, *Sea Change*) and produced by Al Clark, who also produced *Priscilla*.

Australia (2008)

Lady Ashley (Kidman) and Nullah (Walters) share a moment

The ancestors created songs for everything. For every rock and tree; they're all linked. And Galapa, the magic man, sings them in order. He'll sing us to water, even across the Never Never.

– Drover

Director: Baz Luhrmann
Writers: Baz Luhrmann, Stuart Beattie, Ronald Harwood, Richard Flanagan
Producers: Baz Luhrmann, G Mac Brown, Catherine Knapman
Cast includes: Nicole Kidman, Hugh Jackman, David Wenham, Brandon Walters, Bryan Brown, David Gulpilil, Jack Thompson

ABOUT THE FILM

The term 'epic' isn't bandied around too often in Australian film industry circles – probably due to the fact that the average budget for local productions is equal to the craft service kitty of your average B-grade Hollywood action flick. So when Baz Luhrmann announced this $130-million movie production behemoth, it was no surprise that this grandiose project quickly became the most anticipated Australian film of all time. I mean, it's called *Australia* for crying out loud, how could it not be massive?

The plot revolves around delicate Englishwoman Lady Sarah Ashley (Kidman), who travels from her homeland to northern Australia to try and convince her aristocratic hubby to sell his failing cattle station, Faraway Downs. She arrives to the news that said hubby has been murdered and decides she has to save the station (and keep it from the clutches of evil King Carney) by driving its cattle all the way to Darwin. This she does, with the help of the ruggedly handsome Drover (Jackman), an orphaned half-caste Aboriginal boy, Nullah, (Walters), and the town drunk (played by the legendary Jack Thompson).

What ensues is a tale of love, action and adventure using the northern Australian landscape as spectacular backdrop – from

Film poster

NICOLE KIDMAN   HUGH JACKMAN

AUSTRALIA

> I'm going to bring
> Faraway Downs
> back to life.
>
> — *Lady Sarah Ashley*

sweeping panoramic shots of the vast, unspoiled outback to the rustic urbanity of early Darwin during the 1942 Japanese bombing.

Although the reviews for *Australia* were somewhat mixed, the film will endure as a love letter to the immense beauty of the Australian outback. Tourism Australia even chipped in, spending an unprecedented $40 million on a companion advertising campaign.

Let's just hope that lady visitors to this great southern land aren't expecting every second male walking down the street to resemble Hugh Jackman's rugged Drover ... that's just not fair on us poor Aussie blokes.

LOCATIONS

AROUND KUNUNURRA
WESTERN AUSTRALIA

The remote outback town of Kununurra lies in the immense East Kimberley region of Western Australia in close proximity to the Northern Territory border. Just a 50-minute drive north-west of the town centre is Carlton Hill Station, an actual working cattle station. It was the location for Faraway Downs, the fictional cattle station central to the film's plot. It's not far from

the eastern banks of the Ord River and the rugged House Roof Hill features as a backdrop in many scenes.

The landscape around Kununurra is quintessential outback: huge, red and gorgeous (as in, full of those imposing gorges, carved out over millennia). Adjacent to Kununurra is the stunning Mirima National Park (the 'mini Bungle Bungles') and south is Lake Argyle in the Carr Boyd Range, which is the largest body of fresh water in Australia – so massive it's actually classed as an inland sea. Though man made, it's quite apt, as Kununurra means 'big waters'.

The breathtaking El Questro Wilderness Park, west of Kununurra, was used as the location for many of the cattle-driving scenes. Other locations shot in the area are Diggers Rest Station, Home Valley Station and Faraway Bay.

VISITOR INFO

Kununurra Visitor Centre
75 Coolibah Dr; (08) 9168 1177 or 1800 586 868; www.kununurratourism.com

Main Roads Western Australia
13 8138 (for information about road conditions)

When to visit
The seasons are 'the wet' and 'the dry'. May is the ideal time to visit, though it's good all year round if you're into watery pursuits.

THINGS TO SEE AND DO

Carlton Hill Station
A privately owned cattle station, this was the location for Faraway Downs, the property owned

by our pale-faced heroine. Disappointment awaits eager beavers flocking to the area to catch a glimpse of the homestead; Faraway Downs was custom-built specifically for the film and dismantled after production. Don't despair, though; Tourism WA is currently working with the Kununurra Visitor Centre and Fox to use the homestead's furnishings at the Argyle Downs Homestead Museum, which is located south of Kununurra.

The nearby Ord River was the location used at the very beginning of the film, where little Nullah witnesses the murder of Lady Ashley's hubby and rides away gracefully on his horse.

Note: there's no public access to Carlton Hill, except on Macka's Barra Tours, which includes overnight camping at the station.

Home Valley Station

Home Valley Station occupies a massive 280 000 hectares of rugged Australian bushland 120 clicks west of Kununurra. It encompasses the iconic Cockburn Range, the 600-metre-tall red rock fortress that was the backdrop for several of the epic cattle drive scenes.

One of the final scenes of the film has the buff Drover and his fair Lady Ashley crossing the Pentecost River on their way back to Faraway Downs; local wags have since renamed this spot 'Kidman's Crossing'.

The scenes at the start of the film with the Drover and Lady Ashley driving to Faraway Downs by truck were also shot on Home Valley Station.

The station offers a range of accommodation, from luxury to roughin' it–style Aussie camping, and a bar and grill with entertainment. They also offer a heap of outback tours, including a special *Australia* movie tour – thankfully

Hidden Valley and the Ord River

minus the dangerous 400-head cattle stampede. *Via Gibb River Rd (four-wheel drive access only); (08) 9161 4322; www.hvstation.com.au*

Digger's Rest Station

About 70 kilometres west of Kununurra, Digger's Rest Station is another working cattle station featured in some of the film's cattle-driving scenes. The Drover and Lady Ashley shared their first romantic locking of lips here under a boab tree along the King River. Boabs are unique to the Kimberley – some of the individual trees are almost 1500 years old, making them the oldest living things in Australia.

The station housed around 90 of the hard-working cast and crew for several weeks as they shot around the property. In proud Aussie tradition – and despite the soaring temperatures – the cast and crew used to gather for a hit of backyard cricket around the homestead. *King River Rd, off Great Northern Hwy; (08) 9161 1029; diggersreststation.com.au*

El Questro Wilderness Park

The enormous, unspoilt frontier that is El Questro covers almost a million acres. The eastern part of the park (around Kununurra) was used for several of the cattle-driving shoots, including the large cattle stampede and the drought scenes. After the bulldust had settled, the park also features in some glorious aerial panoramic shots.

A variety of scenic and adventure tours are offered. There are accommodation options at El Questro Station, the Homestead and Emma Gorge, and each has restaurant options that won't let you get away without trying the local beef or barramundi (or both). *Gibb River Rd, off Great Northern Hwy; (08) 9169 1777; www.elquestro.com.au*

Faraway Bay

Their catch phrase of 'You've never been this far away' couldn't ring any truer. Only accessible by air, the spectacular Faraway Bay is around 70 minutes by plane from Kununurra. The dramatic, rip-roaring twin waterfalls on the King George River feature in the film. The camp has eight rustic bush cabins. Activities include swimming, fishing, croc spotting, visiting unique Bradshaw Aboriginal rock art nearby or just lazing in a hammock with a good book. Return flights from Kununurra to Faraway Bay are included in the accommodation package. Open April to October inclusive. *(08) 9169 1214 or 0417 986 614; farawaybay.com.au*

Celebrity Tree Park

On the shores of Lake Kununurra is an arboretum where trees have been planted by the likes of John Farnham, Her Royal Highness Princess Anne, Rolf Harris and, most recently, director extraordinaire Baz Luhrmann. It's as close to being knighted as there is in this country. Entry is free; not a great deal to see. *Via Old Darwin Road*

Kelly's Knob Lookout

At 191 metres, it's the highest spot to be at sunset. Don't forget your esky and picnic blanket. *Off Kelly Rd, Kununurra*

WHERE TO STAY

Hotel Kununurra

Comfortable hotel in the heart of town with friendly staff. Budget and premium rooms, free in-house movies and complimentary airport transfers. Feel free to get rowdy, sports fans, as you can cheer on [insert favourite sports team here] in the attached sports lounge. Yelling at the flat screen encouraged. *37 Messmate Way; (08) 9168 0400; www.hotelkununurra.com.au*

Diversion Dam and the winding blue Ord River

Digger's Rest Station

Bunkhouse and bush hut accommodation available at one of the major shooting locations. Jackman, David Wenham and David Gulpilil stayed here during filming; each left their autograph on the homestead walls. *Via King River Rd, off Great Northern Hwy; (08) 9161 1029; diggersreststation.com.au*

El Questro Wilderness Park

This award-winning park offers a variety of different outback accommodation experiences: the Homestead, with six luxury suites fit for royalty, Emma Gorge Resort, with safari-style tented cabins, and the Station, with bungalows and camping facilities, all with dining options. *Gibb River Rd, off Great Northern Hwy; (08) 9169 1777; www.elquestro.com.au*

Kimberley Croc Lodge

Beaut cheap stay for holidaymakers spending a lengthy amount of time in Kununurra, with discounted long-term rates. Offers backpacker dorms and private single and double rooms. The refreshing pool is a godsend when the mercury's rising. *2 River Fig Ave, Kununurra; (08) 9168 1411; www.kimberleycourt.com.au*

CARAVANS AND MOTORHOMES

Discovery Holiday Parks

Powered and unpowered caravan sites, camping and holiday units on the banks of Lake Kununurra. Tonnes of facilities, including pool and internet kiosk. *Lakeview Dr; (08) 9168 1031; lake-kununurra.wa.big4.com.au*

Ivanhoe Village Caravan Resort

An award-winning resort with ensuite powered sites, camping and resort cabins with private balconies. *Cnr Ivanhoe Rd and Coolibah St; (08) 9169 1995; www.ivanhoevillageresort.com*

CAMPING

Kununurra Agricultural Society Showgrounds

Pet-friendly camping 600 metres from town. *Cnr Ivanhoe Rd and Coolibah Dr*

Lower Ord River

Terrific camping sites at Buttons Crossing, Mambi Island and Skull Rock, all downstream from Lake Kununurra. Note that saltwater crocodiles frequent the area and they really don't like to be patted. *Access via Parry Creek Rd on the western side and Weaber Plains Rd on the eastern side*

WHERE TO EAT

Dusty Bar and Grill

An outback gem on Home Valley Station decorated with authentic station memorabilia (more dusty than the grill). Menu options feature Aussie bush tucker ingredients (herbs, seeds, fruits and flowers) – you're guaranteed to feel more Australian after eating here. *Gibb River Rd; (08) 9161 4322; www.hvstation.com.au*

Pump House Restaurant

Converted from an actual irrigation pumphouse, this corrugated-iron-shed eatery naturally boasts beautiful Ord River views and retains the original massive pumps, gantry and switchboards. Stunning at sunset. Open for breakfast, lunch and dinner; free wi-fi an added bonus. Closed Monday. *Lot 3005 Lakeview Dr, Kununurra; (08) 9169 3222; www.ordpumphouse.com.au*

Kelly's Bar and Grill

The Kununurra Country Club Resort offers relaxed dining with a sophisticated Australian menu (including croc and roo) paired with local wines. Nic and hubby Keith ate here several times during filming. *47 Coolibah Dr, Kununurra; (08) 9168 1024; www.kununurracountryclub.com.au*

TOURS

Home Valley (HV8) Station and *Australia* Movie Tour

A fun-filled insight into the operation of a working cattle station, the four-wheel-drive tour stops at two locations where the movie was shot: stand at 'Luhrmann's Lookout' right near 'Jackman's Jump', where you will be able to see 'Kidman's Crossing'. If you're staying at the station, you can watch the film in the comfort of your own Grass Castle luxury suite. *Via Gibb River Rd; (08) 9161 4322; www.hvstation.com.au*

El Questro's Big Day Out Tour

A one-day four-wheel-drive tour taking in a number of key locations from the film, including the cattle stampede scene, Emma Gorge and the Pentecost River. *Gibb River Rd, off Great Northern Hwy; (08) 9169 1777; www.elquestro.com.au/homestead/play/toursActivities-en.html*

Macka's Barra Camp

The Lower Ord River is hailed as one of the best barramundi fishing spots in all of Australia and Macka will show you where. On the extended tour you get to stay overnight at Carlton Hill Station, which is otherwise closed to the public. *(08) 9169 1759; www.mackasbarra.com.au*

Horse treks and trail rides at Diggers Rest Station

Saddle up and re-enact the drove while enjoying the stunning Kimberley scenery from horseback. Sorry ladies, muscle-clad drover Jackman is back in Hollywood and will not be leading these treks, but you will be in the capable hands of the good people at Diggers Rest. Choose from one-hour to full-day trail rides or two- to eleven-day horse treks. Novice riders, remember your ice pack – you'll need it. *Via King River Rd; (08) 9161 1029; diggersreststation.com.au*

Faraway Bay River Cruise

Spend the day on the *Diamond Lass* exploring the beautiful King George River, including King George Falls, the twin waterfalls featured in the movie. *(08) 9169 1214 or 0417 986 614; farawaybay.com.au*

Did you know?

Such was their faith in Baz Luhrmann that Nicole Kidman and Hugh Jackman agreed to star in the movie before even reading the script.

BOWEN QUEENSLAND

In the far north of Queensland, level with the top of the Whitsunday Islands is Bowen – dubbed 'Bowenwood' these days by some of the locals. Situated within 5 kilometres of several pristine beaches and bays, Bowen is that charming costal town that brings flashbacks of magical childhood holidays; you just want to stay forever. The town is principally known for its mango production – it's pretty hard to miss the Big Mango on your way into town.

For *Australia*, Bowen was dressed up to play pre-war Darwin complete with faux stockyards and Chinese opium dens created especially for the film. The scenes in which Lady Ashley and the Drover herd the cattle onto the ship in Darwin were, in fact, shot on Bowen's striking waterfront. Over 600 locals were used as extras in the film, while most of the others provided many vital services to the crew.

VISITOR INFO

Bowen Visitor Information Centre

Bruce Hwy (next to the Big Mango);
(07) 4786 4222; www.tourismbowen.com.au

THINGS TO SEE AND DO

Bowen Jetty

Bowen's large jetty is the key reason Luhrmann chose to shoot the film here; it's one of the only places in Australia that could be used to realistically portray the Darwin Harbour in wartime. (McDonalds, McMansions and late-model cars in Darwin itself might have spoiled

> Mrs Boss! We gotta get those fat cheeky bulls into that big bloody metal ship!
>
> – *Nullah*

The main reason Baz Luhrmann chose Bowen for production – its jetty

the mood.) Over 700 shorthorn cattle and 33 stock and quarter horses were used in the epic cattle-run scenes.

The jetty is an ideal place to chillax with a fishing line or chow down on some locally fried barra and chips as you watch the sun set. The main beach at Bowen just near the jetty was used as the location for Mission Beach, the tiny island where they ship Nullah and the other 'half castes'. Today the Bowen beach and foreshore are unrecognisable as the area has undergone a huge refurbishment since the filming. *South end of town, off Santa Barbara Pde*

Police station

Located on Dalrymple Street, this 'historic' cop shop is actually a movie set – the only one remaining in Bowen from the production. Over 16 hectares of land around the police station were used to recreate 1940s Darwin, said to be one of the largest outdoor movie sets ever built. *Dalrymple St*

Summergarden Theatre, aka editing central during production

Summergarden Theatre

A Deco-style movie house modelled on those found in 1930s Southern California. Luhrmann and his team used the theatre to view raw footage (called 'rushes' in the biz) and edit scenes during production. The theatre also hosted the simultaneous world premiere of the film, along with Sydney, Darwin and Kununurra. The theatre screens new movies and presents stage performances. *40 Murroona Rd; (07) 4785 1241; bowensummergardencinemas.com*

Grandview Hotel

The exterior of this popular pub was transformed to replicate old shops on Main Street in Darwin. The facade of the hotel can be seen in a few scenes, including when Lady Ashley and the Drover drive the cattle through town and in some of the bombing scenes. The Grandview came alive in a different way when the cameras were packed away, doing what a good pub does best and filling the bellies of the cast and crew with hot meals and cold brews. One magical night, Nic's hubby, country music star Keith Urban, gave an impromptu boot-scootin' concert in the beer garden for over 500 elated cast and crew members. *5 Herbert St; (07) 4786 4022*

Customs house

Heavily featured in the film, both the interior and exterior of this building were used as the headquarters of the Carney Cattle Company. The building currently houses the local Department of Transport customer service centre. *Opposite the Grandview Hotel, cnr Herbert and Dalrymple sts*

Bays and beaches

Some magnificent spots for swimming, snorkelling and fishing surround Bowen. Rose and Horseshoe bays are connected by a walking track with panoramic views of the ocean, while Coral Bay is a great spot for a secluded swim. On his days off, Hugh and family were often spotted splashing around in Horseshoe Bay. Most likely the other blokes on that beach felt a tad inadequate when topless Hugh was around.

Big Mango

You can't miss this gigantic fruit, a tribute to the Kensington Mango, which has been grown locally since 1880. It's next door to the Bowen Visitor Information Centre, which has a shop selling brain-freeze-worthy mango sorbet and irresistibly kitschy *Australia* stubby holders. *4 km south of Bowen on the Bruce Hwy; (07) 4786 4222*

Murals

Twenty-five or so historical murals created by local and national artists depict the history of the region. Every two years a new mural is commissioned. There are weekly walking tours.

WHERE TO STAY

Rose Bay Resort

Stunning modern apartments located directly on Rose Bay, a secluded beach just north of the main township. Many of the cast stayed here during production, including King Carney himself, Bryan Brown. Affordable studio, one- and two-bedroom apartments, all with ocean views. Affable owners Paul and Colleen will take good care of you. *2 Pandanus St; (07) 4786 9000; www.rosebayresort.com.au*

Bluewater Harbour Motel

Motel in name, but offers hotel facilities. Up-scale garden, business and family rooms all with modern amenities. Many have sung the praises of the locally caught seafood and delish homemade cheesecakes in the attached restaurant. *1 Powell St; (07) 4786 6289; bluewatermotel.com.au*

Castle Motor Lodge

Motel accommodation in a quiet location for those trying to save a few pennies; there are 32 comfy rooms, including family rooms that sleep up to seven people. Restaurant and bar on site. *6 Don St; (07) 4786 1322; www.castlemotorlodge. com.au*

The police station is the only remaining movie set in town

CARAVANS AND MOTORHOMES

Harbour Lights Caravan Park

Numerous powered caravan sites, holiday cottages and deluxe villas adjacent to the harbour and beach. *40 Santa Barbara Pde; (07) 4786 1565; www.bowencaravanpark.com.au*

Did you know?

Bowen Village Caravan Park

An eco-friendly park on 30 acres with powered and unpowered sites, plus a Water Park pool just out of the town centre. *18540 Bruce Hwy; (07) 4786 1366; www.bvcp.com.au*

BIG4 Bowen Coral Coast Beachfront Holiday Park

Right on the beachfront, the park offers powered sites and luxury villas with spas, a community pool, recreation lounge, golf course and free barbecue facilities. *Cnr Horseshoe and The Soldiers rds; (07) 4785 1262; coral-coast-holiday-park.qld.big4.com.au*

WHERE TO EAT

Jochheim's Pies

The seven-decades-young owner of this quaint pie shop changed the course of Australian movie-making history. On a location-scouting trip, Baz Lurhmann got to chatting with Merle Jochheim, something of a town historian, in mid-2006. She gave the director the lowdown on Bowen's history – she should know, her great-great-grandfather was Captain Daniel Sinclair, who founded the town in 1859. Merle didn't realise who she was talking to at the time, but she soon made *The Courier-Mail* newspaper with the headline: 'Pie Lady Seals Movie Deal'.

Merle's connection with *Australia* didn't stop there. Jochheim Pies became a second home for the cast and crew during the two months of shooting in Bowen. Jackman and his son Oscar were frequent customers and they even stepped behind the counter a couple of times to try their hands at baking pies.

Today you can try the flaky nirvana that is the Jackman Special, a 'Hunky Aussie Beef' pie, while during production you could have partaken in a Baz Baguette or the Kidmango White Chocolate Cheesecake. The bakery walls are lined with historic photos of Bowen and a swag of clippings, photographs and autographs from the film's cast and crew. If you're lucky enough to catch Merle in the shop, she's more than willing to spin a yarn or two about the time when 'Hollywood' came to town. *49 George St; (07) 4786 1227*

360 on the Hill

In Flagstaff Hill's interpretive centre, this modest cafe offers casual meals and panoramic views to die for. Nic and Keith thought so, anyway. During production, Keith hired out the whole

Merle and her grandson Joel outside her pie shop

> If you've got no
> love in your heart,
> you've got nothing ...
> No dreaming, no
> story, nothing.
>
> — *Magarri*

While Luhrmann chose to shoot many of *Australia*'s Darwin scenes in Bowen (because Darwin was too built up to replicate the era), the Territory's capital city still features in some scenes. The historic Stokes Hill Wharf, once the focus of a prominent port catering to sailing vessels and steamers, is now home to a number of restaurants and bars. It was used in the scenes when our lovely Lady Ashley arrives from England and also doubled in certain parts as the real Darwin wharf.

VISITOR INFO

Darwin Visitor Centre (Tourism Top End)

6 Bennett St; (08) 8980 6000 or 1300 138 886; www.tourismtopend.com.au

THINGS TO SEE AND DO

Stokes Hill Wharf

The feature Darwin location used in the film, the wharf and its surrounds were used in the scene when Lady Ashley arrives in Darwin for the first time on a Qantas Flying Boat. Yes, boats could fly back then!

The scenes involving the schooner shipping Nullah to and from Mission Island were also shot at the wharf. Segments of scenes involving a very small section on the wharf with some cattle and vehicles were also shot there. Other scenes supposedly shot on the wharf were actually filmed at a sound stage and Fox Studios in Sydney. Yes, moviemaking is complicated!

Most arrivals these days are seeking fish and chips or ice-cream and feed their leftovers to the fat fish off the side. You can even safely ride a boogie board at the wave pool.

joint for a romantic dinner under the stars to celebrate Nic's 40th birthday. *Margaret Reynolds Dr; (07) 4786 6360*

The Cove International

Hit the ground floor of the Coral Cove Apartments for spectacular views of Horseshoe Bay and scrummy Asian and modern Australian nosh. *Horseshoe Bay Rd; (07) 4791 2050; www.coralcoveapartments.com.au*

DARWIN NORTHERN TERRITORY

Regarded as Australia's northern outpost, Darwin's proximity to Asia and manifest Aboriginal history and culture make it one of the world's most interesting cities.

City centre

The bustling heart of Darwin is bursting with attractions, from Crocosaurus Cove in Mitchell Street to shopping at Smith Street Mall, and the Northern Territory Chinese Museum and Chinese Temple on Woods Street. Follow the exotic aroma of incense to find the latter. A leisurely walk through Bicentennial Park on the Esplanade is the perfect way to spend a sunny afternoon.

State Square

This precinct boasts a fresh mix of new and old, from the modern Parliament House and Supreme Court buildings to the elegant Government House, a reminder of the city's colonial days. Survivor's Lookout gives panoramic views of Darwin Harbour and Stokes Hill Wharf.

Mindil Beach Sunset Markets

The town's most popular tourist attraction, this market operates every Thursday and Sunday evening from 5pm during the dry season. Feast on a multitude of tastes from the Asia–Pacific and beyond, browse Aboriginal art, handmade crafts and watch the live performances and fire twirlers. *The Esplanade; (08) 8981 3454; www.mindil.com.au*

SKYCITY Casino

Raise the stakes with blackjack or poker and feed your inner card shark in this spectacular city casino. (Or retreat to your room for a few hands of 'Go Fish' if gambling doesn't float your boat.) A tempting selection of excellent restaurants will arouse your taste buds and several bars can quench that Top End thirst. *Gilruth Ave; (08) 8943 8888; www.skycitydarwin.com.au*

Cullen Bay Marina

A popular dining and recreation area; take your pick from a smorgasbord of restaurants overlooking the busy marina. *cullenbaymarina.com.au*

WHERE TO STAY

Banyan View Lodge

Dirt-cheap hostel offering shared dorms and private ensuite rooms with air-con to escape the muggy Darwin nights. Enjoy a splash and snag or two with other travellers in the relaxing pool and barbecue area. *Gardens Hill Cres; (08) 8981 8850; www.moonshadowvillas.com*

Palms City Resort

Affordable and centrally located on the Esplanade, its villas and motel rooms are set in beautifully landscaped tropical gardens. *The Esplanade; (08) 8982 9200; www.citypalms.com*

Moonshadow Villas

Voted one of the best resorts in all of Australia, this five-star accommodation option with a who's who guest list has gorgeous villas amid lush rainforest by sandstone waterfall pools. Dig deep. *119 Mitchell St; (08) 8981 8644; www.banyanviewlodge.com.au*

CARAVANS AND MOTORHOMES

Hidden Valley Tourist Park

Just south of the Darwin CBD, this tropical park has ensuite powered sites, lodges and villas and a boutique cafe offering the famous Valley Big Brekky. You won't have to eat all day after that. *25 Hidden Valley Rd, Berrimah; (08) 8947 1422; www.hiddenvalleytouristpark.com.au*

Darwin FreeSpirit Resort

Further south of the Darwin CBD is this family park, which offers a range of accommodation options, from premium caravan sites to poolside spa villas. Float and eat in the poolside cafe and bistro and enjoy the live evening entertainment. *901 Stuart Hwy, Holtze; (08) 8935 0888; www.darwinfreespiritresort.com.au*

WHERE TO EAT

Lizards Outdoor Bar and Grill

Embrace the muggy Darwin air and enjoy some cheap mains surrounded by lush fig trees and tropical palms. Any of the seafood, steak and salad choices, complemented by icy-cold brews, will hit the spot! *Daly St; (08) 8981 6511*

Darwin from the air

The Jetty Restaurant

Situated on Stokes Hill Wharf, as to be expected, the speciality here is seafood. In addition to the à la carte menu, you can't go wrong with the topnotch seafood buffet. *Stokes Hill Wharf; (08) 8942 1500*

Waterfront Bistro

An eatery at the Darwin Sailing Club, with beautiful views of Fannie Bay, offering a scrumptious range of international and modern-Australian cuisine. *Atkins Dr; (08) 8981 1700; www.dwnsail.com.au*

CINEMA

Deckchair Cinema

How often have you had to slather yourself in Aeroguard to watch a screening of the latest action flick? Mosquitoes are just half the fun of this unique reclining outdoor cinema experience. The Deckchair screens new releases and some classic flicks as well. Hot food available

A balmy evening at the Deckchair Cinema

seven nights a week, including the themed Tastes of India and Timor nights. *Jervois Rd; (08) 8981 0700; www.deckchaircinema.com*

TOURS

Darwin Tour Tub

Hop-on, hop-off bus tours of the city. Hop off at Stokes Hill Wharf and try to envision just what was involved for Baz and his crew to transform this location into early 1940s Darwin – you'll certainly have to use your imagination. *(08) 8985 6322; www.tourtub.com.au*

Darwin Harbour Cruises

Barbecue lunch, and sunset and dinner cruises departing from Stokes Hill Wharf. *(08) 8942 3131; www.darwinharbourcruises.com.au*

STRICKLAND HOUSE
SYDNEY, NEW SOUTH WALES

The white sand of Horseshoe Bay in Bowen

This 1850s heritage-listed property was used as Darwin's Government House in the film. The most memorable scene shot here was the gala scene, when the Drover and Lady Ashley share a sloppy, romantic kiss in the rain. The grounds of the house contain a two-storey coach house and horse stables. There are terrific views of the house from the Hermitage Reserve walking track in Sydney Harbour National Park. *52 Vaucluse St, Vaucluse*

CAMELOT, ELDERSLIE
SYDNEY, NEW SOUTH WALES

On the western outskirts of Sydney is the majestic Camelot residence, originally known as Kirkham House (so don't bother looking for Arthur). The stables and grounds were used as Lady Ashley's posh residence in England early in the film. Tours of the house are by appointment only (groups only, generally minimum 15 people). *Kirkham La, Elderslie; (02) 4658 1370*

Did you know?

Australia was unfairly snubbed by the AFI Awards, not even being nominated for Best Film. But it was nominated for six other awards, taking home Best Costume Design, Best Production Design and Best Visual Effects.

Two poor-fella rums, Ivan.

— *Drover*

No women. Ladies lounge next door.

— *Ivan*

She's no lady, Ivan. She just drove a mob of cattle across the Never Never. She deserves a drink like any man.

— *Old drunk*

Q & A Phillip Roope, location manager for *Australia*

Phillip Roope has been working as a location scout for almost 20 years. His local and international credits include *Two Hands* (1999), *The Beach* (2000), *Tomorrow Never Dies* (1997), *The Man Who Sued God* (2001), *Superman Returns* (2006) and the acclaimed TV series *Underbelly*. His latest production was the Mad Max sequel, *Fury Road* (due for release in 2012).

Q: *How did you first get into the field of location scouting?*

A: It's a strange story, really, I used to be a teacher. **My way into film was through my dog – I had a dog that sang.** It was just a party trick: put her on my lap and make her sing and I'd sing along with her (I haven't got a bad voice). We did it at a city hotel and everyone thought it was great, they threw money and whistled. Someone stepped out of the audience and said would you like to do that on TV. So we hit the airwaves. For a very short period of time we were on *Hey Hey It's Saturday*, *New Faces*, *The Don Lane Show*, *The Mike Walsh Show* – this was the early '80s – *Simon Townsend's Wonderworld* and whatever else you can think of.

After that I thought [it would be] great material for a short film, so I made a short film. That led into a feature film, called *Molly,* starring a ten-year-old Claudia Karvan, Garry McDonald and Ruth Cracknell. That film was made in 1983 and got me into the film industry. I did some tutoring of children on set as well ... I looked after the 'feral children' on *Mad Max 3* for a while.

On the film about my dog, Molly, I had about six or seven roles, one of which was location manager. That was the role I enjoyed the most. I had no idea when I started what it was all about. Back in those days it was a lot easier to roll up somewhere and park a few trucks and start filming. But nowadays it's almost impossible to do that. It's hard to think back now of how we actually did it without mobile phones and email, but somehow trucks rolled up, people got out, streets were closed off and filming was done.

Q: *What's the process of scouting locations? How did it work for* Australia?

A: Basically you read the script and form your own ideas. Then you meet the director and set designer and get a more detailed idea of the brief. You then think [about] where those things may be situated. Maybe you have a few photos on file that might back up what you've said. You show those to the designer or the director. Then you get on a plane or in a car and go there and come back with a series of shots, maps and videos that show how the area might work with the script.

And then they'll say things like, 'That's good, but maybe we could have the mountains a bit higher.'

In TV it's a very quick process, because you might be filming there in the next week or so. But on feature films, especially if they're quite large, it's usually a long and drawn out process. **For a feature film you have to find your 'A' locations first. For *Australia*, for example, your 'A' locations would be a wharf, Darwin and where the homestead is going to be built.** You have to find them first and everything else will fall around them. Baz wanted to film in the north. But there are also other considerations – **about 300 people have to travel out to a location and be accommodated, fed and watered. Your filming location can only be 50 to 60 kilometres – maximum 80 to 90 kilometres – from a major town.**

For *Australia*, the homestead's starting point was Kununurra, because other than Broome it was really the only town that could cope with that number of people. So I worked out from Kununurra and drove absolutely every road within a radius of 100 kilometres. In the case of the homestead, it had to be between a river and some feature that was interesting, so the starting point was this big outcrop of rock on Carlton Hill, which is huge and had its own character. It was near the Ord River, with beauty and crocodiles and all of that. Baz said he would like to explore that area even further, so he came up. Basically we knew that the movie's homestead was going to be in that area and finally picked the exact location of the house.

So then you start to find your 'B' and 'C' locations around that area. Then you have to go through the process of actually locking in all the permissions.

Q: *How long was the location scouting process? What were the major challenges?*

A: From beginning to end, location scouting took about 18 months. A lot of the locations weren't locked in until a relatively short period before they shot the film. Up there most properties are owned by the Crown and occupied under pastoral leases. And then there are Indigenous rights. There might also be national parks or other organisations [that] are interested in the treatment of the land. **You could be dealing with four different bodies to get permission to shoot.** [Each] of those takes ages, so four of them together is just miles of paperwork, off-site visits and getting agreements for things that aren't even done in the end!

We were told that it's *never ever* rained in June in Kununurra or the Kimberley, because the wet season usually starts in December and finishes towards the end of April. Then it's clear blue and quite cool for the rest of the winter. **We brought four inches of rain with us in June, which was the first time since 1889!** That was during the construction phase at Kununurra; while filming was happening in Bowen. The decision was made to go to Darwin, where rain wouldn't affect anything, then go back to Sydney and do some studio stuff, and then go back up to Kununurra when it got dry. But that's not the most economical way to work. It put everything out of synch. Strangely enough, film crews seem to go to a place and bring rain.

Q: *You dressed up Bowen to look like 1940s Darwin. Was that the plan all along?*

A: There are no areas [in Darwin] you could use and it's far too busy really. The only thing that was good in Darwin was the wharf itself, which is remarkable because it's so high and underneath the wharf the water is an incredible aqua colour. Baz wanted to film there mainly because of the colour of the water.

We did a search for wharfs around Australia and came up with the most idle big wharf in Australia, which was the wharf at Bowen. It had been a main wharf, but the main loading area had moved up the coast a bit. Just next to the wharf was a big open area, which was about to be developed. It was perfect. So we had to hold the developer off – he's a very nice man. **It would be very hard to repeat**

that, if not impossible, to get a very long, big jetty and right next to the jetty a big open area of level land with nothing on it and then a street behind it that looked like old Darwin anyway. It was a pretty remarkable combination of things!

Q: *What was Baz was like to work with?*

A: To work with Baz is being part of a great team. He's incredibly energetic, full of enthusiasm and draws people into the whole thing. He's a great communicator and a great motivator. It's an exciting process. He and Catherine [Martin, his wife] are just totally inclusive and they bring the best out in people. **You're part of a team, you're involved and it's fun. Out of all the films I've worked on, this was the most fun.**

Q: *Is it more difficult to lock down city locations than country areas?*

A: I think I go against the grain in that, I think it's actually easier … because we've done it for so long we're sure how it works. **When you know how something works, it doesn't frighten you.** We've just done the last two *Underbelly* TV productions and were shooting full-on Kings Cross and full-on city, inner-city locations. While that is absolutely scary, for most of it we were dealing with pretty much the same person the whole time. You keep a dialogue going and you have a bit of a sense of what can be done and what can't be done.

Q: *Did you feel any trepidation choosing locations in Kings Cross for* Two Hands?

A: Absolutely! For *Two Hands*, we shot there for four nights. Gregor [Jordan, writer and director]

was worried about security. I had no idea, having never shot there. So I walked up for a look around and I saw a big Samoan chap working security at the Westpac bank right in the middle of the Cross. You very rarely see someone as big as Bobby. **I thought if Westpac have him as a security guy he must be pretty reliable. So I went up to him and said, 'How would you go about securing a shoot here for four nights, Bobby?'** And he said, 'I'd hire me. I'll do the night shift and I know all the bouncers. You give me money for being the supervisor and we pay the bouncers either side of you and down the street a bit $50 a night.' We didn't have a single problem.

Q: *What are your favourite film locations in Australia?*

A: I'd have to say the location for *The Man Who Sued God* – Bermagui. It was just this sleepy little southern coastal town that hasn't changed that much because it's off the main highway. It's just absolutely beautiful – seaside fishing and mountains. **Bowen was really great and friendly. I love country towns**, especially if they haven't changed much … places like Carcoar, in New South Wales, that haven't changed a lot and probably never will.

I love Sydney as well. I call Sydney home. I don't think there would be too many people who would know it better, but it still keeps revealing itself. Mainly because it's so broken up and divided by coves and the harbour and waterways … you go down some road and you're standing in some part of the harbour you've never been before and you're lost and can't think where the city would be and think, 'My God. I've never been down here before.' **Sydney still has some surprises.**

Babe (1995)

Farmer Hoggett guesses the weight of our cute hero

That'll do pig. That'll do.

— *Farmer Hoggett*

Director: Chris Noonan
Writer: Chris Noonan
Producers: George Miller, Doug Mitchell
Cast includes: James Cromwell, Magda Szubanski, Christine Cavanaugh (voice), Hugo Weaving (voice), Miriam Margolyes (voice)

ABOUT THE FILM

No film in the history of Australian cinema has captured the audience's heart and imagination quite like *Babe*. The film is also more than likely responsible for a spike in vegetarian converts and a drop in bacon sales during the mid-'90s.

This loveable romp tells the story of an orphaned piglet named Babe (voiced by Christine Cavanaugh) – the little porker with the gift of the gab – who defied his own destiny and dared to be different.

After his mother is tragically sent to the slaughterhouse, Babe is taken under the wing of wise sheepdog Fly (Margolyes), who Babe quickly emulates by herding sheep himself. Despite being ridiculed by a cross-section of quirky barnyard animals, Babe is undeterred and does such a first-rate job of sheep herding that farmer Arthur Hoggett (Cromwell) enters him into the National Grand Challenge Sheepdog Trials. This pleases Babe no end, as the alternative was being eaten for Christmas lunch. The rest, as they say, is Australian cinema history.

The success of *Babe* wasn't just limited to Australian shores; the movie grossed over US$250 million worldwide. This lobbed it into the slot of second most popular live-action Australian film to date, behind *Crocodile Dundee*. The film was nominated for a slew of Academy Awards, including Best Picture, Best Supporting Actor (Cromwell) and Best Director

Babe enjoys the rising sun

> Baa-ram-ewe! Baa-ram-ewe! To your breed, your fleece, your clan be true! Sheep be true! Baa-ram-ewe!
>
> — *Babe*

The Hoggett Farm site as seen from Fountaindale Road

(Noonan). However, it went home with only one award, which was for Best Visual Effects, beating *Apollo 13*. At the time of publication, Babe was the last G-rated film to be nominated for Best Picture at the Academy Awards.

As for public opinion, *Babe* stands as the best-reviewed Australian movie of all time, according to the popular movie reviews website RottenTomatoes.com, which rates the film an astonishing '98% fresh'.

Babe's raging success brought on the inevitable sequel, *Babe: Pig in the City* (1998), directed by George Miller. It didn't scale the dizzy heights of the original, but was still considered a success. Few people know that *Babe* was actually adapted from a book called *The Sheep-Pig*, written by British author Dick King-Smith.

LOCATIONS

ROBERTSON
NEW SOUTH WALES

The small town of Robertson, straddling Macquarie's Pass in the New South Wales Southern Highland region, was thrust into the tourism spotlight in 1995 when *Babe* became an international mega-hit. The film was shot primarily on a farm in the quiet township, famous for being Australia's most prolific potato-growing area. There's even a big potato on Main Street to hammer the point home.

While the legacy of the film still hovers around the town, Robertson has moved on from *Babe* and established itself as a quaint country township worth a visit, talking pigs aside. The picturesque rolling hills and rich-red volcanic basalt soil, known simply as 'Robertson soil', is unlike anywhere else in Australia.

The town was named after former New South Wales premier, Sir John Robertson. Other claims to fame include being the hometown of Australian cricketer Brett Lee and rugby star Nathan Hindmarsh.

There's plenty to see and do in and around town, from the Old Time Music Museum to the rainforests of Robertson Nature Reserve. Stay a while and don't forget to bag some fresh-dug local spuds. Towns around Robertson, including Exeter, Berrima and Kangaroo Valley, were also used as shooting locations for the film.

VISITOR INFO

Southern Highlands Visitor Information
62–70 Main St, Mittagong; (02) 4871 2888; www.southern-highlands.com.au

THINGS TO SEE AND DO

Hoggett Farm
Much of the film's action takes place at the fictional farm owned by Arthur and Esme Hoggett (Szubanski), including the house and outlying barn. The real farm is named 'Prospect'. Head down Fountaindale Road, go over the railway line and past the row of houses on the right and slow down. Through a gap in the trees, you'll be able to spy the location. You're in for some disappointment if you're hoping to catch a glimpse of Babe's home; the farmhouse and barn were purpose-built for the film and torn down at the end of filming.

Note: Prospect farm is a private property – no entry without permission.

Also off Fountaindale Road is the site where they shot the climactic National Grand Challenge Sheepdog Trials competition – it's on the left-hand side, just over the railway line. The original choice for the location was Chevalier College near Bowral, but location manager Peter Lawless

If you're craving something starchy, Robertson is the place

discovered this beautiful spot at the last minute. Picket fences and a grandstand were built to make the space look like an old English oval, which, in the film, was called the King Smith Showground (a homage to the author of the book). *Off Fountaindale Rd*

Robertson Showground Pavilion
This large pavilion was the base for hundreds of extras, who used the area for costume changes. The large mob of extras appeared mainly in early scenes at the country fair and the final sheep-herding-competition scenes. The Robertson Agricultural and Horticultural Show is held here annually in March. It features agricultural and commercial displays, billy tea and damper making demonstrations, woolly sheep rides and a fireworks display. The show has been running for over 130 years. *Kangaloon Rd*

The Big Potato
Woombye has the Big Pineapple, Coffs Harbour has the Big Banana and Robertson is the proud

home of the Giant Spud! Located at the eastern end of town on Main Street, this mammoth ball of starchy goodness (quite hollow inside, but go with it) was built in 1977 by local potato grower Jim Mauger. It was created to house a potato information centre, but due to lack of funding the centre never came to fruition. The potato stands 10 metres tall and 4 metres wide. It was modelled on the Sebago potato.

In 2010, a group of local pranksters dressed up the spud as Mr Potato Head and affectionately called him 'Robbo Spud Face'. *Main St*

Kev Neel's Old Time Music Machines

This unique music museum displays (and plays) antique gramophones and other music memorabilia from the 1800s. Step outside with a cuppa for breathtaking views of the Illawarra coastline. *Illawarra Hwy; (02) 4885 1562*

Robertson Nature Reserve

Don't be fooled by the unassuming entrance – inside is a wondrous rainforest habitat,

Exeter's charming General Store

a remnant of the famous Yarrawa Brush. Stroll though the sub-tropical, warm and cool-temperature rainforests, with towering trees, low-hanging vines and abundant birdlife. *Entrance at South St*

Exeter

This small village was a location for a couple of major scenes in the film. The country fair at the beginning of the movie, where Farmer Hoggett correctly guesses Babe's weight (16 pounds, 2 ounces, in case you were wondering), was shot on a private property on the edge of town.

The Exeter Village Hall was used for the scene when farmer Hoggett is informed by the Sheepdog Association judges that Babe can compete in the trials. The hall sits diagonally opposite the Exeter General Store on Middle Road. Exeter is 30 kilometres west of Robertson.

Kangaroo Valley

'The most beautiful valley in all of Australia', Kangaroo Valley is to be found just 32 kilometres south of Robertson. The picturesque spot was used for a scene where Farmer Hoggett and Babe watch a sheep farmer trial his dog. The rich green pastures of this serene paradise and its great cafes, galleries and cosy B&Bs attract Sydneysiders for weekend getaways.

Bowral

A charming rural town 25 or so kilometres north-west of Robertson, Bowral honours its famous son, Sir Donald Bradman – otherwise known as 'The Don', the greatest batsman of all time – with the Cricket International Hall of Fame. Bowral also holds an annual Tulip Festival each September.

Journey to Bowral from Robertson via Kangaloon Road, which was used as a location towards the end of the film featuring dog Rex (Weaving), as he runs back and forth to Hoggett Farm in an attempt to get the secret password from the mob of stubborn sheep.

Just a few kilometres north of Bowral is the tiny speck of a town called Braemer. The interior of a large warehouse near Gillies and Draper streets was used at the very beginning of the film when Babe's adoring mum is snatched away from him and taken to the slaughterhouse.

Berrima

Established in 1831, this picturesque valley town played a small, yet significant part in the *Babe* production. The facade of part of the Blue Southern Cement Works on Taylor Avenue was used in the opening scenes when Babe's mother is hauled away by the large 'Meats' truck. Berrima is an enchanting townscape, resplendent with beautifully preserved Georgian sandstone homes and inns, and old historic churches. Take a self-guided walk around the village or stop in for a bite at one of the many cafes.

Belmore Falls

Located in the Robertson section of Morton National Park, around 10 kilometres south-west of the township, this natural wonder plunges almost 80 metres into two separate rockpools. There are walking tracks and picnic facilities here. Around 5 kilometres further south-west is Fitzroy Falls, another stunning sandstone waterfall with spectacular lookouts. *Fitzroy Falls Visitor Centre, Nowra Rd, Fitzroy Falls; (02) 4887 7270; www.environment.nsw.gov.au/NationalParks*

Did you know?

Veteran British actress Miriam Margolyes, who was the voice of Fly in the film, fell in love so much with Robertson that a few years after the film she purchased a property in town.

Illawarra Fly Treetop Walk

Travel east of Robertson if you want to fly without taking off. The 500-metre walkway is 25 metres above the ground, with a 45-metre high tower, giving visitors an aerial view of the Southern Highlands and the rainforest below. Unforgettable vistas of Lake Illawarra and the Pacific Ocean. Avoid if heights give you the heebie jeebies. *182 Knights Hill Rd, Knights Hill; (02) 4885 1010 or 1300 362 881; www.illawarrafly.com*

Budderoo National Park

This 7120-hectare park, with borders just 10 kilometres south-east of Robertson, encompasses impressive rainforests, sandstone heaths and woodlands. The Robertson section of the park features Carrington Falls, a 50-metre waterfall with adjacent walking track. On the eastern edge of the park, in Jamberoo, is the award-winning Minnamurra Rainforest Centre with elevated walking tracks showcasing the rainforests that covered this whole area eons ago. *Minnamurra Rainforest Centre, 345 Minnamurra Falls Rd, Jamberoo; (02) 4236 0469*

WHERE TO STAY

Fountaindale Grand Manor

Formerly Ranelagh House, in 1925 this exquisite country manor had the prestigious title of 'most luxurious hotel in the Commonwealth'. Not much has changed within the property, set in 14 acres of well-tended gardens, still offering some of the best hospitality in rural New South Wales. Choose from affordable heritage rooms to king suites. The manor is a hugely popular location for weddings and is not far from Prospect Farm, where much of *Babe* was shot. *Cnr Fountaindale Rd and Illawarra Hwy; (02) 4885 1111; www.fountaindale.com.au*

Lloran Log Cabins

Cosy cabins in the peaceful and tranquil surrounds of the Robertson bushland. Choose from three cottages on offer, including The Hobbit House, a separate cottage with its own fenced garden (but no Golum). *Yeola Rd; (02) 4885 1376; www.highlandsnsw.com.au/lloran/index.html*

Twin Falls Bush Cottages

Located on 50 acres of unspoilt bushland near Fitzroy Falls in Morton National Park, there are five eco-friendly hexagonal cedar cottages with all the essentials. Bushwalk through the surrounding national park, attack the mountain-bike track or have a hit of tennis. *Throsby Rd, Fitzroy Falls; (02) 4887 7333; www.fitzroyfalls.com*

CAMPING

Budderoo National Park

Around 8 kilometres east of Robertson there's a small camping area at stunning Carrington Falls. An ideal spot for swimming, picnics and outdoor activities such as rock climbing and abseiling. *Access off Jamberoo Mountain Rd; details available from Fitzroy Falls Visitor Centre, Nowra Rd, Fitzroy Falls; (02) 4887 7270; www.environment.nsw.gov.au/NationalParks*

WHERE TO EAT

The Famous Robertson Pie Shop

There's homemade flaky deliciousness aplenty at the Robbo Pie Shop with a selection of 24 mouth-watering pies as well as delicious tarts and other heavenly pastries on display. Guilt ensues when you order the beef, bacon and cheese pie; guilt quickly dissipates when you take a bite. *Illawarra Hwy; (02) 4885 1330*

Did you know?

James Cromwell was a vegetarian before he started work on the movie; by the end he decided to become a fully fledged vegan.

Cromwell, as Farmer Hoggett, had only 171 words of dialogue in the entire film, 61 of which were sung. It has been said that he chose the role because of the minimal lines, yet in *Babe*, Cromwell had more screen time than any of his other films.

The Old Robertson Cheese Factory

Established in 1936 by the local dairy farming community, this vibrant country food outlet has been a town stalwart for decades. The dedicated cheese room has over 70 varieties of cheese and the cafe serves up fantastic antipasto platters. Gelati is made on the premises, though thankfully not in cheese flavours. Homewares and gifts can also be purchased. *107 Illawarra Hwy; (02) 4885 1133*

Pizzas in the Mist

Hugely popular Italian restaurant in the heart of Robertson that was nominated Best Pizza Restaurant on the South Coast in 2009. Good luck choosing from the 28 wood-fired pizzas, including the Garlic Lobster and Robertson Spud. *42 Hoddle St; (02) 4885 1799; www.pizzasinthemist.com.au*

Did you know?

Due to the fact that baby pigs grow at an alarmingly fast rate, 48 pigs were used for the filming of *Babe*. Over 1000 animals featured in the film and 56 animal trainers were employed on set.

Exeter General Store

While good for essential grocery shopping, this quirky general store also has a gourmet cafe with delightful seasonal menus and homemade cakes. Pick up a second-hand book for your journey. *Middle Rd; (02) 4883 4289*

CINEMA

Empire Theatre

Located in Bowral, this award-winning cinema opened in 1915 – one of the earliest built in Australia – and is still one of the best independent theatres in all of Australia. Four modern cinemas screen new releases. *327 Bong Bong St, Bowral; (02) 4861 4676; empirecinema.com.au*

See pages 180–1 for an interview with Babe *location manager Peter Lawless.*

Dairy heaven: The Old Robertson Cheese Factory

Aussies at the Oscars, part 1

For such a tiny country, Australia has produced an extraordinary number of Academy Award winners. Here is a list of the Australian films and the people who took home that shiny golden man – or came so agonisingly close.

KOKODA FRONT LINE (1942)

Ken Hall and Damien Parer won Best Documentary. The film is a harrowing look at the Australian campaign in New Guinea featuring real-life combat footage.

THE BISMARCK CONVOY SMASHED (1943)

Nominated for Best Documentary Short. A graphic short film documenting the Battle of the Bismarck Sea.

SCHOOL IN THE MAILBOX (1947)

Nominated for Best Documentary Short. The film shows how Australians triumphed over distance to educate the children of the outback by correspondence.

LEISURE (1976)

Bruce Petty and Suzanne Baker won Best Short Film. A 13-minute animated short by newspaper cartoonist Bruce Petty about the importance of leisure time in society. Petty still works as a satirist and won an AFI Award in 2007 for his documentary *Global Haywire*.

MY BRILLIANT CAREER (1979)

Anna Senior was nominated for Best Costume Design. Senior also worked as a costume designer on *Breaker Morant*, winning an AFI Award for it. She was also costume designer on *Phar Lap* (1983) and *The Odd Angry Shot* (1979), as well as working in wardrobe on *Don's Party* (1976).

BREAKER MORANT (1980)

Bruce Beresford, Jonathan Hardy and David Stevens were nominated for Best Adapted Screenplay; the winner was *Ordinary People*.

CROCODILE DUNDEE (1986)

Paul Hogan, Ken Shadie and John Cornell were nominated for Best Original Screenplay. It was up against two Oliver Stone films, *Platoon* and *Salvador*, but lost out to the Woody Allen film *Hannah and Her Sisters*.

THE ADVENTURES OF PRISCILLA, QUEEN OF THE DESERT (1994)

Lizzie Gardiner and Tim Chappel won Best Costume Design. Gardiner and Chappel beat out the gun-slinging western apparel in *Maverick* and the 1920s New York attire in Woody Allen's *Bullets Over Broadway*.

BABE (1995)

John Cox won Best Visual Effects. It became the most successful Australian film at the Oscars with seven nominations. Beaten for Best Picture by *Braveheart*. James Cromwell, nominated for Best Supporting Actor, lost to Kevin Spacey in *The Usual Suspects*.

SHINE (1996)

Geoffrey Rush won Best Actor. It received six other nominations. Joined *Babe* as the most nominated Australian movie. *The English Patient* dominated the awards, beating *Shine* for Best Picture and Best Director. Rush has received three further nominations for *Shakespeare in Love* (1998), *Quills* (2000) and *The King's Speech* (2010).

OSCAR AND LUCINDA (1997)

Janet Patterson was nominated for Best Costume Design. However, there was no stopping the *Titanic* train, which collected a record-breaking 11 Academy Awards. Patterson has received three other nominations for costume design for *The Piano* (1993), *Portrait of a Lady* (1996) and *Bright Star* (2009).

MOULIN ROUGE! (2001)

Catherine Martin and Angus Strathie won Best Costume Design. Catherine Martin and Brigitte Broch also won Best Art Direction and thus this became the most successful Australian film at the Academy Awards. It received six other nominations, including Best Actress (Nicole Kidman) and Best Picture.

INJA (2002)

Steven Pasvolsky and Joe Weatherstone were nominated for Best Live Action Short Film. Set in South Africa just before the end of apartheid, this 17-minute short tells a tale of a young boy and his dog, and the implications of cruelty when they reunite years later.

HARVEY KRUMPET (2003)

Adam Elliott won Best Animated Short. The famous claymation short about Tourette's riddled oddball Harvey Krumpet shot Elliot to national fame.

BIRTHDAY BOY (2004)

Sejong Park and Andrew Gregory were nominated for Best Animated Short. A charming animated short film about a little boy living through the Korean War in the early 1950s.

THE SAVIOUR (2006)

Peter Templeman and Stuart Parkyn were nominated for Best Live Action Short. This story of religion and relationships won the Best Narrative Short at the Slamdance Film Festival (the second year in a row for Templeman to garner this gong).

MIRACLE FISH (2010)

Luke Doolan and Drew Bailey were nominated for Best Live Action Short. An eight-year-old boy wishes for everyone in his school to go away and wakes to find his wish granted.

See pages 236–7 for more Oscar winners.

Breaker Morant (1980)

Lieutenant Morant (Woodward) and a soldier take a break

Shoot straight, you bastards.
Don't make a mess of it.

— *Lieutenant Harry Morant*

Director: Bruce Beresford
Writers: Bruce Beresford, Jonathan Hardy and David Stevens
Producer: Matthew Carroll
Cast includes: Edward Woodward, Bryan Brown, Jack Thompson, Lewis Fitz-Gerald and Charles (Bud) Tingwell

ABOUT THE FILM

In an interview with *Filmink* magazine in 2009, actor Lewis Fitz-Gerald noted that at the time, 'the Australian film industry was in such a state that *Breaker Morant* was almost expected to be one of the last films ever made'. Hindsight tells us that this was not, thankfully, the case. Hindsight even indicates that the film might have actually saved our entire film industry.

Set in the South African Transvaal Republic in 1901 during the Second Boer War, *Breaker Morant* centres around three Australian soldiers of the Bushveldt Carbineers – Lieutenant Harry Morant (Woodward), Lieutenant Peter Handcock (Brown) and Lieutenant George Witton (Fitz-Gerald) – who are put on trial for the murder of Boer prisoners. The film is based on true events and the memoir *Scapegoats of the Empire*, which was written by George Witton, the youngest of the men to be court-martialled.

Bruce Beresford's examination of the ambiguous morality of war was received with great accolades both here and abroad. He managed to craft a tale that is so specific to the soldiers in the Boer quagmire of the early 1900s, yet so ethically relevant to any war in the history of time.

Sergeant Major Drummond (Ray Meagher) testifies in court

The film was another notch in the belt for actor-on-the-rise Bryan Brown and cemented Jack Thompson as one of our finest screen thespians. He was extraordinary in the role of Major Thomas, the lawyer sent to defend the three charged men. Thompson won the Best Supporting Actor award at the 1980 Cannes Film Festival for his role. Edward Woodward was also marvellous in the title role of Morant.

The film won a record ten AFI Awards and was nominated for an Academy Award for Best Adapted Screenplay.

LOCATIONS

BURRA SOUTH AUSTRALIA

Burra was founded in 1845 when copper was found in the area, though many of the get-rich-quick dreamers scarpered for the booming goldfields of Victoria in the 1870s. The township, thanks to a thoughtful and loyal community, has retained its charm and elegance over the years, and remains as one of South Australia's most thoroughly fascinating historic municipalities. There are many grand heritage buildings to visit as well as museums and notable mine shafts left over from mining days.

Burra was the major location used in the filming of *Breaker Morant*. The production took around four weeks to shoot. The Redruth Gaol, heavily featured in the film, is the most famous site in town. Various other locations in and around Burra were also used. Burra is about 155 kilometres north of Adelaide.

The barbarities of war are seldom committed by abnormal men. The tragedy of war is that these horrors are committed by normal men in abnormal situations.

— *Major Thomas*

Harry 'Breaker' Morant – so nicknamed for his skill with horses

VISITOR INFO

Burra Visitor Information Centre

2 Market Sq; (08) 8892 2154; www.visitburra.com

THINGS TO SEE AND DO

Redruth Gaol

This heritage-listed building was erected in 1856 and was the state's first country jail to be built outside of Adelaide. It was mainly used to house rowdy drunks and was closed in 1894, to reopen three years later as a reformatory for young (hopefully sober) girls. It closed after the girls rioted in 1922.

The location was used for all the interior and exterior gaol scenes involving the condemned Australian prisoners. Aside from a little wear and tear, the facade of Redruth has remained virtually unchanged since the film was shot here over 30 years ago.

In November 2009, the gaol hosted a 30th anniversary screening of the film. It was a tremendous celebration of the classic tale and a moving tribute to stars Edward Woodward and Charles 'Bud' Tingwell, who tragically passed away in the months leading up to it. *Tregony St; access to Redruth Gaol can be gained using the Burra*

Market Square in the heart of Burra

Heritage Passport, which gets you entry to 49 historic sites in town, or you can purchase the key to just the gaol; passports available from Burra Visitor Information Centre

Market Square

Bang in the centre of town, Market Square was used as the location for the movie's town scenes set in Pietersburg. The unmistakeable vermilion Rotunda still stands; this was the spot in the film where the military band played.

Did you know?

Breaker Morant was adapted from a play written by Kenneth G Ross. The play was produced by the Melbourne Theatre Company and premiered in February 1978 at the Athenaeum Theatre.

The interior at Redruth Gaol

Though the horns and drums of the band are long gone, Market Square is still the heart of Burra. It has a variety of places to eat and some interesting attractions, including the Market Square Museum and the Diprotodon Fossil Display. *Market St*

Heathmont Estate

This historic 1882 homestead featured in the scene when Major Thomas receives a visit from Major Bolton (Rod Mullinar) and they have a chat on the verandah about the trial. The inside lounge and dining rooms of the homestead were also used in the production, for the scene when the poor old Boer prisoner with the heavenly pipes is forced to belt out a tune in front of the dinner party. Talk about singing for your supper!

Heathmont is a private property, so you can only view it from the outside. *Vineyard Tce*

The sun sets once again on Burra Historic Mine

Bon Accord Mine Complex

A National Trust museum, the blacksmith's shop played itself in the film. It has a working forge and the museum displays mining relics and old ore samples. Visitors can imagine what Burra was like in the 1850s. Guided tours are available five days a week; check visitor centre for times. *Cnr West and Linkson sts*

Cactus Farm

This farm, around half a kilometre before you reach the main town of Burra (to the right off the Barrier Highway coming from Adelaide), was the setting for the Boer ambush scenes. The farm is a private property, so no entry without permission. *Barrier Hwy*

Outskirts of Burra

East of Burra, just off Mullaby Road heading towards the town of Baldina was the site of the infamous Morant and Handcock execution scene. Follow the road until you reach a group of farm buildings and look for tracks to the east into bare hills to find the location for the scene. Locals refer to the spot as One Tree Hill.

The area is quite remote and the production team had to use four-wheel-drive vehicles borrowed from the army to get all the camera and lighting equipment to the spot. In fact, the army provided more than vehicles – a platoon of heavy artillery soldiers played the British soldiers in the execution squad. Ironically, these soldiers had never used the British Lee-Enfield rifles used throughout the British Empire for half a century and had to be taught how to carry and shoot the rifles correctly.

Keep heading down Mullaby Road and you'll reach the cliffs used as the location for a flashback scene involving Morant and his fellow soldiers. *Off Mullaby Rd*

WHERE TO STAY

Burra Hotel

The great thing about staying in a pub is that a cold pot is only a staircase away. This historic hotel, built in 1847, offers budget accommodation overlooking Market Square. Single, double and family rooms available. *5 Market Sq; (08) 8892 2389*

Burra Heritage Cottages

Built in 1856 (the same year as the gaol), this is 19th-century Australia meets the modern day. The row cottages offer a homely place to doze by a crackling fire with all mod cons added. Just a short walk from Redruth Gaol. *8/10 Truro St; (08) 8892 2461; www.burraheritagecottages.com.au*

Burra Motor Inn

Modern motel comfort with 20 spacious rooms along the Burra Creek. There's a heated indoor swimming pool and the fully licensed Jumbuck's restaurant on site. *Market St; (08) 8892 2777; www.burramotorinn.websyte.com.au*

CARAVANS AND MOTORHOMES

Burra Caravan Park

Situated on the banks of the Burra Creek, wake up to the glorious (or not, depending on your mood) sounds of native birds at one of the 28 powered sites. Plenty of unpowered camping spots, too. *12 Bridge Tce; (08) 8892 2442*

CAMPING

Burra Creek Gorge

A camping area 26 kilometres south of Burra with prolific birdlife in the area, not to mention great trout and yabby fishing in the creek. *Access via Robertson Rd off Burra–Morgan Rd*

Mallee camping area

In the Redbanks Reserve, 15 kilometres east of Burra, with an abundance of roos hopping around. *Access off Eastern Rd*

WHERE TO EAT

Polly's Tea Rooms

An old-school town deserves some old-school tucker. Old-fashioned Cornish pasties, scones straight from the oven, and cakes and tarts, all complemented with boutique teas and coffees. *11 Commercial St*

Royal Exchange Hotel

Serving traditional pub grub seven days a week. (Similarly hearty pub meals can also be had at the Burra Hotel, Bon Accord Hotel, Commercial Hotel and Kooringa Hotel. Why not stay a while and try them all.) *1 Best Pl; (08) 8892 2392*

The Royal Exchange Hotel – great place for a cold brew

Did you know?

A few actors were considered for the role of Harry 'Breaker' Morant, including Rod Steiger (*In the Heat of the Night, On the Waterfront*), Terence Donovan (*The Man from Snowy River*) and Alan Bates (*Zorba The Greek, Hamlet*). The part was initially offered to Bates, who turned it down. Woodward happily accepted the part.

Burra Fresh

The place to go for lunch on the run, choose from tasty baguettes, quiches and country pies, and wet your whistle with a freshly squeezed juice. Local fruit and vegies on sale. *16 Market St; (08) 8892 2168*

Redruth Gaol is virtually unchanged since the film

OTHER LOCATIONS

ROSTREVOR COLLEGE
ADELAIDE, SOUTH AUSTRALIA

This catholic boys boarding school is located around 8 kilometres west of the Adelaide CBD in the suburb of Woodforde. Rostrevor House, a pristine two-storey white building on the school's premises, was used for the exterior shot of Lord Kitchener's headquarters in the film. The house was built in 1876 and revamped in 1900. The interior scenes in Lord Kitchener's residence were actually filmed inside a private Heritage Trust home in the suburb of Kensington, east of Adelaide. The Loreto Convent in Marryatville and Sacred Heart College in Somerton Park, both suburbs in Adelaide, were also used as locations for Lord Kitchener's headquarters. *Glen Stuart Rd, Woodforde; (08) 8364 8200; www.rostrevor.sa.edu.au*

SOUTH AUSTRALIAN FILM CORPORATION STUDIO ADELAIDE, SOUTH AUSTRALIA

The now defunct SAFC Studio in the suburb of Norwood was used for all the trial scenes in the film. The courtroom set was constructed from scratch. The shooting of these scenes took five days. The SAFC Studio was a public cinema until being converted into a sound stage and used by various South Australian productions. *At the top end of The Parade near Union St*

Q & A Elspeth Radford, actress and set nurse for *Breaker Morant*

Many Burra locals played a vital part in the making of *Breaker Morant*. Initially vying for a gig as a horserider on the production, Elspeth was cast by Bruce Beresford to play Lt Handcock's wife opposite Bryan Brown. She was also employed as a trained nurse on set. Elspeth runs the clothing store, Saltbush, in Burra.

Q: *Tell me about being cast as Handcock's wife?*

A: They did a try-out for the horsemen and horsewomen and I went along. We all had horses and could ride and they wanted lots of locals involved in those parts. I was really disappointed I didn't get that, but then they said that they had a part they wanted me to play – Handcock's wife.

Q: *Were there many other locals cast in the film?*

A: Yes, lots and lots. **Basically all the extras were locals – everyone from the local grocer to an older lady who had a farm out east.** There was a big street scene where they covered the street with dirt and had all the locals filling the street. All the horsemen were locals. My other cap was as a trained nurse, so I worked as a nurse on set for a couple of weeks when they were doing a lot of stunt work up at the gaol.

Q: *What was it like for you acting opposite Bryan Brown (albeit briefly)?*

A: I was nervous, I'm not an actor! Bruce Beresford was very patient. Everyone was very patient and good about it. It was a very small part. The baby [the Handcocks' child] was played by the child of a friend of ours.

Q: *Did the experience give you the acting bug?*

A: No, totally the opposite! **After being involved in the film, I really admire actors, because they spend most of their time standing around and waiting.** I had an enormous amount of admiration, but no wish to go down that path.

Q: *How long was the production in town for?*

A: The first weekend in May they held the try-outs for the horseriding. Not long after that, Heath Harris (horse stunt coordinator) came to Burra to train all the horses so they weren't gun shy. He'd go up and down these rows of horses cracking a stock whip until they wouldn't flinch. The animal training was extraordinary – watching him with his horses trained on cue to lie down and die was amazing.

The pre-production took a long time. The jail scenes took well over two weeks to shoot. **For the filming itself, they were here for over a month. Only the outdoor stuff was done here, but it was a bitterly cold winter.** Everyone was starting very early in the morning and finishing late – huge hours for all the people involved.

Q: *Was there a buzz in town during production? Did everyone embrace the cast and crew?*

A: Absolutely! **Edward Woodward stayed at the house of a friend of ours because there wasn't a lot of accommodation in town.** It was pretty basic pub accommodation at the time. It's very different now, there's a lot of very nice accommodation in town. Another thing that was terrific for the locals was all these extra people in town spending money. That's great for any small country town!

Q: *What was it like seeing the film for the first time, seeing the town, people you know and yourself on screen?*

A: It was good, everyone was so excited. It was our little town and we'd all done a little bit to be part of it. And it was a super movie, it really is a super movie.

Q: *Did you notice an influx of visitors coming to town after the film was released?*

A: After it was released, there was quite a bit of publicity because it won an award at Cannes. A lot of people came to the town to see where it was shot. We need another film like that!

Did you know?

One of the most important scenes in the history of Australian cinema is the execution of Lt Harry Morant and Lt Peter Handcock. The men hold hands as they are marched to the place where they are to be shot. In the film, this moment was improvised by Edward Woodward and Bryan Brown. It wasn't until much later that they discovered that the real Morant and Handcock had also held hands in that manner prior to their execution.

AND ANOTHER THING ...

WORLD'S FIRST FEATURE FILM AN AUSSIE!

The world's first dramatic feature film was *The Story of the Kelly Gang*, filmed in Melbourne (including St Kilda, Eltham, Greensborough, Heidelberg, Mitcham and Rosanna) and released in 1906.

It was accompanied by live narration and sound effects to heighten the drama. Originally 60 minutes long, most of it has been lost; currently 17 minutes survive.

It's said that one of the Kelly gang's suits of armour was used in the film. Though the Australian public loved the new genre of bushranger films, the boys in blue weren't too keen – screening of any bushranger film was banned in South Australia in 1911 and Victoria in 1912 and production of them was banned in New South Wales in 1912.

You can watch parts of the film here: aso.gov.au/titles/features/story-kelly-gang/

Aussie sports movies

BODYLINE (1984)

While technically a seven-part miniseries that aired on Network Ten, this retelling of the 1932–33 Ashes series in England is one of the best (and only) Australian-made productions about cricket. The title of the series, which stars Gary Sweet (as Don Bradman) and Hugo Weaving, refers to the bruising bowling tactics devised by the English cricket team in the hopes of knocking off Bradman and co (they did, winning the Ashes 4–1). The film was shot at various locations in Sydney.

PHAR LAP (1983)

This sporting celluloid classic about Australia's most famous racehorse (who, like many of our stars, was actually born a Kiwi) used a variety of locations around New South Wales and Victoria. A racecourse and grandstand in Towong in Victoria was used for some of the racing scenes, while locations in Sydney included Le Perouse, Bare Island, Centennial Park and Kurnell. The latter was also used as a location for *Mad Max: Beyond Thunderdome*. The film was written by David Williamson and directed by Simon Wincer, who also directed *The Cup* (2011). Phar Lap's real-life trainer, Tommy Woodcock (played by Tom Burlinson) had a small cameo in the film as a horse trainer.

THE CLUB (1980)

Melbourne is an Aussie Rules footy town and *The Club* is its *Citizen Kane*. Starring Jack Thompson, Graham Kennedy and John Howard, the film delves into the politics and comedy of the real-life Collingwood Football Club. The main location for shooting was Abbotsford and – within Abbotsford, not far from Collingwood – the club's home ground at Victoria Park was used as the main location for all the football scenes. While it still stands (albeit a little run down), the real Collingwood Football Club played their last game at Victoria Park in 1999.

SWIMMING UPSTREAM (2003)

Based on the true story of swimmer Tony Fingleton, who won a silver medal at the 1962 Commonwealth Games, this film stars Jesse Spencer, Geoffrey Rush and Judy Davis. The film delves into Tony's teenage years and his dealings with his troubled family. It was shot at numerous locations, including the North Sydney Olympic Pool in Milsons Point and the Spring Hill Baths in Brisbane. Fortitude Valley in Brisbane was another location, as was Perth. After his swimming career, Tony Fingleton attended Harvard University and ended up a screenwriter; he wrote the 1991 Rik Mayall comedy *Drop Dead Fred*. Fittingly, he also penned the screenplay for *Swimming Upstream*, adapted from his own autobiography.

STRICTLY BALLROOM (1992)

They call it dancesport, so go with this film's inclusion here, readers! Baz Luhrmann's feature film debut was a delightful romp packed with over-the-top dance numbers (how can we forget the Bogo Pogo), sparkly, frilly frocks and Paul Mercurio showing off his buff bod in a white tank top. Most of the film was shot in Sydney, including the suburbs of Marrickville and Pyrmont. The St George's Theatre in Yarraville, in Melbourne's west, was used as the location for the ballroom of the dance finals at the end of the film. Unfortunately, this theatre was torn down in 2008 to make way for an apartment complex.

CRACKERJACK (2002)

The highest-grossing Australian comedy of 2002 tells the story of lazy larrikin Jack, played by Mick Molloy, who joins a lawn bowls club in order to access a free parking space near his work. When the club hits financial trouble, Jack is forced to compete in bowls tournaments in order to save it. The Melbourne Bowling Club, just off Chapel Street in the Melbourne suburb of Windsor, was the major location used in the film. The scenes at the final tournament were, however, shot at the Corowa Bowls Club in the Sydney suburb of the same name. Mick Molloy co-wrote the AFI-nominated script with his brother Richard.

THE CUP (2011)

There hasn't been more of a dramatic Melbourne Cup than Media Puzzle's 2002 victory, when champion jockey Damien Oliver rode the horse to victory only days after the tragic death of his brother in a riding fall. The emotional tale, retold by *Phar Lap* director Simon Wincer, stars Stephen Curry, Brendan Gleeson and Daniel Macpherson and was shot on location at Flemington Racecourse. The seaside satellite city of Geelong, south-west of Melbourne, was another location; the production took over Geelong Racecourse and 13th Beach. The film also stars Bill Hunter as legendary trainer Bart Cummings.

THE COOLANGATTA GOLD (1984)

This family drama tells a story of sibling rivalry and the rocky relationship between a father and son. It was set around Australia's most famous endurance race (held every year in November), the Coolangatta Gold. The event attracts Australia's best ironmen and ironwomen, who power through an incredibly gruelling course of 23 kilometres on a surf ski, 3.5 kilometres ocean swimming, 6 kilometres board paddling and then 14 kilometres of beach running that takes over four hours to complete. The event is a return trip from Surfers Paradise, going through Coolangatta, Currumbin and Burleigh. The shooting of the film coincided with the inaugural running of the event and stars Colin Friels, Grant Kenny (a former Olympian), Joss McWilliams and Nick Tate. It was released under the title *The Gold and the Glory* in the US.

Crocodile Dundee (1986)

That's not a knife ... That's a knife.
– Mick Dundee

Director: Peter Faiman
Writers: John Cornell, Paul Hogan, Ken Shadie
Producer: John Cornell
Cast includes: Paul Hogan, Linda Kozlowski, John Meillon, David Gulpilil

Mick Dundee (Hogan) and Sue (Kozlowski) camp in the outback

ABOUT THE FILM

You know you've reached dizzy heights when you're parodied by *The Simpsons*, which happened to *Crocodile Dundee* in 1995. In an episode titled 'Bart vs. Australia', the family takes a trip Down Under. Bart is sitting with his sister Lisa. As he shows her small pocket knife, a blonde, ocker Aussie appears and spouts the famous line, 'You call that a knife? This is a knife.' He then brandishes a spoon, which Bart quickly recognises as, well, a spoon. The bloke then replies, 'I see you've played knifey-spoony before.'

The story of legendary outback folk hero Mick Dundee is by far the most successful film Australia has ever produced. Based on the exploits of real-life bushman Rodney Ansell, the film was made for just under $9 million – a small fortune back in those days. It didn't take long for *Crocodile Dundee* to become a worldwide sensation, a cultural phenomenon such as never before seen in this country.

The film grossed just under $175 million in the US in 1986, making it the second biggest film of the year, just behind Tom Cruise's *Top Gun*. By the end of 1986, it had reached the the number one position of Australia's highest grossing live-action film, making a staggering $328 million. (To put this into perspective, the next highest-grossing Australian film, *Babe*, made US$254 million globally.)

Paul Hogan made the character of Mick Dundee his own, bringing a warm, larrikin charm to the role. Starting with the hugely popular 'Shrimp on the Barbie' tourism campaign, which had hit international screens in the early '80s, Hogan became the decade's international ocker face of Australia. Considering this, it's surprising that Hoges didn't strike while the iron was smoking hot.

To date, Hogan has only acted in seven films since *Crocodile Dundee*, including the two sequels *Crocodile Dundee II* (a relative hit) and *Crocodile Dundee in Los Angeles* (definitely one to forget).

Dundee in his element

Mick shows some battle scars to Sue when they first meet at the Walkabout Hotel

LOCATIONS

Kakadu National Park
Northern Territory

Kakadu National Park is one of the most fascinating natural wonders on the planet. Words can't do it justice. Covering almost 20 000 square kilometres (close to 5 million acres), it's one of Australia's most important cultural, natural and traditional sites and even scored a possie on the UNESCO World Heritage List. Home to Indigenous people for over 50 000 years, Kakadu is a place of rare beauty in the northern part of the Territory, with some of the most spectacular landscapes you will ever lay your eyes on. It's packed with all kinds of flora, monsoonal forests, tidal mudflats and some very rare and endangered wildlife species.

Numerous sites around Kakadu were used for Mick's exploits in the film. These include Ubirr Rock, one of the most fascinating Aboriginal rock-art sites, and Gunlom Falls, just one of the many spectacular waterfalls in the park.

Note: certain areas of the park are not accessible during the wet season (November to April), so plan accordingly.

VISITOR INFO

Bowali Visitor Centre
Kakadu Hwy (outside of Jabiru); (08) 8938 1120; www.kakadu.com.au

Warradjan Aboriginal Cultural Centre
Kakadu Hwy, Jim Jim; (08) 8979 0145

Kakadu Park Pass

To enter Kakadu National Park, you must have a Kakadu Park Pass. These passes cost $25 and allow access to all sections of the park. All Northern Territory residents and children under 16 are exempt. Passes can be purchased from the Bowali Visitor Centre and other major tourism centres, including Tourism Top End in Darwin, Gagudju Lodge and Katherine Visitor Information Centre.

THINGS TO SEE AND DO

Gunlom Falls

This 30-metre waterfall, also known as UDP Falls or Waterfall Creek, is easily the most recognisable location from *Crocodile Dundee*. The waterfall was the backdrop for Mick and

Well, you see, Aborigines don't own the land. They belong to it. It's like their mother. See those rocks? Been standing there for 600 million years. Still be there when you and I are gone. So arguing over who owns them is like two fleas arguing over who owns the dog they live on.

– *Mick Dundee*

Sue's (Kozlowski) first romantic encounter and where Mick channels his inner bushman and catches a fish with a spear. The couple also has an absorbing conversation here about bush tucker.

Located in the Mary River area of the park, Gunlom Falls is one of the most popular swimming spots in Kakadu; the crashing white water is an absolute sight to behold when the waterfall is roaring, although access to Gunlom Falls is restricted during the wet season. There's a magnificent lookout at the top of the falls and some pools for a dip, but be careful as the climb is steep so wear sensible shoes (blokes, no thongs; ladies, no high heels). *Access via Kakadu Hwy from the south entrance of the park*

Nourlangie Rock

One of the most significant Aboriginal rock-art sites in Australia was used as the backdrop for Mick and Sue's first morning in the outback, where Mick gives himself a close shave with his big old bowie knife.

The paintings in the shelters at the base of the rock can be viewed during a 1.5-kilometre circular walk from the car park. These paintings depict the rich history and myths of the Indigenous people who have inhabited the area for thousands of years, and include creation ancestor and Lightning Man paintings. There's an adventurous climb to the Gunwarddehwardde lookout, which provides

DID YOU KNOW?

Rodney Ansell, the inspiration behind Mick Dundee (though Hoges denies it), first grabbed the headlines in 1977 when he was rescued after being stranded in the Northern Territory outback for two months. His boat capsized near the Victoria River and he and his two cattle dogs survived by hunting wild cattle for food. Tragically, he made the headlines again in 1999 when he was gunned down and killed in a shootout with police.

some amazing views of the rock as well as the surrounding escarpment.

Nourlangie Rock is just south of the town of Jabiru in the north-eastern part of the park. Jabiru is the major town centre for the thousands of tourists that come to the park each year. The town was originally built in 1982 to service the nearby uranium mine and has accommodation, a restaurant, cafe and other amenities. *Access via Kakadu Hwy south from Jabiru, signposted*

Ubirr Rock

In the far north-east of the park, by the East Alligator River, Ubirr's rock art is mostly from the last 1500 years. The Ubirr Lookout was a major location in the film; it was one of the first places that Mick takes Sue on their outback expedition.

The magnificent views are even better in real life than on celluloid – splendid panoramic vistas of the wilderness landscape surrounding the Nardab floodplain. It's a moderate 250-metre climb to the lookout and takes about 30 minutes. The sites are accessed via a 1-kilometre circular walking track from the car park. They include the Rainbow Serpent and the Narmaggan Sisters, two of the more significant Aboriginal rock-art sites in all of Australia. *Access via a sealed road off the Arnhem Hwy, around 40 km north of Jabiru*

Ja Ja

Located on the infamous Jabiluka Mineral Lease, the area of Ja Ja was used for numerous scenes in the film. The lagoon about 3 kilometres south of Ja Ja was the setting for the postcard-perfect scenes in the boat when Wally (Meillon) transports Sue and Mick. This area was also used for the scene on the second night, when Mick and Sue camp in the wilderness and Mick sneaks off to participate in an Aboriginal dance ritual. About 5 kilometres north of Ja Ja, along Oenpelli Road, Mick and Sue camp on the first night and Mick catches a snake with his bare hands.

While filming around Ja Ja, the cast and crew stayed in an old miner's camp, which has since been torn down. The Ja Ja area is not open to the public. Your best bet is a helicopter tour, which takes you over Ja Ja and the surrounding areas. *Off Oenpelli Rd, north-east of Jabiru*

Jim Jim Falls

The Sydney Opera House, Uluṟu (Ayers Rock), a boxing kangaroo, a cuddly koala ... well, these are classic Australiana images, and you should add Jim Jim Falls to that list. The towering 200-metre-tall rip-roaring waterfall is the colossus you've seen in TV tourism commercials and calendars.

Located in the south-east section of the park, the wet season is the time to visit Jim Jim and see it thundering. Vehicle access to the falls during the wet season is absolutely impossible, so you'll have to fork out for speccy helicopter or light-plane views, which are certainly worth the coin.

In the dry season, the area can be accessed by four-wheel drive, but due to the lack of rain there may be no falls – perhaps a trickle – though the plunge pool is still refreshing (when there are no crocs in residence – a good incentive to always follow the signs).

Further south of Jim Jim Falls is Twins Falls, another significant waterfall. *Jim Jim Falls access Rd (dry season only), off Kakadu Hwy; four-wheel drive essential*

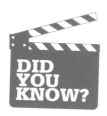

DID YOU KNOW?

While most of the reaction to the release of the film was positive, a few rogue journos and critics panned the film for not accurately representing Australia.

Good ol' Hoges hit back, responding by saying 'What are we going to do, put a nice sensible hard-working accountant in a film and say: "Here's a typical Australian, hard-working, industrious". Everyone would yawn and say "Never go to Australia".'

Yellow Water Wetlands

In the South Alligator River floodplain, the tranquil wetlands are home to some of the most remarkable and stunning wilderness you'll find in the park. An essential addition to your itinerary is a Yellow Water Cruise, which takes in the abundant birdlife (more than 60 species), flora (lovely lilies) and fauna (including frisky crocs roaming the waters). There's also a terrific Yellow Water Walk, while the nearby Warradjan Aboriginal Cultural Centre tells the stories of thousands of years of Indigenous heritage.

Yellow Water is south-west of Jabiru just outside of Cooinda. *Various tour companies run cruises from Yellow Water; Gagudju Dreaming is one of the best (see 'Tours' for more information)*

Yellow Water billabong at sunset in Kakadu National Park

Mamukala Wetlands

These wetlands, in the South Alligator region of the park, are paradise for bird lovers. Marvel at the thousands of migratory magpie geese gathering to feed (September and October). There's a boat ramp and picnic area on the banks of the South Alligator River, while there's great camping in the area throughout the dry season for those with a four-wheel drive. *Access from Kakadu Hwy, 30 km south-west of Jabiru*

Jim Jim Falls in Kakadu National Park

WHERE TO STAY

Holiday Inn Resort Gagudju Crocodile

In Croc Dundee spirit, you can't pass up the opportunity to stay at a hotel shaped like a crocodile. The deluxe hotel was once a finalist at the prestigious Quaternario Architectural Awards in Venice. This hotel offers modern rooms with a gym, Olympic-size swimming pool, and restaurant and bar. Best of all, you get to stay in a crocodile! *Flinders St, Jabiru; (08) 8979 9000; www.holidayinn.com/hotels/us/en/JABGG/hoteldetail*

Aurora Kakadu Hotel

Unwind, relax, and enjoy the tropical surrounds and the fresh Kakadu air. From this comfortable accommodation on the doorstep of the national park, you don't have to go far to get in touch with the wildlife – cute local wallabies and corellas frequent the hotel grounds. Restaurant and gift shop on site. *Arnhem Hwy, South Alligator; (08) 8979 0166; www.auroraresorts.com.au*

Lakeside Park Kakadu

Affordable cosy cabins and bush bungalows set among palm trees and lush greenery. Ensuite van sites also available. *27 Lakeside Dr, Jabiru; (08) 8979 3144; www.lakeviewkakadu.com.au*

Green Pygmy-geese in a billabong in Kakadu National Park

Mick caught taking a bath in the New York Hotel

CARAVANS AND MOTORHOMES

Kakadu Lodge and Caravan Park

This enormous park offers 200 spacious caravan sites as well as studio, one- and two-bedroom cabins and a large unpowered camping area. Lagoon-style pool and poolside bar to cool off in. *Jabiru Dr, Jabiru; (08) 8979 2422; www.auroraresorts.com.au*

Goymarr Tourist Park

In the southern region of the park, Goymarr (formerly known as the Mary River Roadhouse) is operated by the Werrenbun Aboriginal Association. It has powered and unpowered sites, motel and budget rooms and two self-contained cabins. Roadhouse and visitor information centre on site. *Kakadu Hwy, Mary River; (08) 8975 4564; www.goymarrkakadu.com*

CAMPING

As expected, Kakadu National Park is a camper's delight. There are over 20 camping sites throughout the park, ranging from self-sufficient to sites with full amenities. Highlights include the Merl camping area near Ubirr Rock, Gunlom camping area, Muirella Park near Nourlangie Rock and the Jim Jim Billabong camping area. *Contact the Bowali Visitor Centre for more details; www.kakadu.com.au*

WHERE TO EAT

Barra Bistro

Sensational open-air eatery perfect for a casual lunch or a dinner with some mates. Why not tackle the Taste of Kakadu platter, which includes delicious crocodile spring rolls and kangaroo skewers. Enjoy live entertainment between May and October. *Gagudju Lodge, Kakadu Hwy, Cooinda; (08) 8979 0145; www.gagudju-dreaming.com*

Kakadu Bakery

Quick and cheap tucker at this country bakery, serving fresh sandwiches and a variety of cakes and pastries. *Gregory Pl, Jabiru; (08) 8979 2320*

Jabiru Plaza Cafe and Take Away

Casual cafe open seven days for breakfast, lunch and dinner. *Jabiru Shopping Plaza, Tasman Cr; (08) 8979 2570*

TOURS

Guided Ranger Tours

Kakadu National Park offers free ranger guided tours, including daily rock-art site talks, walks, cultural activities and evening slide shows (dry season only, May to October). *Contact the Bowali Visitor Centre for more details; www.kakadu.com.au*

How do you like your goanna? Medium? Well done?
– Mick Dundee

Gagudju Dreaming

An award-winning tour company specialising in wetland cruises, four-wheel-drive treks and Aboriginal cultural experiences. Their three-day Yellow Water cruise begins in Darwin and ends with a sunrise cruise followed by breakfast in Cooinda. Tours offered year-round. *1800 500 401; www.gagudju-dreaming.com*

North Australian Helicopters

Scenic flights over Kakadu National Park and surrounds. Their East Alligator/Magela Floodplains Tour takes in Ubirr Rock and the Ja Ja area. *Victoria Hwy, Katherine; (08) 8972 1666 or 1800 621 717; www.northaustralianhelicopters.com.au*

Animal Tracks Safaris

Award-winning day safaris combing wildlife, Indigenous history and culture and the gathering of bush tucker. *Cooinda Lodge, Kakadu Hwy; (08) 8979 0145; animaltracks.com.au*

Adventure Tours Australia

Guided one-day to extended tours of the Kakadu National Park, including safaris, four-wheel-drive activities, camping and adventure tours. *(08) 8132 8230 or 1800 068 886; www.adventuretours.com.au*

Kakadu Air

Heli adventures and scenic flights taking in every square inch of the park – the pilots might even take the doors off! You have to shell out to see it this way, but you won't regret it. *(08) 8941 9611 or 1800 089 113; www.kakaduair.com.au*

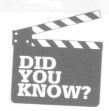

DID YOU KNOW?

Early in the film, there's a scene when Sue talks on the phone from a high-rise Sydney apartment, with the classic steel frame of the Harbour Bridge prominent in the background.

Many people don't know that Paul Hogan actually worked as a maintenance rigger on the construction of the bridge in the early '70s.

McKinlay Queensland

This tiny township in north-west Queensland between the towns of Mt Isa and Winton was made famous for playing Walkabout Creek in *Crocodile Dundee*.

The town was named after the adept explorer, John McKinlay, who led the South Australian Relief Expedition to find Burke and Wills when they went missing in 1861. He didn't find them, but they named a river and this town after him regardless.

McKinlay is located on top of one of the world's largest underground aquifers and is also home to some of Australia's most progressive primary producers and leading miners.

The famous pub where we first meet Mick Dundee still stands and is a hugely popular tourist destination.

VISITOR INFO

Julia Creek Visitor Information

Cnr Burke and Julia sts, Julia Creek;
(07) 4746 7690; www.mckinlay.qld.gov.au

THINGS TO SEE AND DO

Walkabout Creek Hotel

Pubs are like churches in Australia – we go there regularly to seek solace, the flowing frothy beer is our sacramental wine and prayers are offered by murmuring sports fans urging their respective teams over the line. With that being the case, it's safe to say that the Walkabout Creek Hotel is our Vatican.

Built in 1900, it used to be known as the Federal Hotel, but a name change in December 1986 was appropriate after thousands of tourists began to flock here. The Walkabout was moved from its original location on Middleton Street to the main part of the highway in 1996.

While the joint has undergone some minor changes, fans will be utterly pleased to know that the pub is still completely recognisable from the film. Additions to the pub's interior include film-related paraphernalia on the walls. The exterior may look a tad different, though; set dressers put a facade over the roof and painted the outside of the pub to make it look older and more decrepit for the film.

Inside, you'll find friendly locals, some of the coldest beer on tap and all the classic counter meals. There's also very basic accommodation on the second level. Amen. *Cnr Kirby and Wilde sts; (07) 4746 8424*

South of McKinlay

One of the aerial shots used in the film's opening credits was filmed a few kilometres south of town (the shot with the two small water silos and the flocks of birds gliding through the air). The area is called the McKinlay Town Common.

Mick feels like a fish out of water at a party in New York with Sue

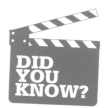

Walkabout Creek Hotel in McKinlay

DID YOU KNOW? Despite the passing of 25 years and the release of countless fantastic films since, *Crocodile Dundee* is still the second highest grossing film at Australian box offices.

The other aerial shots in the opening credits were taken between Cloncurry and Mt Isa, west of McKinlay.

McKinlay Library

The smallest public library in Queensland is open Thursdays 11am to 3pm. It's tough to make ends meet just being a librarian in McKinlay! *Middleton St; (07) 4746 8848*

Julia Creek

This traditional sheep and cattle grazing, and mining area is less than 100 kilometres north-east of McKinlay and definitely worth a visit. It hosts the annual Dirt and Dust Festival (www.dirtndust.com) in April, one of the biggest country festivals in all of Oz. The festival includes horseraces, a ute muster, bull riding contests, a triathlon and the Australia's Best Butt competition. Cheeky or what! Other attractions worth a visit are the Duncan MacIntyre Museum, the Opera House and the Nature Trail. *North of McKinlay via McKinlay–Gilliat Rd*

Kynuna

This tiny outback town is most famous for its links with legendary Aussie bush poet Banjo Paterson. Sit under the shade of the coolibah tree at the Combo River Conservation Park (16 kilometres east of town), the rural setting that inspired the classic song 'Waltzing Matilda'. *South-east of McKinlay on Landsborough Hwy*

WHERE TO STAY

Walkabout Creek Hotel

Tell 'em Mick sent ya. The famous pub offers 14 basic air-conditioned rooms with shared bathroom facilities. There are also eight powered caravan sites. *Cnr Kirby and Wilde sts, McKinlay; (07) 4746 8424*

Gannons Hotel/Motel

Gannons Hotel was built in 1925 but burnt down only five years later. Rebuilt in 1932, it's lasted a little longer the second time around. The hotel featured in the film *A Town Like Alice*, which was shot in the area in 1956. Spacious rooms with ensuite and pay-TV channels. Counter meals at the bar and dining room, including Angus and Wagyu steaks. *36 Burke St, Julia Creek; (07) 4746 7103; www.gannonshotelmotel.com.au*

CARAVANS AND MOTORHOMES

Julia Creek Caravan Park

Numerous powered campsites as well as four cabins, barbecue facilities and a naturally heated artesian spa to soothe those achy breaky travelling joints. *Old Normanton Rd, Julia Creek; (07) 4746 7108*

Kynuna Roadhouse and Caravan Park

24 powered and unpowered sites, large grassy camping areas and four single cabins. Meals available at the roadhouse. *Matilda Hwy, Kynuna; (07) 4746 8683*

WHERE TO EAT

McKinlay Roadhouse

Typical roadhouse grub: dine-in or takeaway hot and cold food, including a large selection of drinks, ice-creams and various snacks to satisfy the cravings. *Matilda Hwy, McKinlay; (07) 4746 8472*

JT's on Burke

Located in Julia Creek, this casual cafe offers dine-in and takeaway hot and cold food. *Burke St, Julia Creek; (07) 4746 7678*

That's not a statue ...
That's a statue!

Girraween Lagoon
Howard Springs, Northern Territory

Located on Girraween Road in Howard Springs (just south of Darwin), this large body of water was the location for the scene when Sue foolishly goes for a dip and nearly gets her head bitten off by a disgruntled croc. Be careful, crocs do occasionally hang out at the lagoon, depending on rains.

Holsworthy Army Base
Sydney, New South Wales

These barracks in the outer south-west of Sydney were used for the scenes involving the drunken poachers who shoot kangaroos near Mick and Sue's camp.

Philip Street Sydney, New South Wales

Located right next to the botanic gardens, the Penthouse at The Quay apartment building on Philip Street was used at the start of the film to portray Sue's apartment overlooking Sydney Harbour.

New York City USA

A large chunk of the film was shot on location in Manhattan, New York City. The hotel that Mick stays in is the Plaza Hotel on Fifth Avenue, while filming also took place at Greenwich Village, the East Village, Central Park and the 9th Avenue Subway Station.

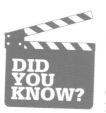

DID YOU KNOW? Paul Hogan says the idea for *Crocodile Dundee* came to him when he visited New York City and felt like a complete fish out of water.

International films shot in Australia

Mick Dundee brought croc wrestling, snakeskin vests and bush tucker to the rest of the world. Now let's look at what has come the other way.

THE MATRIX (1999)

Probably the most famous international production ever shot in Australia. All the locations for *The Matrix* were in Sydney. The top of AON Tower at 201 Kent Street in the CBD was the site of the famous scene when Neo dodges the bullets. The Allianz Building on Market Street was used for the helicopter crash scenes. The underground subway scenes at the climax of the film were shot at Rozelle and Redfern train stations, while the restaurant where Cypher meets Agent Smith for dinner was played by Forty One Restaurant in Chifley Tower on Chifley Square. Fox Studios in Moore Park was also used for many scenes.

ON THE BEACH (1959)

This production was a major coup for the city of Melbourne – in the '50s it didn't get much bigger than Gregory Peck, Ava Gardner and Fred Astaire coming to shoot a film about the end of the world. The film was shot in the outer suburbs of Berwick and Frankston. Platform 1 on Frankston Railway Station (since demolished) was used for a scene. Young Street in Frankston was the location for another scene. Berwick was a new development at the time and some of the streets being built were named after people associated with the film, including Kramer Drive named for the film's director, Stanley Kramer.

THE THIN RED LINE (1998)

The stellar cast for this harrowing and bloody recreation of the battle of Guadalcanal in World War II included George Clooney, Sean Penn, Adrien Brody and John Cusack. The film was shot predominantly in the Daintree rainforest in far north Queensland, its lush tropical greenery a near-perfect replica for the real location in the Solomon Islands. Other locations used in the area included Cairns, Port Douglas and Mossman. The film was nominated for seven Academy Awards.

GHOST RIDER (2007)

The city of Melbourne helped bring this international blockbuster, based on the popular Marvel Comics antihero, to life. The story of vigilante motorcyclist Johnny Blaze, played by Nicholas Cage, used numerous spots in and around the city. Etihad Stadium in the Docklands was used for Blaze's daring helicopter jump. Flagstaff Train Station and the Melbourne Cemetery on Lygon Street are two other recognisable locations. Central City Studios was used for much of the studio work and outside of Melbourne, locations included Bacchus Marsh, Little River and Geelong.

FOOL'S GOLD (2008)

This adventure rom-com, starring Matthew McConaughey and Kate Hudson as deep sea treasure hunters, was shot in Queensland. Hamilton Island, Fraser Island, Hervey Bay and Port Douglas were the gorgeous backdrops used for the film. Some scenes were filmed at locations in Brisbane, including the Brisbane City Botanic Gardens and Queensland University of Technology. Warner Bros. Studio at Movie World on the Gold Coast was also used.

CHARLOTTE'S WEB (2006)

This remake of the immensely popular children's classic (1952 book and 1973 animated feature) starred 11-year-old Dakota Fanning and the Victorian countryside. The tiny town of Greendale, about an hour's drive north-west of Melbourne, was the setting for the country farm, while Heidelberg Park in the suburb of Heidelberg, in Melbourne's east, was used for the carnival scenes. The seaside inner-city suburb of Williamstown was also prominently featured.

SUPERMAN RETURNS (2006)

The return of the caped crusader also meant the return of Sydney to the international film stage. This mammoth production, directed by Bryan Singer and starring Brandon Routh and Kate Bosworth, was shot in numerous locations around Sydney. Elizabeth Street and Martin Place in the CBD were used as the streets of Metropolis. The Rivendell Hospital in Concord West was used as Lex Luthor's mansion, while the Art Gallery of New South Wales was made up to look like the Metropolis Museum. Lois Lane's house was shot in the suburb of Sylvania Waters, while the town of Smallville was shot in Tamworth.

ABBA: THE MOVIE (1977)

A huge cult hit among ABBA fans, this film delves into the lives of the Swedish superband on tour in Australia in the mid-'70s. Directed by Lasse Hallstrom, the script was said to be conceived on a plane on the way to Australia to film it, if that makes any sense at all. Filming took place in most of the major capital cities, including concert footage at Sidney Myer Music Bowl in Melbourne and Football Park (now AAMI Stadium) in Adelaide.

MISSION: IMPOSSIBLE II (2000)

Being chosen for the sequel to the action-adventure flick starring Tom Cruise was yet another coup for Sydney on the world film stage. Darling Harbour featured prominently in the film, as did the Royal Randwick Racecourse and Governor Phillip Tower. Probably the most recognisable location was Bare Island, which is south-east of the CBD, near the northern tip of Botany Bay. Climactic scenes, including the exhilarating motorcycle chase at the end of the film, were shot on the island. Broken Hill and Silverton also featured in the film.

THE KILLER ELITE (2011)

The latest big Hollywood film to be shot in Australia is the remake of a 1975 film, *The Killer Elite*, which starred James Caan and Robert Duvall. Version 2.0 stars Robert De Niro, Clive Owen and Jason Statham. The plot revolves around a former Navy Seal dragged out of retirement to help save a friend. The film was shot in 2010 in various locations around Melbourne, as well as the Yarra Valley just outside the city.

PITCH BLACK (2000)

A sci-fi action flick starring Vin Diesel and Radha Mitchell as space travellers stranded on a lifeless and uninhabitable sun-scorched planet. Hmm ... where to shoot it? Coober Pedy, of course. A spaceship prop was left behind and sits outside the opal cave shop on Hutchinson Street. While the temperature looks beyond hot on screen, it was actually filmed during winter when the temperatures were extremely cold.

JAWS (1975)

Da-dum, da-dum, da-dum ... It's a little-known fact about the early Spielberg flick that scared the bejesus out of every single beachgoer in 1975 that part of the film was actually shot in Australia. Some of the underwater footage of the frightening, sharp-toothed predator was filmed in the Southern Ocean and at Dangerous Reef, a body of water just off the South Australian coast near Port Lincoln. Director Steven Spielberg has recently brought productions back to our shores; the 2010 Emmy-winning miniseries *The Pacific* was shot in Queensland and Victoria and his US$150-million TV series *TERRA Nova* (2011) was shot in south-east Queensland.

SALAAM NAMASTE (2005)

Who doesn't love choreographed dance numbers, brightly coloured outfits and characters that inexplicably break out into song at the drop of a hat. Yep, it doesn't get any cheesier than the cinema of Bollywood. Since the late '90s, Australia has been a hotbed for many Bollywood productions. *Saalam Namaste* is the first Indian film to have been shot entirely in Australia. The film used locations around Melbourne, including Federation Square and the General Post Office, as well as the Great Ocean Road and Mornington Peninsula in Victoria's south.

NIM'S ISLAND (2008)

This family-friendly adventure romp blurs the lines between the real and fantasy worlds when precocious young girl Nim (*Little Miss Sunshine*'s Abigail Breslin) must rely on an agoraphobic author (Jodie Foster) to save her adventurer father (Gerard Butler). Though set in the South Pacific, the film was shot entirely in Queensland, with parts of Port Douglas, Hinchinbrook Island and Bowen (yes! Bowenwood!) used for the shoot. The role of Selkie the sea lion in the film was played by Spud and Friday, two friendly pinnipeds who call Sea World home. The film grossed over US$100 million worldwide.

Gallipoli (1981)

The famous Gallipoli Beach near Coffin Bay

I'll see you when I see you.

— *Archy*

Not if I see you first.

— *Frank*

Director: Peter Weir
Writer: David Williamson
Producers: Patricia Lovell, Robert Stigwood
Cast includes: Mel Gibson, Mark Lee,
Bill Hunter, Bill Kerr, Peter Ford

ABOUT THE FILM

Just a year after the release of *Breaker Morant* – an enduring classic in its own right – Peter Weir delivered what many people view as the greatest film this country has ever produced. Divided into three fairly distinct acts, *Gallipoli* begins in Western Australia, where track sprinters Archy (Lee) and Frank (Gibson) meet and quickly become best mates. The two naive country boys decide to travel to Perth to enlist (illegally, as they are underage) in the Light Horse Brigade to fight in World War I.

The fresh-faced soldiers are quickly shipped off to Cairo, where they undergo basic training and enjoy their last days of freedom before being thrown into the desperate pits of trench warfare.

The final chapter takes place in Anzac Cove on the Gallipoli Peninsula during the fateful Battle of Lone Pine and the doomed Battle of the Nek. This real-life tragedy took place in August 1915 and hundreds of young soldiers lost their lives at the hands of the Turkish soldiers.

Much like *Breaker Morant*, *Gallipoli* is so specifically Australian in its telling of the ANZAC legacy and the brave fight put up by the Diggers in World War I, yet its themes of mateship, loss of innocence and coming of age are also universal. All elements of the movie work magnificently together, from the strong mateship between Aussie larrikins Frank and Archy, to the differing cross-continental landscapes, and the realism and drama of the

Archy (Lee) and Frank (Gibson) do a little sightseeing on arrival in Egypt

All right men ... we're going. But I want you all to remember who you are. You are the 10th Light Horse! Men from Western Australia. Don't forget it. Good luck.

— *Major Barton*

final battle scenes. *Gallipoli* truly is a masterpiece of Australian cinema.

Mel Gibson admits that it launched his career. Weir came up with the idea to make the film after visiting the real war site in Turkey, while en route to London for the premiere of *Picnic at Hanging Rock*. The project took three years to secure funding. In 2008, 27 years after its release, AFI voters hailed the film as one of the top five Aussie flicks of all time.

LOCATIONS

COFFIN BAY
SOUTH AUSTRALIA

The sleepy South Australian holiday town of Coffin Bay lies at the southern tip of the Eyre Peninsula, approximately 700 kilometres west of Adelaide over the Spencer Gulf. There's nothing morbid about its name, the town was named after a bloke, not a box. Matthew Flinders honoured his mate Isaac Coffin with a shout out as he sailed by.

With a population of around 650 people, this quiet, fairly modest fishing village explodes during the summer months with a flood

Frank races to deliver a message during battle

of tourists streaming towards the beaches for the amazing boating, sailing, swimming, waterskiing and fishing. Yet it still retains the unspoilt character of days gone by and holidays of our youth.

Coffin Bay was once known as the oyster capital of Australia, but serious dredging over the years has severely damaged the industry – and the zinc intake of Coffin Bay oyster aficionados. Luckily, the beautiful azure waters still produce some of the best cultivated oysters in the country. The town lies in close proximity to Gallipoli Beach, one of the most famous locations in Australian cinema. This stretch of sand was used to recreate the ANZACs' landing on Gallipoli Beach in Turkey and the inauspicious Battle of the Nek.

VISITOR INFO

Coffin Bay Visitor Centre
Beachcomber Agencies, The Esplanade; (08) 8685 4057; www.coffinbay.net

THINGS TO SEE AND DO

Gallipoli Beach
North-east of Coffin Bay, just past Mt Dutton Bay, is Gallipoli Beach. This was the location for one of the grandest and most complex set of scenes ever captured on Australian film. Hundreds of extras were used on the beach, the sand dunes, the rocks, in the trenches and dug-outs, many of them trained and drilled like real soldiers to increase the authenticity of the footage. The battle scenes took approximately four weeks to shoot and the results are a magnificent real-time war re-creation.

The beach itself is a great spot for boating, swimming and fishing, with King George whiting usually the main catch of the day. Gallipoli Beach was originally part of Farm Beach, but the section was renamed by the council in honour of the production. Farm Beach is a quirky strip of sand to visit in the summer months when many fishermen use their old 'farm' tractors to launch their boats into the water. *Gallipoli Beach is approximately 40 km north-west of Coffin Bay; access via a dirt road at the north end of Farm Beach, adjacent to the car park*

Yallunda Flat Showground
This small rural centre to the east of Coffin Bay and close to Tumby Bay was the location for two pivotal scenes in *Gallipoli*. The local showgrounds were used to replicate the Perth track meet where Archy and Frank first compete against each other. The same showground was used again later when Archy and Frank enlist in the army.

Sand dunes in Coffin Bay National Park

The annual Yallunda Flat Show is one of the highlights of the region's calendar with sheep shearing and giant pumpkin and scarecrow competitions. It's held on the Monday of the Labour Day long weekend in early October. *Bratten Way, Yallunda Flat; (08) 8688 4252; www.sacountryshows.com*

Coffin Bay National Park

This diverse 31 000 hectare park is strewn with towering sandstone cliffs and gigantic dunes, fringed by pounding surf beaches and waterways. There are too many highlights to enjoy, from four-wheel driving along Gunyah Beach, to walking the trails at Yangie Bay, Black Springs and the Whidbey Wilderness Area. There's some excellent fishing at any of the beaches and waterways, and wilderness camping in plenty of spots throughout. Sea birds breed here and the place goes bloomin' crazy with wildflowers in spring. *Entrance via Long Beach Rd; entry and camping fees apply; contact Department for Environment and Heritage West Region Office, 75 Liverpool St, Port Lincoln; (08) 8688 3111; www.environment.sa.gov.au/parks/sanpr/coffinbay*

Oyster Walk

More than just a short stroll, this lengthy 12-kilometre walk along the foreshore and bushland explores many of the town's historical sites including Old Oyster Town. Take a day and stop along the way for a barbecue, picnic, fishing or swimming. *Brochure from visitor centre or through website at www.coffinbay.net/pdf/Oyster-Walk-brochure.pdf*

Mt Dutton Bay

Just off the Flinders Highway on the way to Farm Beach is Mt Dutton Bay. Visit the woolshed museum, which displays many items relating to local history. The woolshed was once a thriving shearing station, with 14 hard-working shearers processing up to 20 000 sheep a year – you get an aching back just thinking of it! While you're in the 'hood, check out the adjoining State Heritage–listed jetty, a fully restored relic of the town. *Off Flinders Hwy just past the town of Wangary*

WHERE TO STAY

Coffin Bay Beach Units

Five fully self-contained units right on the shores of the beach. Each unit sleeps up to six people. *347–351 Esplanade; (08) 8685 4173; www.coffinbay.net/accommodation/beach_units.htm*

Modra's Apartments

Spacious, modern and affordable studio and family units just a short walk to the beach and boat ramp. Perfectly located to explore the Eyre Peninsula and only a short drive to Yallunda Flat. *2 Yaringa Ave, Tumby Bay; (08) 8688 2087; www.tumbybaysideholidayunits.com.au*

Shelly Beach Lodge

On over 100 acres of stunning bushland in Mt Dutton Bay, this eco-friendly

Scenic walk near Almonta Beach, Coffin Bay NP

pine-panelled lodge runs on solar and wind power. With the stunning views of the waterfront from the bedrooms and balcony, you'll feel like the last person on earth. *Lot 22 Shelly Beach Rd, Mt Dutton Bay; (08) 8685 4192; www.shboo.com.au*

CARAVANS AND MOTORHOMES

Coffin Bay Caravan Park

Centrally located park with 130 powered and unpowered sites, an ensuite cabin and a three-bedroom cottage. *91 The Esplanade; (08) 8685 4170; www.coffinbay.net/caravanpark*

CAMPING

Coffin Bay National Park

There are camping sites at Yangie Bay, Big Yangie, Black Springs, Morgans Landing, The Pool and Sensation Beach. Access and rules differ for various campgrounds, so check and plan accordingly. *Entry and camping fees apply; contact Department for Environment and Heritage West Region Office, 75 Liverpool St, Port Lincoln; (08) 8688 3111; www.environment.sa.gov.au/parks/sanpr/coffinbay*

WHERE TO EAT

The Oysterbeds

Does it get any better than slurping Australia's tastiest oysters while taking in such gorgeous waterside views? Open Wednesday to Sunday (closed in winter). *61 The Esplanade; (08) 8685 4000; www.oysterbeds.com.au*

Soldiers arrive at Gallipoli

Did you know?

In the film, British Colonel Robinson is the man that gives the orders at the Battle of the Nek, sealing the tragic fate of the Australian troops. In reality, it was an Australian officer who gave the orders. Weir subsequently came to regret the decision to play out the story like that.

Coffin Bay Pizza and Homemade Foods

Freshly made pizza, pies, cakes and pastries, open Wednesday to Sunday. *Shop 4/61 The Esplanade; (08) 8685 5042*

BELTANA SOUTH AUSTRALIA

Right in the heart of the Flinders Ranges, 500 kilometres north of Adelaide, Beltana is a special and unique outback settlement town. Be careful not to confuse Beltana with a ghost town – though so many of the houses look abandoned, there are about 80 people living here (up from a low of nine in 1984), so take care where you wander. Note the 'keep out' signs posted by people sick of hapless home-invading tourists disturbing their afternoon in front of *Deal Or No Deal*.

Beltana became a State Heritage area in 1987, probably due to its stubborn refusal to lay down and die, even after the miners left, the train station moved and the brewery, hospital, school and cop shop closed down. The area has a rich multicultural history, with people of Aboriginal, South Asian and European descent having once resided here.

The charming heritage townscape is dotted with distinguished buildings, from the Old Beltana Hotel to the railway station complex. The town was the location for the Hamilton Homestead in the beginning of the film, its desolation and ageing buildings providing an excellent replica for the small towns in the outback of Western Australia.

To the west of Beltana are the salt plains of Lake Torrens, another key filming location.

VISITOR INFO

Leigh Creek Visitor Centre
13 Black Oak Dr; (08) 8675 2723;
www.users.on.net/~lcvic

How fast can you run?

– Jack

As fast as a leopard.

– Archy

How fast are you going to run?

– Jack

As fast as a leopard!

– Archy

Remains of the boiler-chimney for an old copper mine near Beltana

THINGS TO SEE AND DO

Beltana Station

This historic station covers over 410 000 acres and was once the home of the thriving Beltana Pastoral Company. One of the outstations on the land was used as the exterior of Hamilton Homestead. The scenes inside the homestead were actually shot inside Beltana Homestead.

The surrounding arid landscape was used in the opening scenes of the film where Archy trains for the track meet and when he dares the sneering cattleman that he can beat him home on foot. The homestead still stands today, though the outstation was dismantled for its materials many years ago.

Historical buildings

Beltana town has a number of old buildings worth a look. Most of these buildings are now privately owned, so don't mosey on in without permission. Buildings worth a gander are the old police station, railway station, post and telegraph office, school and church. All buildings can be seen on a short stroll around town.

On a four-wheel-drive track to Mt Hack, east of Beltana

Lake Torrens

The vast salt flat of Lake Torrens lies around 30 kilometres west of Beltana. The lake itself is over 240 kilometres long. It probably shouldn't be called a lake – it's only been filled with water once in the last 150 years! The lack of any H_2O made it the perfect spot to replicate the Western Australian desert when Archy and Frank boldly cross by foot to enlist in the army. Four-wheel drive is recommended to access the lake, permits required. *For permits contact (08) 8204 1910; www.environment.sa.gov.au*

WHERE TO STAY

Leigh Creek Tavern

Modest motel and cabin accommodation. Mosey on down to the beer garden for a cold beer and some hearty pub grub. *Oak Black Dr; (08) 8675 2025*

CARAVANS AND MOTORHOMES

Leigh Creek Caravan Park

Powered and unpowered sites with cabins from basic to a little more fancy. Socialise with other holiday folk at the camp kitchen and communal TV and lounge area. *Acacia Dr; (08) 8675 2016; www.leighcreekcaravanpark.com*

Copley Caravan Park

An award-winning park with powered sites, camping areas and cabins in the quiet and tranquil surrounds of Copley. *100 Railway West Tce; (08) 8675 2288; www.copleycaravan.com.au*

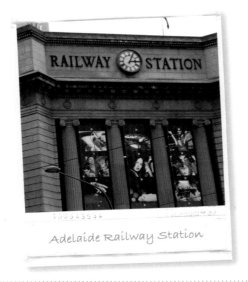
Adelaide Railway Station

WHERE TO EAT

Copley Bush Bakery and Quandong Cafe

There's nothing better than strolling through a quiet country town and being hit with the irresistible aroma of pies and cakes fresh out of the oven. This bakery is arguably the best in the Flinders Ranges, with yummy quandong pies (made with a native fruit) to try, as well as homemade jams and meat sauces for sale. *Railway Tce, Copley; (08) 8675 2683*

Did you know?

Gallipoli cost $2.8 million to make, which – at the time – made it the most expensive Australian film ever produced.

Beltana Roadhouse

Fair-dinkum roadhouse offering delicious Beltana Burgers and pies, cold drinks and snacks for those on the go plus maps and town information. *Main St; (08) 8675 2744*

OTHER LOCATIONS

ADELAIDE RAILWAY STATION SOUTH AUSTRALIA

The busy station on North Terrace in the Adelaide CBD was used to recreate Perth Railway Station for *Gallipoli*. The station, which has been operating since 1856, has around 40 000 people passing through on any given weekday.

Attached to the station is the former Marble Hall, a grand old domed waiting room, which was the location for the ballroom party that Archy and Frank crashed the night before sailing off to Gallipoli. The hall has been refurbished since the film and now houses SKYCITY Casino's gaming area. *North Tce*

QUORN SOUTH AUSTRALIA

The scene of Frank and his buddies camping out by the train tracks was filmed just outside this small township in the Flinders Ranges, next to the Pichi Richi Railway – a historic steam locomotive that carries passengers from Quorn to Port Augusta. The short Pichi Richi Explorer trip is a return service to Woolshed Flat departing from Quorn (Sundays); the Afghan

Express is the longer return trip from Port Augusta (Saturdays).

See pages 208–9 for a feature on other films shot in the Flinders Ranges.

CAIRO EGYPT

All the Egypt scenes were actually shot on location in Cairo, from the football game in front of the pyramids to the bazaar scenes. When asked why the entire film wasn't shot in Egypt, Weir said it was too difficult to get Anglo-Saxon extras, of which there were almost 4000 used in the film.

Director Peter Weir and crew members shooting in Egypt

AND ANOTHER THING ...

THE POPULARITY OF CINEMA

- Although T.J. West was the first man to construct a purpose-built hall for screening movies in 1906, it was entrepreneur J.D. Williams who opened Australia's first continuous cinema in Sydney in 1909. Tickets were threepence for an adult and a penny for a child.

- In 1928, the first 'talkies' were introduced, seeing a 70 per cent rise in cinema admissions. This didn't last, with the depression soon hitting. By 1931, many movie houses were laying off staff due to poor attendances.

- The advent of World War II, surprisingly, saw an increase in cinema admissions. People wanted to escape the harsh realities of war and watching movies was the answer.

- The first drive-in cinema was opened in Burwood, Melbourne in 1954. Two years later Australia had 23 drive-ins. By the late 1950s, general cinema attendance was down due to the introduction of television.

- By 1977, there were 884 cinemas across Australia. Over 24 millions cinema tickets were sold that year.

- 2001 and 2002 were the highest attended years in Australian cinema history, with over 92.5 million tickets sold, which roughly translates to just over 4 admissions per person.

Numbers and information courtesy of Screen Australia, www.screenaustralia.gov.au/gtp/wchistsince1900.html

Q & A Russell Boyd, cinematographer for *Gallipoli*

Russell has been the Director of Photography on some of the greatest Australian films, including *Picnic at Hanging Rock, Gallipoli* and *Crocodile Dundee*. He has collaborated with director Peter Weir on many other feature films, including *Master and Commander: The Far Side of the World*, for which he won an Academy Award in 2004.

Q: *Gallipoli is an Australian classic. Was this the biggest movie you'd undertaken?*

A: Yes it was! **It was certainly big in scale, we had over a hundred extras in the wide shot of Gallipoli Cove on the beach, maybe two. It was an exercise in logistics.** We could get our lighting and equipment down on the beach, but we couldn't get a generator down there, it was just too heavy. So we had to run cables all the way down from the top of the sand ridges to the beach. In those days, lighting equipment was not nearly as powerful, so we didn't have a whole lot of light there. For the night exteriors on the beach, we had every single lamp burning. It still worked out okay actually.

Q: *Would a film like Gallipoli be much easier to film today?*

A: I don't know whether I would say *easier* because directors have gotten used to all the equipment and demand a lot more these days. **No matter how big a budget, how much equipment you can afford or how much time you've got to do it ... the job expands to fit or exceed the parameters.** No film is easy, the bigger the budgets, the more the demands made on you.

Q: *What was it like shooting in Egypt for Gallipoli and, in general, travelling overseas to shoot movies?*

A: One of the great things I've had working in film over a long career is the travel that's involved – you get to see a lot of the world. Egypt was a terrific place to be an observer, I enjoy countries that are quite exotic or unique, different to Australia.

One thing stands out in my memory about shooting in Egypt. We were getting ready to shoot the exterior scenes in the market. It was teeming with people, paid extras and non-paid extras; it was very crowded. We were setting up a shot first thing in the morning and **this little kid led a sheep into the marketplace. I thought, 'Oh, isn't that lovely, this kid is bringing his pet sheep'. Then he pulled out this big knife and slit its throat.**

Q: *What was it like working with a young Mel Gibson?*

A: He's a scallywag! Over the years I worked with him quite a bit. **Mel's definitely a bit of a larrikin, but a terrific guy.** He doesn't like a lot of cerebral stuff from a director and I don't think Peter gave him that kind of thing anyway. He doesn't like to talk about character a lot, he just likes to hear that cameras are rolling and then he gets into it. I heard him say that once when we were doing *Forever Young*.

Q: *Did you have any idea how strongly* Gallipoli *would resonate with Australians?*

A: It certainly did resonate with me, even when I first read the script. Gallipoli is close to my heart. **I don't have any relatives that fought there, but I certainly felt – and still do – that it was part of our nation's coming of age.** I'm not a big fan of war in any way, I'm very much anti-war, so I knew how important the story was, and I thought Peter was a terrific director to tell a terrific story. It's got all sorts of stuff in it, right from the beginning when the boys cross the desert. **It's a very emotional film. I still feel it's one of the real icons of the Australian film industry.**

Q: *Do you approach shooting in a busy city like New York (for* Crocodile Dundee*) differently to shooting in a remote place like Kakadu National Park? Do you prefer one over the other?*

A: I love New York and I love Kakadu, so there's no preference. **I just let the location dictate how we shoot it.** I don't go in with a preconceived idea.

I seem to remember in *Crocodile Dundee* we tended to use wider-angled lenses in Kakadu and use slightly longer lenses in New York to compress it a bit. I think locations are an important element of the story. Kakadu was made for *Crocodile Dundee*, or Dundee was made for Kakadu.

Q: *When shooting* Crocodile Dundee, *could you foresee just how massive this film was going to be?*

A: **I had an inkling it would be big. It was a very funny script and the timing was perfect.** John Cornell (Hogan's writing partner) is a very savvy marketing person. Hoges had just done the 'Throw Another Shrimp on the Barbie' series of commercials that were all over America, so they thought now was the time to hit. I think Hoges had the script in his head for a while. It was a real coup.

Q: *Are there any Australian landscapes or spots you would love to shoot one day?*

A: I always love to go back to the outback. And the Great Ocean Road area down in Victoria. I would like to shoot on the north-west coast of Western Australia, the Kimberley area north of Broome – I would love to experience that whole area. I like all the capital cities too.

See the continuation of this interview on pages 194–5.

Aussie directors abroad

You have to admit that for such a small country, we contribute a lot on the world stage in the areas of science and technology, sports and, of course, film. And it's not just our actors that Hollywood loves.

BRUCE BERESFORD (1940–)

Director of such Aussie classics as *Breaker Morant* (1980), *Don's Party* (1976) and *The Club* (1980), Beresford has also had great success as a director in the US. In 1984 he directed Robert Duval to an Academy Award in the drama *Tender Mercies*, a film for which he received an Oscar nomination for Best Director. His other more popular films include *Crimes of the Heart* (1986), *Driving Miss Daisy* (1989), *Double Jeopardy* (1999) and *Evelyn* (2002). His latest film is a comedy entitled *Peace, Love & Understanding* starring Jane Fonda and Catherine Keener.

PETER WEIR (1944–)

The man behind *Picnic at Hanging Rock* (1975) and *Gallipoli* (1981) took his directing skills halfway across the world with an enormous amount of success. His first Hollywood feature was *Witness* (1985) starring Harrison Ford, which won a couple of Oscars from eight nominations, including Best Director. His other well-known films include *Dead Poets Society* (1989), *The Truman Show* (1997) and *Master and Commander: The Far Side of the World* (2003). Weir himself has been nominated for six Academy Awards. His latest film *The Way Back* (2010), which he also wrote, is about a group of soldiers who escape from a Siberian gulag in 1940.

PHILLIP NOYCE (1950–)

While some of Noyce's early films will go down as classics of Australian cinema – *Newsfront* (1978) and *Dead Calm* (1989) – it's his Hollywood resume that is most impressive. *Patriot Games* (1992), *Clear and Present Danger* (1994), *The Bone Collector* (1998), *The Quiet American* (2000), *Catch a Fire* (2007) and *Salt* (2010) are all Noyce vehicles. He also has a plethora of projects in pre-production and development, including an adaptation of the Philip Roth novel *American Pastoral*. Of all his directing accomplishments, Noyce still lists *Rabbit-proof Fence* (2002) as the movie he is most proud of.

ALEX PROYAS (1963–)

Proyas' first feature film was the independent sci-fi thriller *Spirits of the Air, Gremlins of the Clouds*, which was nominated for two AFI Awards in 1988. His second feature film and his first Hollywood project was the 1994 fantasy thriller *The Crow*. The production was marred by the tragic death of lead actor Brandon Lee. His biggest film to date is the

Will Smith action thriller *I, Robot* (2004), which grossed $343 million worldwide. Proyas has returned to Australia to direct numerous times and his credits include the Aussie comedy *Garage Days* (2002), *Dark City* (1998) and *Knowing* (2009). Though born in Greece, he became an Aussie at age three when his family moved here.

JAMES MCTEIGUE (1967–)

McTeigue cut his teeth as assistant director on numerous Australian productions, including *Country Life* (1994), *Looking for Alibrandi* (2000) and The Matrix trilogy. His first feature film, shot mainly in London, was the very excellent 2005 comic adaptation *V For Vendetta*, starring Hugo Weaving and Natalie Portman. His credits since include directing Nicole Kidman in *The Invasion* (2007) and *Ninja Assassin* (2009), starring South Korean megastar and occasional actor Rain. Next on the slate for McTeigue is *The Raven*, a movie about the poet Edgar Allan Poe.

ROBERT LUKETIC (1973–)

The Sydney-born Victorian College of the Arts graduate has quite a strange resume. He blipped onto the radar of Tinseltown big wigs with his award-winning short film *Titsiana Booberini* (1997), which led to a job directing Reese Witherspoon in the smash-hit comedy *Legally Blonde* (2001). A string of films since has made him one of Hollywood's leading rom-com directors – his credits include *Win a Date with Tad Hamilton!* (2003), *Monster-in-Law* (2005), *The Ugly Truth* (2009) and *The Killers* (2010). The strange part? Luketic has never directed a feature-length film in Australia.

ROGER DONALDSON (1945–)

Though many may not recognise his name, the Australian-born director (and now New Zealander) has arguably the most impressive overseas resume of any of his ilk. He broke onto the scene with *The Bounty* (1984), a remake of *Mutiny of the Bounty* (1935, 1962), starring Mel Gibson and Anthony Hopkins, which earned a Palme d'Or nomination at Cannes. Other Donaldson-helmed films include *No Way Out* (1987), *Cocktail* (1988), *Dante's Peak* (1997), *Thirteen Days* (2000), *The Recruit* (2003), *The World's Fastest Indian* (2005), *The Bank Job* (2008) and *The Hungry Rabbit Jumps* (2010).

FRED SCHEPISI (1939–)

One of the pioneering directors of the Australian film industry, Schepisi blew away local audiences with *The Devil's Playground* (1976) and *The Chant of Jimmie Blacksmith* (1978). He quickly decided to take his talents to Hollywood, with his first foray into American cinema being the 1982 western *Barbarosa*, starring Gary Busey and musician Willie Nelson. Schepisi went on to direct a spate of hugely successful films, including *Roxanne* (1987), *The Russia House* (1990), *Six Degrees of Separation* (1993), *IQ* (1994) and *Fierce Creatures* (1997). He returned to Australia to shoot *The Eye of the Storm* (2011), which stars Geoffrey Rush, Judy Davis and Charlotte Rampling.

Japanese Story (2003)

Hiromitsu (Tsunashima) and Sandy (Collette) hydrate in the Pilbara

Director: Sue Brooks
Writer: Alison Tilson
Producer: Sue Maslin
Cast includes: Toni Collette, Gotaro Tsunashima, Matthew Dyktnyski, Lynette Curran, Yumiko Tanaka

ABOUT THE FILM

In 2003, cinema lovers were fawning over *Lost in Translation*, the very excellent Sofia Coppola–directed film about two American souls lost in the foreign world of Tokyo, Japan. While it deservedly won Oscars and Golden Globes, a little-known Australian film about a very similar – yet, at the same time, very different – clash of cultures, was flying under the radar in cinemas across the land.

Japanese Story centres around Sandy Edwards (Collette), a cranky Perth-based geologist who is forced to chaperone Japanese businessman Hiromitsu Tachibana (Tsunashima) across the vast mining plains of Western Australia. What begins as an uncomfortable and frustrating situation quickly evolves into a mutual tussle against the harsh and unforgiving terrain of the Pilbara desert. This battle with the outback bonds our two urbanite protagonists, who briefly explore a love story against the natural beauty of the rust-red landscape.

The second collaboration between director Sue Brooks, screenwriter Alison Tilson and producer Sue Maslin (the first was 1997's *Road to Nhill*), *Japanese Story* was accepted in the *Un Certain Regard* category at the 2003 Cannes Film Festival.

The film is a beautifully drawn-out tale of love and loss balanced with humour, elegance and tragedy. The film's theme of what lies underneath the surface is superbly matched by the untouched, authentic backdrop of the Pilbara, a terrain renowned for its mysterious layers.

It comes as no big surprise that Collette is outstanding as Sandy, while Tsunashima puts in a deft performance as the foreign man figuratively and spiritually lost in a foreign land.

The movie is scored by a brilliant musical composition by Elizabeth Drake and directed to near perfection by Brooks. *Japanese Story* won eight AFI Awards.

Sandy and Hiromitsu, stranded by a breakdown, try to get comfy for the night

I am not traipsing around the bloody desert with some Japanese prick who doesn't know his ass from his elbow and wants a glorified tour guide. I'm a geologist, not a bloody geisha.
— *Sandy*

The Pilbara Western Australia

The Pilbara is 500 000 square kilometres of sheer, unfiltered splendour in the north-west of Australia. Said to be almost 2.8 billion years old, the region is known for being one of the world's most prolific iron ore mining areas. The attractions of the region are divided into distinct areas: the seaboard towns of Port Hedland and Karratha, the awe-inspiring natural wonders of Karijini and Millstream–Chichester national parks, Hamersley Range between these two national parks, and unspeakably large tracts of deserts: the Great Sandy, the Little Sandy, the Gibson and the Tanami.

The small town of Marble Bar, just 150 kilometres south-east of Port Hedland, is literally hot property – in the 1920s it set the world record for 161 consecutive days of temperatures over 100 degrees Fahrenheit (37.8 degrees Celsius). The heat must have gone to the person responsible for naming town's head 'cause there ain't even any marble there – it's jasper, a type of quartz!

The majority of *Japanese Story* was filmed on location in the Pilbara region.

VISITOR INFO

Karratha Visitor Centre
4548 Karratha Rd, Karratha; (08) 9144 4600

Port Hedland Visitor Centre
13 Wedge St, Port Hedland; (08) 9173 1711

Newman Visitor Centre
*Newman Dr, Newman; (08) 9175 2888;
www.newman-wa.org*

Sandy and Hiromitsu relax by Kalgan's Pool

Impressive orange-hued rocks in Millstream–Chichester National Park

Before I came to Australia I was sad. I have heavy obligations. But I must get through it. Here in the desert, a desert … you have shown me something beautiful. Thank you.
– *Hiromitsu*

THINGS TO SEE AND DO

Port Hedland

With a population topping 12000, Port Hedland is one of the most populated towns in the Pilbara. The port here handles the lion's share of Australia's iron ore export tonnage. The scene in which Sandy and Hiromitsu's four-wheel drive gets bogged on the dirt road was shot on the dusty Old Marble Road to the east of Port Hedland on the way to Marble Bar. Access to this road can be a bit tricky and the reality of being bogged is very real, so extreme caution must be taken (supplies: winching kit, charged mobile phone, food and drink, ice blocks, maybe a good book).

Port Hedland offers many interesting attractions, from the open-air Don Rhodes Mining Museum to the self-guided heritage trail around town. It's also a top spot for aquatic activities, including some of the best fishing in the region. From October to March you can view the nesting flatback turtles.

Dampier

Around 20 kilometres north-west of Karratha, this small coastal township is the gateway to the fascinating group of uninhabited islands known as the Dampier Archipelago. Dampier Beach was used as a location early in the film for the scene when Sandy, chilling on the sand, slyly cops a look at the topless Hiromitsu emerging from the ocean. Dampier Beach is a haven for aquatic activities, from swimming to boating, while the foreshore is just so inviting it would be poor form to ignore the barbecue and picnic facilities.

Later in the film, when Sandy and Hiromitsu make their way further into the Pilbara, the scene in which the duo sit on the rusty-red jagged rocks was shot on Hearsons Cove Road south-east of Dampier. *Access to the beach and foreshore via Central Ave onto Church Rd to The Esplanade*

Mt Whaleback Mine

By golly, it's big! BHP Whaleback is the largest open-cut iron ore mine in the world. This location outside Newman was used for several scenes in the film. The mine itself, a gigantic, cavernous hole in the ground, must be seen to be believed. The mine runs one-and-a-half-hour tours, which depart from the Newman Visitor Centre. Long sleeves and pants are required on the tour and no thongs (the thong ban is a tough call, but rules are rules). Minimum of four people per tour.

The Newman Airport was used in the scene when Sandy first meets Hiromitsu. *Newman Visitor Centre, cnr Fortescue Ave and Newman Dr; (08) 8175 2888; www.newman-wa.org*

Kalgan's Pool

The famous waterhole where Hiromitsu dives into the shallow waters was shot at Kalgan's Pool, 54 kilometres north-east of Newman. This picturesque waterhole, shadowed by tall cliffs and gum trees, can only be accessed via four-wheel drive. The track to access Kalgan's Pool can get flooded; always walk the crossing to check the depth before driving across. It's an excellent spot for bush camping and a sensible dip when the rain has been plentiful. *Access via Marble Bar Rd; permit required to access the area available from Newman Visitor Centre*

Mt Herbert Lookout

The stunning lookout at the top of Mt Herbert was used in the scene when the suddenly smitten Sandy and Hiromitsu take in the gorgeous panorama of the savannah lands. Mt Herbert is located in the rich green oasis of Millstream–Chichester National Park, a wonder of rolling hills, snappy white-barked gum trees and lush wetlands. The moderate Class 3 climb to the summit of Mt Herbert is around 600 metres and is a 25-minute return trip. The national park is a great base for

The isolated Pilbara landscape

camping, picnicking and swimming. *Access via Roebourne–Wittenoom Rd south of Karratha, a comfortable two-hour drive; (08) 9184 5144*

Karratha

Karratha means 'good country' – the original inhabitants certainly named it well. The town was initially built on land from a cattle station of the same name. Since 1968, the town has played home to the hard-working miners digging for iron ore out in Hamersley Range and natural gas workers out on the north-west shelf.

Today, Karratha is also a designated base camp for travellers exploring the Pilbara region, including Millstream–Chichester National Park. The Karratha International Hotel was used for the scenes of Sandy and Hiromitsu's first raunchy romp plus the inevitably awkward morning-after breakfast scene. *Karratha Visitor Centre, 4548 Karratha Rd; (08) 9144 4600*

Harding River

This body of water by the ghost town of Cossack was the location for the scene when Sandy and Hiromitsu paddle out in the small boat. Cossack used to be a thriving pearling town up until 1881 when a severe cyclone damaged much of the area and destroyed the industry.

The town is around 50 kilometres east of Karratha. Check out the Tien Tsin Lookout for sweeping views of the coast. Budget travellers can stay in the old police barracks – could be fun to sleep in a cop shop without being arrested first! *Access via Cossack Rd*

Roebourne

Established in 1866, Roebourne is the oldest town in the Pilbara area and was once the centre for mining and pastoral industries in the region. The scene when a totally traumatised Sandy, with Hiromitsu's body in the trunk, asks for help from a local was shot outside the Victoria Hotel on Roe Street.

WHERE TO STAY

Karratha International Hotel

This smart and sassy hotel was a major filming location. It has a couple of restaurants and several bars (poolside, cocktail and saloon). The teriyaki duck wood-fired pizza served by the pool is as good as it sounds. *Cnr Hillview and Millstream rds; (08) 9187 3333; www.karrathainternational.com.au*

Hotel All Seasons Port Hedland

This Accor hotel has 65 rooms, many with ocean views. Grab a quiet meal at their bistro. The nearby Port Hedland Racecourse holds country race meetings six times a year. *Cnr Lukis and McGregor sts, Port Hedland; (08) 9173 1511; www.accorhotels.com*

Dampier Mermaid Hotel and Motel

With such spectacular sea views overlooking King Bay and Hampton Harbour you won't notice the daggy bedspread. Tough choice ... sports bar or beer garden (with all-you-can-eat barbecue on Sundays). *The Esplanade, Dampier; (08) 9183 1222; www.dampiermermaid.com.au*

Mia Mia Hotel

Affordable luxury: pristine standard rooms and VIP apartments newly decorated in outback tones with a gym, restaurant (you can phone them for takeaway fish and chips and burgers). *32 Kalgan Dr, Newman; (08) 9175 8400; www.miamia.com.au*

CARAVANS AND MOTORHOMES

Pilbara Holiday Park

Nice park in Karratha with paved powered sites, camping, cabin and chalet accommodation, pool, recreation room and barbecue facilities. *Rosemary Rd, Karratha; (08) 9185 1855; www.aspenparks.com.au*

Newman Caravan Park

Powered sites with barbecue facilities and a playground for the kids. *Kalgan Dr; (08) 9175 1428*

Port Hedland Caravan Park

Powered sites with modest cabin accommodation; a perfect spot for fishing, boating and birdwatching. *945 Great Northern Hwy, Port Hedland; (08) 9172 2525*

Cooke Point Holiday Park

Resort park accommodation catering for everyone from backpackers to business travellers. Powered sites along with studio rooms, holiday and motel units. Located on the picturesque Pretty Pool inlet in Port Hedland. *2 Taylor St, Port Hedland; (08) 9173 1271; www.aspenparks.com.au*

CAMPING

Dampier Archipelago

Swimming in crystal-blue waters and sleeping under a starry night sky – please, take me there! Numerous beach camping spots are scattered

Red rocks and flare towers near Dampier in the Pilbara region

Sandy tries to stay warm and contemplates their predicament

throughout the 42 islands, including on the West Lewis and East Lewis islands. Self-sufficient campers only. *Access via boat from Dampier; boat hire and tour information available from the Karratha Visitor Centre*

Millstream–Chichester National Park

A variety of brilliant bush camping spots, including the Crossing Pool and Homestead camping areas. Caravan and vehicle access. *Access via Roebourne–Wittenoom Rd*

Roebourne

Great bush camping spots around the Roebourne region, including Cleaverville, Forty Mile, Fortescue River Mouth and the Balla Balla camping areas. Caravan and vehicle access to all sites. *All accessed via North West Coastal Hwy*

In Australia, you have a lot of space. No people. In Japan, we have many people, no space.
– *Hiromitsu*

WHERE TO EAT

Capricorn Roadhouse

This particular roadhouse was used for the scene when Sandy and Hiromitsu return to civilisation after their bogging ordeal. They share a meal and Hiromitsu explains the Japanese word 'hai' to Sandy. The location was also used for an exterior shot later in the film of Sandy filling up her vehicle with petrol. The roadhouse offers standard hot snacks such as pies and sausage rolls. *Great Northern Hwy, Newman; (08) 9175 1535*

Pilbara Room Restaurant

Billing itself as 'THE place to dine' in Port Hedland, the menu heaves with fresh seafood, prime meat cuts and local produce. Pre-dinner libations at the cocktail bar essential. Also serves breakfast. *Webster St, Port Hedland; (08) 9173 1044; www.porthedland. wa.hospitalityinns.com.au*

Universal Chinese Restaurant

Spring rolls and dim sims aplenty at this typical Asian restaurant; locals recommend the satay beef and Mongolian lamb to fill your belly after a long day of sightseeing. *1 Balmoral Rd, Karratha; (08) 9185 4333*

Moby's Kitchen

Legendary seafood joint in Point Samson, just near Roebourne. Kids run up an appetite on the lawn out front while adults park their bums on the benches. Freshly caught fish and crustaceans cooked and available for beachside dining or takeaway. *Bartley Crt, Point Samson; (08) 9187 1435*

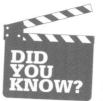

DID YOU KNOW? *Japanese Story* **was not the first Australian production featuring Japanese actor Gotaro Tsunashima. He played the role of Lieutenant Aso in the acclaimed ABC television drama** *Changi* **in 2001.**

Perth Western Australia

Said to be the sunniest city in all of Australia, Perth's isolation from the rest of the country adds to its spacious and relaxed charm. The town has everything you could ever want from urban living – a bustling CBD, gorgeous parks, stunning beaches and an enviable food and wine scene.

Perth earned the nickname 'The City of Lights' when residents lit their houses and streetlights for astronaut John Glenn when he orbited the earth in 1968. In 2010 *The Economist* magazine voted Perth as one of the most liveable

Writer Alison Tilson, director Sue Brooks and producer Sue Maslin at the Mt Whaleback Mine

cities in the world. All the city scenes involving Sandy were shot in Perth.

VISITOR INFO

Western Australia Visitor Centre

*Albert Facey House, cnr Forrest Pl
and Wellington St; (08) 9483 1111;
www.wavisitorcentre.com*

THINGS TO SEE AND DO

Burswood Entertainment Complex

This complex on the banks of the Swan River is one of the major tourist attractions of the city. Burswood consists of a world-class casino, hotel, convention centre, golf course, day spa and the Burswood Dome indoor stadium, which is the venue for the Hopman Cup tennis tournament in January.

The scenes towards the end of the film involving Hiromitsu's wife Yukiko (Tanaka) were shot in the hotel's penthouse suite. It's an embarrassment of riches at Burswood, from poker marathons to sensational restaurants and bars, a swing of the three-iron on a sunny Sunday morning to ballet, opera, musical theatre and concerts – it's all here. *Great Eastern Hwy; (08) 9362 7777; www.burswood.com.au*

Perth Airport

Travellers arriving in the city by air won't have to go far to see one of the film's locations. The Qantas domestic arrivals and departures gate of the airport was used in the final scenes when Sandy and her work colleague, Bill (Dyktynski), farewell Yukiko. This is also the location for the poignant scene when Sandy reads the letter left behind for her by Hiromitsu. *2 George Wiencke Dr; (08) 9478 8888; www.perthairport.com*

Swanbourne

A house in this coastal suburb, just past Claremont in the city's south-west, featured in the scenes with Sandy and her Mum (Curran). It has great beaches and is close to the famous sands of Cottesloe Beach.

Kings Park and Botanic Garden

High on the list of must-see Perth attractions, Kings Park is just south-west of the Perth CBD. This 400 hectare natural bushland reserve right on the Swan River is scattered with landscaped gardens, lakes, playgrounds, shaded picnic spots and cafes. They have a wildflower festival in September and an open-air cinema in summer. A little slice of heaven in the big smoke. *Fraser Ave; (08) 9480 3600; www.bgpa.wa.gov.au*

Perth Mint

Money, money, money. It is indeed a rich man's world at Australia's oldest operating mint. Visit this turn-of-the-century building to see Australia's largest gold nugget collection, featuring the Normandy Nugget – the second largest gold nugget in the world – weighing a whopping 25.5 kilograms. There's also the world's largest gold bar exhibition, guided talks and you can watch molten gold being poured. Hands off the merchandise! *310 Hay St, East Perth; (08) 9421 7223; www.perthmint.com.au*

Crowds pack Cottesloe Beach during summer

Perth's Kings Park and Botanic Gardens

Crew members working to get a shot

Fremantle

Not far south-west of Perth is the bustling port city of Fremantle – or Freo as it's known by most locals. With beautiful 19th-century streetscapes lined with grand old buildings and heritage houses, this major boat and fishing centre at the mouth of the Swan River has something for everyone. Visit the Western Australian Maritime Museum for a journey back into the state's boating past, grab a bargain at the famous Fremantle Markets or just sip a latte and let the refreshing afternoon breeze, known as the 'Fremantle Doctor', blow out the cobwebs. Films shot in Fremantle include *Thunderstruck* (2004), *Last Train to Freo* (2006), *Two Fists, One Heart* (2008) and *Bran Nue Dae* (2010). *Fremantle Visitor Centre, Kings Sq, High St; (08) 9431 7878; www.fremantlewa.com.au*

WHERE TO STAY

Miss Maud Swedish Hotel

A little bit of Sweden goes a long way. Boutique Scandinavian-themed pub hotel that's a Perth institution. Come for the comfy rooms and friendly staff (maybe some in traditional Swedish getup), but don't miss the free smorgasbord breakfast heaving with 65 dishes. Located in the CBD. *97 Murray St; (08) 9325 3900; www.missmaudhotel.com.au*

Intercontinental Perth Burswood

All the luxury you would expect from a high-class casino hotel. High-end suites have private terraces with Perth skyline views. Worth the splurge! *Cnr Bolton Ave and Great Eastern Hwy; (08) 9362 8888 or 1800 999 667; www.ichotelsgroup.com/intercontinental*

Swanbourne Guest House

This small four-star lodging in a beachy suburb offers comfy garden and terrace rooms. Enjoy the nearby Creswell Park and Lake Claremont as well as Swanbourne's beaches. *5 Myera St, Swanbourne; (08) 9383 1981; www.swanbourneguesthouse.com.au*

CARAVANS AND MOTORHOMES

Perth Vineyards Holiday Park

Around 14 kilometres north-east of the Perth CBD on the Upper Swan River, this park offers powered sites, camping, cabin and chalet accommodation. Base yourself here to explore the wineries on your doorstep. *91 Benara Rd, Caversham; (08) 9279 6700; www.aspenparks.com.au*

Perth Central Caravan Park

Only a ten-minute drive to Perth city, this park offers powered and tent sites, as well as one- and two-bedroom cabins. *34 Central Ave, Ascot; (08) 9277 1704; www.perthcentral.com.au*

WHERE TO EAT

Victoria Station Steakhouse

This house of meat at the Burswood Entertainment Complex is sure to satisfy the carnivores. Open for breakfast (continental buffet), lunch and dinner. Burswood also has seven other dining choices, from the fancier Alure and Sirocco restaurants to the informal Carvers buffet and Snax. *Located near the main casino entrance; Great Eastern Hwy; (08) 9362 7551; www.burswood.com.au*

The Naked Fig Cafe

Alfresco dining with 180-degree ocean views – what a way to spend a balmy night on Perth's sunset coast. Open for breakfast, lunch and dinner, but sunset is best, for obvious reasons! Tuesday is vego night and Wednesday is curry night. Free wi-fi. *278 Marine Pde, Swanbourne; (08) 9384 1222; www.nakedfig.com.au*

Belgian Beer Cafe

Hoegaarden, Stella Artois and Leffe Blond (Belgian beer) are what it's all about. Open for lunch and dinner, the classic pub fare includes pork schnitzel served with sautéed cabbage and succulent T-bone steaks, but most popular are the pomme frites with Belgian mayonnaise and the moules (mussels) done three ways. 'Oyster Hour' is Monday to Friday from 5.30 to 6.30pm. Let's get promiscuous! *Cnr King and Murray sts, Perth; (08) 9321 4094; www.belgianbeer.com.au*

FILM FESTIVAL

The Revelation Perth International Film Festival

Held annually in July, the festival showcases local and international features, as well as live-action and animated shorts and documentaries. *www.revelationfilmfest.org*

CINEMAS

Cygnet Cinema

In the suburb of Como in Perth's inner-south this funky Art Deco cinema, built in 1938, still retains its old-world charm. On the third Sunday of every month for 'Classics of the Silver Screen' they screen old silent films and some of the earliest 'talkies'. *16 Preston St, Como; (08) 9367 1663; www.cygnetcinema.com.au*

Piccadilly Cinema

This 70-year-old grand Art Deco movie house is the only cinema in the Perth CBD. Screens new releases. *700 Hay St; (08) 9322 3577; www.piccadillycinemas.com*

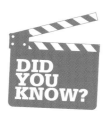

DID YOU KNOW? **Some of the film was 'lost in translation' when it premiered at the Cannes Film Festival in 2003. The movie was received with a standing ovation, though one of the scenes received an inappropriate reaction. The audience laughed when Hiromitsu dived into the waterhole and didn't come back up. The European audience, unfamiliar with the dangers of such an act, thought the character was pulling a joke on Sandy.**

Q & A **Sue Maslin, producer of** *Japanese Story*

Sue Maslin is an award-winning feature film and documentary producer. Her first major feature film, *Road to Nhill*, won the Best Film award at the Thessaloniki International Film Festival in 1997 (the leading film festival in south-east Europe). She has also produced fascinating documentaries, including *The Edge of The Possible*, the story of the Sydney Opera House.

Q: How did you get involved in *Japanese Story*?

A: Sue Brooks, Alison Tilson and I had previously made a feature film together, called *Road to Nhill*, which was also set in the country (out in a little town called Pyramid Hill in northern Victoria). We had set up Gecko Films and had an interest in making feature films together. *Japanese Story* was a project that Alison had written and we started talking about it when *Road to Nhill* was completed. **I read the script and was just completely blown away, I've never read anything that was so astoundingly unexpected.**

At first I thought, 'I know where this is going'. It was about two very unlikely characters who are thrown together in the Australian desert and, of course, in the face of adversity they're going to find out things about each other and fall in love. **But nothing prepared me for the direction that the story took.** It really did take my breath away, I just thought it was the most extraordinary and beautiful script.

So the three of us wanted to try and create a cinema experience for the audience that would be similar, that would really say something about how we live our lives.

We think we know what's going to happen and we are always surprised when the rug gets pulled from under our feet and we're thrown into uncharted territory. That's really what *Japanese Story* **was about, made so much more beautiful by the fact that we were able to set it in the Pilbara.**

Q: The Pilbara is tough terrain. Were you always set on shooting the majority of this film there or did you explore other options?

A: Like every filmmaker before us who has sought to make films in the Australian desert, we took one look at the remote locations, the costs involved and the difficulties of filming in the desert and realised that it was going to be very tough. We went and looked at other options; this is the reason why most Australian desert films end up being shot either in the Flinders Ranges or around Broken Hill. Time and time again, the settings end up being there because there's infrastructure to support the films in those locations. Of course we went and checked those locations and took a good look around South Australia, but **we just kept coming back to the fact that the landscape we wanted to set the story against had to be incredibly elemental and incredibly big and strange.**

We drove thousands of kilometres from Perth up to the Pilbara area. It takes days of driving. You drive 700 kilometres a day and nothing changes. We set out from the coast, from Karratha, and drove inland towards Newman, which is at the heart of the Pilbara. We drove for about six or seven hours and at the end of the day, the sun was setting in the west and it lit up these iron ore ranges in brilliants reds. Set against the intense blue sky, you realise you're in the most extraordinary landscape. **It has that incredible effect on everyone who**

goes there. **We just fell in love with it, it was truly elemental.** We went back on three different occasions and talked to different mining companies about the possibility of shooting there. You can imagine what it was like ... three middle-aged women rolling up and saying, 'Hey, we'd like to take over your mine for filming.' We also talked to the local Indigenous communities, we talked to the locals and tried to work out how it might be possible to realise this dream of setting *Japanese Story* where it belonged.

Q: What lies beneath the surface is a central theme of the film. The Pilbara, being 2.8 billion years old, is a place renowned for what's underneath. Was this another reason to shoot there, to have that true authenticity?

A: In each of the films that we've done together, **authenticity is an incredibly important part of the storytelling**. You want audiences to believe in the emotional journey and the integrity of the story. And that's a lot easier if you're not having to cheat everything. In *Japanese Story*, the landscape was really another character in that story. There's nothing that happens to Hiromitsu and Sandy that's not in some way influenced or dictated by the landscape. So it was important that we did get the landscape right; thematically it's very important. Alison often talks about 'the alchemy of the story', the transformation at the heart of iron ore becoming steel and how it underpins everything we need for daily life. **There's a metaphorical level at work here, we just wanted to set the story where it belonged and that's in this iron ore–rich landscape.**

Q: What were some of the challenges of scouting the locations in the Pilbara?

A: The vastness of the landscape and distances involved! One of the great rules of filmmaking is to try and minimise the amount of time you spend changing locations and setups so you have much more time with the camera and the actors. However, we knew this was effectively a road movie, so the two characters were going to need to move across vast distances and become immersed in different places. It meant that the three of us were on the road a lot – **we travelled thousands and thousands of kilometres in order to find the locations**. Then, when we found a perfect location – such as that beautiful waterhole for a pivotal scene in the film – we had to drive a four-wheel drive through riverbeds just to get there! In fact, we came across another four-wheel drive that had got bogged in a riverbed and we had to winch them out. **There were no effective roads to get to that location, so we had to build a road.** By then, because we had spent so much time up in that area and getting to know the locals, they were terrific and really helpful. The local shire engineer turned around and said, 'No worries. When do you need the road built by?' And they built the road for us!

Q: Did you find locations you wanted to use but couldn't for logistical reasons?

A: We did find some magnificently cinematic locations in the Karijini National Park, which is a series of deep river gorges that cut straight down thousands of feet into the rock. Such stunning locations, but the logistics of actually getting cameras, crew and performers into that space was just not viable.

Finding the right iron ore mine required a bit of negotiation. **It's not a straightforward thing to take a film crew into a working mine, let alone the biggest open-cut iron ore mine in the Southern Hemisphere.**

Q: Was it hard getting approval to shoot at the BHP iron ore mine in Newman?

A: What it took was the building of a relationship between a mining company and a film production company. There's no shortcut to that, it took months, over the course of a year. We had a wonderful media liaison person to deal with. She really assisted us in putting our case to the senior management. And, of course, we needed to meet very stringent safety audits and protocols and scheduling requirements.

None of this can prepare you for the very first time you see an open-cut mine. It's shocking, there's no other word for it. It's awe-inspiring. It can also be very upsetting – that was the case for some of our cast and crew. It's a very giant hole in the earth that has excavated rock shipped out 24 hours a day, seven days a week, 365 days a year. It is visually spectacular.

We were given every assistance by BHP to the extent that they were eventually asking us when they should time an explosion for us and they made sure they did a pretty good explosion.

Q: The shoot must have been difficult for the crew. What challenges did the production face?

A: One of the main challenges was being exposed for long hours in a landscape with a lot of wind, a lot of red dirt and a lot of sun. The real challenge was that if anything went wrong there was no backup. It wasn't a matter of just getting an extra generator or camera lens couriered over. Every department had to have not just one or two, but three backups of every single item of sound, lighting gear, cameras lenses, camera equipment, camera bodies, all of that. So that meant shipping truckloads of equipment to the other side of the continent. We did it on ships. We put trucks full of equipment on ships in Melbourne and they came off in Perth and then the crew drove the 2500 kilometres north. It was quite a substantial logistics exercise.

Another challenge was all these city-based cast and crew experiencing what

it's like to be in the desert. It's a profound experience. There were those of us who just loved it, revelled in the quietness and all of that space. And there were others for whom it was quite confronting and frightening. That was a personal challenge for a number of people, but most people really came to love it.

In terms of the more immediate production challenges, one of the first things we did was to recognise the danger of being in that location, the huge distances that people were driving and so on. Many feature films have ended in tragedy or terrible accidents. **On the very first day with full cast and crew we got the local copper to come in and read the riot act, to talk about all the things that could possibly go wrong – from dehydration to hitting a camel in the middle of the road at night.** He did such a good job that the entire make-up and wardrobe department decided there and then that they weren't going to drive for the rest of the film shoot! So we had to bring in an extra driver. We were very grateful that we completed the shoot with no major injuries and everyone got home safely.

Q: As a producer, is it hard balancing the safety of the cast and crew while trying to get the best shots?

A: It does add a dimension to the shoot. At the end of the day, **Australian crews and cast are just renowned for their 'can-do' attitude** and their absolute commitment to getting the best possible production values up on the screen. **We really are blessed in this country – the spirit, the adventurousness, the creative risk-taking that's common in Australians.** We will just push and push to get that great performance or that perfect setting for a scene.

I can tell you, it was unbelievably uncomfortable for Toni and Gotaro to be swimming in that waterhole – the water was freezing! Despite all the gear we had set up to give them warmth and comfort, when they got out of the water it was not much fun, particularly when they had to do it a second time round. But they did it. And the cast and crew, as always, were just incredible in the lengths that they all went to in order to make the best possible film. Sue Brooks [the director] managed the whole shoot with a broken bone in her foot. That's stamina!

Q: How did Toni and Gotaro handle the conditions?

A: It was a tough shoot for the actors. Gotaro, first of all, had to learn English to the level that he was able to deliver a fantastic performance, which he did. It was his first experience ever in Australia, let alone in the Australian desert. **He had to learn a breathing technique that would enable him to play a dead body for a substantial amount of time.** He had to remain relaxed enough to be handled by another actor with a great deal of physicality as she tries to move his body. We brought in a yoga instructor who worked with him and he was absolutely extraordinary in learning a breathing technique that could ensure that.

It was a very big challenge for Toni to do that scene in the waterhole as well. Having to deliver a performance while she's in freezing cold water, through to the physicality of handling the other actor. It was Toni who worked out how to physically manoeuvre his body into the back of the four-wheel drive.

Q: So was that scene written in the script or was it improvised?

A: That was in the script, and again this is part of the authenticity that the director, Sue Brooks and writer, Alison Tilson were striving for. **We didn't want to cheat it and just cut-away like every other film to make it easy. We actually wanted to show the incredible isolation and difficulty faced by an individual and, in this case, a woman,**

having to deal with a tragic accident of this kind. So that meant workshopping trying to move a dead weight, which is a very difficult thing, let alone getting it into a high four-wheel drive. In the rehearsals Sue was working with Toni and at one point Toni said that she couldn't do it and we'd just have to shoot around it. Sue said no, we have to work it out. Anyway, Toni and Sue worked it out and the struggle is breathtaking to watch on film.

Q: Obviously to pull off a movie like this you need a great crew but also an extraordinary director. How did Sue Brooks handle everything that came her way?

A: Sue is an extraordinary director. Her great capacity is to stick to the emotional truth of the script. And it's all in the script – Alison is a gifted scriptwriter and everything you see in that film I can assure you was all there in the script. But to actually realise that on film ... the first challenge was to find the right actors to play those roles. **Sue went to Tokyo three times for casting trips before she found the right Japanese actor.** While she was being pushed for financing and marketing reasons to choose a bigger-name Japanese actor, she knew that Gotaro was absolutely right for the part, even though this was his first film role (he was an experienced theatre actor and had done some TV). Her judgement was absolutely correct on that.

The thing with Sue is her incredible focus. When you're a director and you're in this very difficult location, you've got 70 people around with all sorts of different production requirements and endless questions, it's tough. **It's also very important not to lose sight of the story in the face of this very beautiful environment and not to get carried away with it.** We see so many Australian films that I think get a bit seduced by the landscape and start including all sorts of shots that aren't in service of the story. **It's a real discipline**

not to lose sight of your story and the emotional journey of the characters and stay true to the original script. That's what Sue's real gift is.

Q: The film won several AFI Awards and premiered at Cannes. How gratifying was that for you as the producer?

A: The first thing that's gratifying is actually much earlier, when you come back, after having spent months on location, hoping you really do have the film in the can. And you sit down with your editor – in our case Jill Bilcock, who is one of the best editors in the world. She played us the rough cut of the film – literally our first week back from the shoot – at that point we were in tears with the realisation that there was a film, let alone that this could be a really good film. That was incredibly exciting. As a producer you carry so many responsibilities and anxieties, trying to ensure that everything comes together as you hoped when you first imagined the script up on the big screen. The red carpet experience at Cannes was also very exciting as it was our first audience. The film received a standing ovation that seemed to go on forever!

Q: If you had to do it all over again, would you?

A: Of course! Unless you're prepared to take a few risks, be creatively challenged, go into worlds that you've never been into before, you're not ever really going to take your audiences on a real journey. I think it's the role of storytellers and filmmakers – that, when those lights go down and the curtain opens, we're all going on a journey together into the unknown. And for that reason, I'll always seek out creative challenges, the locations that haven't been filmed and the stories that haven't yet been told.

AND ANOTHER THING ...

DARRYL KERRIGAN OR MICK DUNDEE?

In October 2010, the Australia Day Council of New South Wales commissioned a survey to find out which films and characters Australians feel best represent them as a nation. With 1003 people surveyed, it's not surprising that *The Castle* (1997) received a whopping 37 per cent of the vote for the movie that people feel best represents the real Australia. Other things to note from the survey:

- Darryl Kerrigan, the humble patriarch from *The Castle*, was also voted Australia's favourite film character, getting 23 per cent of the vote, beating Mick Dundee (21 per cent) and Muriel Heslop (17 per cent)

- Cate Blanchett was declared Australia's favourite leading lady with 41 per cent of the vote. Next in line were Nicole Kidman (23 per cent) and Toni Collette (17 per cent).

- It was a no-contest in the favourite actor category, with Hugh Jackman commanding a whopping 54 per cent of the votes. Tailing Hugh was Russell Crowe (17 per cent) and newcomer Sam Worthington (13 per cent).

- In response to a rather strange question, over 37 per cent of people surveyed admitted that Bob Hawke is the politician they would most like to co-star with in a film. The next pollie was John Howard (18 per cent).

Source: 'Survey finds *The Castle* star best represents Australia' by Isabel Hayes, 6/10/10, AAP.

Jindabyne (2006)

> We don't step over bodies to enjoy our leisure activities. Pack of bloody idiots!
> — *Policeman*

Snow gums in Kosciuszko National Park

Director: Ray Lawrence
Writer: Beatrix Christian
Producer: Catherine Jarman
Cast includes: Gabriel Byrne, Laura Linney, John Howard, Deborah-Lee Furness, Chris Haywood, Max Cullen

ABOUT THE FILM

For director Ray Lawrence, following up his 2001 film *Lantana* was going to be a mighty tough task. *Lantana* is regarded by critics and movie buffs as one of the finest motion pictures our industry has ever produced. It won 34 awards, here and abroad, including eight AFI Awards. How the hell do you top that?

It turns out that the answer is easy – you just make *Jindabyne*, an equally stunning, suspense-laden drama starring international acting heavyweights Laura Linney and Gabriel Byrne.

Based on a short story by acclaimed American writer Raymond Carver, *Jindabyne* centres on Stewart Kane (Byrne) an Irishman living in a small town, who discovers the body of a murdered girl while on an annual fishing trip with three of his buddies. The men decide to continue their angling and report the crime on their return to town. Naturally this causes a major stir when the story breaks.

What ensues is a tumultuous period for the men, particularly Stewart in his relationship with his wife Claire (Linney). The film is a magnificent blend of seemingly effortless directing, a taut script and brilliant acting. Linney and Byrne's talent shines in the way they inhabit the lead roles, while the crop of local talent, particularly Furness, is equally as impressive.

Lawrence's depiction of the sleepy town of Jindabyne contrasts strongly with Cate Shortland's portrayal in *Somersault* (2004) – snowy and tourist-filled (though this is really just for a few months each year). *Jindabyne*, however, takes place in the warmer months, when tourists are much lighter on the ground and the surrounding landscape is dry and desolate. It's this isolation that creates tension, gripping the audience for every single frame.

Jindabyne collected nine AFI Award nominations, but astonishingly went home empty-handed.

The movie poster makes a dark impression

OFFICIAL SELECTION
CANNES
2006
DIRECTOR'S FORTNIGHT

WINNER
EDINBURGH IFF
HERALD ANGEL
AWARD

SPECIAL
PRESENTATION
TORONTO IFF
2006

WINNER
FILM CRITICS CIRCLE
OF AUSTRALIA
4 AWARDS

"superb"
★ ★ ★ ★
THE SCOTSMAN

"stunning"
THE GUARDIAN

"haunting"
★ ★ ★ ★
LWLIES

"fantastic"
DAILY MAIL

gabriel byrne   laura linney

jindabyne

from the acclaimed director of "lantana"

IN CINEMAS MAY 25

Jindabyne New South Wales

The gateway to the adventure playground of the Snowy Mountains, Jindabyne is one of the most visited tourist towns in all of New South Wales. In the winter it becomes a mecca for snow bunnies and snowboarding shredders, who use the town as a pit stop for their forays to the four ski resorts found in Kosciuszko National Park. But don't go thinking Jindabyne morphs into a ghost town when the ice melts. While it's obviously quieter, summer brings out the fly-fishers, bushwalkers and campers who enjoy the splendid mountain streams, rivers and lakes, and tranquil mood of this sleepy slice of heaven. The entire film was shot in and around the township of Jindabyne, from Curiosity Rocks in the middle of the stunning Lake Jindabyne to the Discovery Holiday Park and surrounds.

VISITOR INFO

Snowy Region Visitor Information Centre

Kosciuszko Rd, Jindabyne; (02) 6450 5600 or 1800 004 439; www.visitnsw.com/town/ Jindabyne/Snowy_Region_Visitor_Information_ Centre/info.aspx

THINGS TO SEE AND DO

Lake Jindabyne

In 1967, the town of Jindabyne was deliberately flooded and buried under megalitres of water. Seriously, it was! As part of the Snowy Mountains Hydro-Electric Scheme, the entire town was dammed. A few of the buildings were relocated, as well as the all-important residents inhabiting said buildings. The original town now lies under the serene waters of Lake Jindabyne, a location featured several times in the film. The opening fishing scenes of Stewart and his son Tom (Sean Rees-Wemyss) were shot on the banks of the lake, as was Claire's swimming scene and the scene when Tom almost drowns under the not-so-watchful eyes of Caylin-Calandria (Eve Lazzaro). On the northern side, on the banks of the lake, is Curiosity Rocks, the unique stack of large boulders frequently seen in the film.

The Snowy Mountains have some of the most plentiful trout fishing in all of Australia and the lake's brimming with big browns and steel flanked rainbows. The lake is also a great spot for boating, waterskiing and a variety of other watersports; it's a surprise the trout don't find a quieter place to live. There's also walking and cycling to be enjoyed around the foreshore, from Banjo Paterson Park on Kosciuszko Road to the Discovery Holiday Park (formerly Snowline Caravan Park).

Kosciuszko Automotive

Pop in for an engine check and an oil change, though Irish mechanics might be in short supply. Kosciuszko Automotive was used as the location for the garage owned and run by Stewart. It's next door to Steve Williamson's Tackle Shop, where you can purchase bait and fishing equipment, and book your fly-fishing and boat tours. *Kosciuszko Rd (near Alpine Way intersection); (02) 6456 1300*

Kane family home

The property used for the Kane family home is a house on Snowgrass Drive. The production crew hired out the single-storey property for three months, using the interiors and exteriors to shoot scenes. The production crew weren't entirely happy with how the walls of the home looked on camera, so a few buckets of paint later – voila! – different coloured interiors. Rule numero uno in film production, though, is that crews are to leave a location in exactly the same state as they found it. Although the production had every intention of painting the walls back to their original colour after the shoot, property owners Bill and Jane Needham were so thrilled with the paint job they decided to leave it as is. *Snowgrass Dr, Lakewood Estate*

Bicentennial statue of Paul Strzelecki

Next to Lake Jindabyne, this tall statue could be confused with a Keanu Reeves pose from *The Matrix*. This shiny metallic figure commemorates Sir Paul Edmund Strzelecki, an intrepid Polish traveller who explored and surveyed large areas of New South Wales, Victoria and Tasmania. He was one of the first men to climb Australia's highest peak, Mt Kosciuszko, naming it after compatriot and Polish leader Tadeusz Kosciuszko. *Next to Lake Jindabyne*

Kunama Galleries

Just a few kilometres north-east of the main township, this local gallery has more than 200 original paintings on display. Resident artist Alan Grosvenor has been painting in Jindabyne for over 40 years and loves to chat about his town of inspiration. *Cnr Jerrara and Kunama drives, Jindabyne East; (02) 6457 1100; www.alangrosvenor.com.au*

WHERE TO STAY

Sages Haus Bed and Breakfast

Let lovely hosts Sabina and George take care of you in their charming and homely alpine-style bed and breakfast. Cooked winter breakfasts will be sure to warm you up on those chilly Jindabyne mornings and fuel you for the day; continental in summer. *28 Clyde St; (02) 6456 1184; www.sageshaus.com.au*

Fishing on Lake Jindabyne

An aerial shot of the town

We've got more water than bloody Sydney Harbour.
– *Carl*

Curiosity Rocks on the banks of Lake Jindabyne

Lake Jindabyne at sunset

Snowy Backpackers

A no-brainer for young adrenaline junkies using Jindabyne as home base for their daily assaults on the snowy slopes in winter and whitewater rapids in summer. Dorm rooms sleep up to ten people, and there are single, double and family rooms for a little more privacy. Cheaper during the summer months. *7–8 Gippsland St; (02) 6456 1511; www.snowybackpackers.com.au*

Lake Jindabyne Hotel

While the rooms are basic, this three-star hotel/motel more than makes up for it with its gorgeous views of Lake Jindabyne and home-cooked breakfast every morning. Family rooms sleep up to eight people, so it's perfect for groups heading to the slopes. Or ... you know ... if you're a Brady Bunch type of family. *McCluire Circuit (near Kosciusko Rd); (02) 6456 2203; www.lakejindabynehotel.com.au*

Wanderers Retreat

Year-round lodgings with three B&B rooms and two self-contained units. Free wi-fi and scrumptious breakfasts. *54 Gippsland St; (02) 6456 2091; www.wanderersretreat.com.au*

CARAVANS AND MOTORHOMES

Discovery Holiday Park, Jindabyne

Formerly the Snowline Caravan Park, this four-star accommodation was used as a location in the film as the home of Carl (Howard) and Jude (Furness). The park sits on the shores of the gorgeous Lake Jindabyne and is only 3 kilometres from the main township. Discovery offers a vast array of lodging options, from economy Bogong Cabins to deluxe Alpine Villas (if you have a little bit more cash in the pocket and don't want to bring your own sheets). *Kosciuszko Rd (near Alpine Way intersection); (02) 6456 2099; www.discoveryholidayparks. com.au/nsw/snowy_mountains/jindabyne*

CAMPING

Jindabyne Holiday Park

Offers over 80 powered and unpowered camping sites, most of them overlooking the lake. Cabin and caravan accommodation also available. Great position! *Kosciuszko Rd; (02) 6456 2249; www.jindyhp.com.au*

Snowy Wilderness

Four camping sites (with A-frame shelter and swags for hire), as well as cottage, apartment and lodge accommodation. Horseriding,

> In a hidden valley lies a hidden river. There dwells a fish wild and cunning.
> – Stewart

quad-biking and fly-fishing tours also available. *Barry Way; (02) 6457 9700; www.snowywilderness.com.au*

WHERE TO EAT

Supreeya Thai

Adjoining the Discovery Holiday Park, this Thai eatery was used as the restaurant in the scene where Stewart, Claire and the rest of the group share dinner on the eve of the fishing trip. Enjoy yummy stir-fried noodles, red and yellow curries and daily specials by the open fire in winter or on the veranda overlooking the lake in summer. *Kosciuszko Rd (near Alpine Way intersection); (02) 6457 2525*

Mario's Mineshaft

Mario's is a classic modern Italian bistro with gourmet wood-fired pizzas and hearty pasta, meat and seafood dishes. Claustrophobic souls don't stress, Mario's is up on ground level. *Adjacent to the Lakeview Plaza Motel, 2 Snowy River Ave; (02) 6456 2727; www.lakeviewplaza.com.au*

Cafe Susu

On the ground floor of the Snowy Backpackers, a terrific spot for cheap-and-cheerful burgers, salads and curries. *7–8 Gippsland Rd; (02) 6456 1503; www.snowybackpackers.com.au*

CINEMA

Jindabyne Cinema

This small cinema in the Snowy Region Visitor Centre shows a limited selection of new releases. *Kosciuszko Rd; (02) 6450 5600*

DID YOU KNOW?

Actor Gabriel Byrne had two near misses while shooting the film. He was in a minor car accident when a kangaroo hit his car windshield. Days later, while walking through the bush he stepped on a brown snake, but was luckily not bitten by the extremely venomous reptile.

Kosciuszko National Park New South Wales

Kosciuszko National Park is the largest national park in New South Wales (and encroaches on Victoria as well) and one of the must-visit destinations in Australia. Spread over 690 000 hectares, the park covers a wide variety of treeless plains, glistening white snowfields in winter, historic huts and rushing mountain streams. It's impossible to overlook the towering rock that is Mt Kosciuszko, Australia's tallest peak, standing at over 2200 metres high. Okay, so maybe it's a dwarf compared to Everest or Kilimanjaro, but it's *our* biggest, so we've gotta be proud of it. There's a vast assortment of native flora and fauna throughout the park, including the cuddly (koalas) and not-so-cuddly (copperhead snakes) wildlife that can be viewed from the various walking, hiking and bike trails strewn throughout the enormous wilderness.

Historic hut in Kosciuszko National Park

The park played a very important role in the filming of *Jindabyne*; three major locations were chosen here, including the Yarrangobilly River and the Thredbo Diggings campground.

VISITOR INFO

Snowy Region Visitor Information

Kosciuszko Rd, Jindabyne; (02) 6450 5600 or 1800 004 439; www.environment.nsw.gov.au/ NationalParks

New South Wales Road Conditions

13 2701; www.rta.nsw.gov.au

THINGS TO SEE AND DO

Yarrangobilly River

In the northern end of Kosciuszko National Park is the Yarrangobilly River, one of the three rivers used to create the one fictional river in the film. The scenes shot at Yarrangobilly involve Stewart instructing enthusiastic first-time fly-fisherman Billy (Simon Stone) on the correct way to cast for trout. These scenes were supposed to be shot at the end of production, but were dragged forward because of the possibility of the river's water levels rising. Lawrence, the director, is an experienced fly-fisherman himself and wanted the fishing scenes to be as authentic as possible so he brought in a fly-fishing instructor to train the actors.

Aside from the bushland wilderness and tranquil river, the highlight of the area is undoubtedly the Yarrangobilly Caves, a system of limestone caves dating backs millions of years. There are three lit show caves regularly open to visitors interested in guided and self-guided tours of caves, as well as a 27-degrees-Celsius thermal pool (and wading pool for the littlies) if you're getting a bit whiffy. *Yarrangobilly Caves; (02) 6454 9597*

Island Bend

This popular fishing and rafting spot on the Snowy River was the location for the movie's key scene in which the four friends make the gruesome discovery of the young dead girl, Susan (Tatea Reilly). This is also the spot where murderer Gregory (Haywood) throws her lifeless corpse into the water. Island Bend has vehicle-based camping facilities and some excellent fishing. In the unlikely event that you happen to see a floater, don't let life imitate art: call the authorities. *Access via Guthega Rd from Kosciuszko Rd*

Thredbo Diggings

The scene of the smoke funeral for Susan towards the end of film was shot at Thredbo Diggings campground on the banks of the Thredbo River in the far south of Kosciuszko National Park. The area was once sacred ground for Aboriginals and was used as a ceremonial ground and a place for educating children. It's now a popular bush campground with pit toilets. From here the 3-kilometre Bullocks Track Walk takes in a hut built in 1934 (old Dr Bullock's holiday house back in the day). *Signposted access via Alpine Rd*

Skiing and snowboarding

It's called the Snowy Mountains for a reason! Hit the slopes on your board or sticks and discover some muscles you didn't even know you had. Or just stay in and sip on a warm hot chocolate with schnapps or a gluhwein in front of the fireplace. It's all good. Four snowfields are located within Kosciuszko National Park: Perisher, Thredbo and Charlotte's Pass in the south of the park and Mt Selwyn in the north. The resorts fill up quickly in winter, so plan and book early. *For information on location, resort accommodation and equipment hire, visit www. snowymountains.com.au*

Bushwalking

For nature lovers, there are a number of formal and informal walking tracks located throughout the park to get you among the beautiful native wildlife and plant life. These walks range from the breezy Yarrangobilly Caves to River Walk trek (2 kilometres), which starts at the Thermal Pool and takes you upstream, to the more challenging Summit Walk from Charlotte's Pass to Mt Kosciuszko, Australia's tallest peak (9 kilometres each way). As with all walks in the park, remember it's an alpine area and prepare for all weather conditions. *For more information visit www.environment.nsw.gov.au/ NationalParks/parkWalking.aspx?id=N0018*

Cycling

There are plenty of opportunities for cycling enthusiasts within the park, particularly the madder mountain bikers, who take a chairlift at Thredbo and barrel down Cannonball Run as fast as they can. Both the park trails and roads are open to cyclists, however the walking trails are off-limits. Try not to have a head-on collision with a horse, as they have right of way.

The central section of the park is the most popular, with the more popular rides being the day trips from Dead Horse Gap to Cascade Hut and along the old Kosciuszko Road from Charlotte Pass to Rawson Pass. Several operators offer bike tours. *For more information on cycling in Mt Kosciuszko, visit www.environment. nsw.gov.au/NationalParks/parkCycling. aspx?id=N0018*

Fishing

There are dozens of fishing spots within the park, including the Island Bend camping area. Trout is the main game in the region and the season runs from October to mid-June. Some sections of the Thredbo River and Sawpit and Khancoban Creeks are closed to fishing all year round. A fishing licence is needed to fish anywhere (available from New South Wales Fisheries). *NSW Fisheries, 1300 369 365; www. dpi.nsw.gov.au/fisheries/recreational/licence-fee*

WHERE TO STAY

Lake Crackenback Resort

This stunning four-and-a-half-star resort located on the border of Kosciuszko National Park was the base camp for many of the cast and crew on the film. Laura Linney, Gabriel Byrne and Deborah-Lee Furness called Crackenback their home for the three months of shooting.

Blue Lake in Kosciuszko National Park

Rams Head Range
near Perisher

The resort offers beautiful one-, two- and three-bedroom apartments overlooking the water (with over-water balconies), as well as larger two- to four-bedroom mountain chalets. You can access the Thredbo Diggings camp area by foot from the resort, along the 4.5-kilometre (return trip) Bullocks track walk. Plus there's a day spa ... aah. *1650 Alpine Way, Crackenback; (02) 6451 3000 or 1800 020 524; www.lakecrackenback.com.au*

Perisher Valley Hotel

Intimate boutique hotel nestled in the heart of the best ski region in all of Australia. Regular rooms to Alpine- and Mountain-view suites, though you may have to take out a second mortgage to afford a suite. Awesome buffet breakfasts and cocktail bar on site plus a private billiards room. *Kosciuszko Rd, Perisher Valley; (02) 6459 4455; www.perisher.com.au*

Smiggins Hotel

Friendly atmosphere with quick access to the Perisher Resort and shops. Learn-to-ski and board lessons for kids and uncoordinated adults alike. Hotel rooms and cosy chalet-style apartments, both have heated towel rails – using a room-temperature towel in this day and age is just not the done thing! *Kosciuszko Rd, Smiggins Hole; (02) 6457 5375; www.smiggins.com.au*

Thredbo YHA Hostel

Come snow or sun, this hostel offers clean and comfortable accommodation for travellers on a budget – its probably the cheapest accommodation on the hill. Private rooms available. *8 Jack Adams Pathway, Thredbo; (02) 6457 6376; www.yha.com.au/hostels/nsw/snowy-mountains/thredbo*

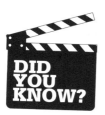

DID YOU KNOW? **Director Ray Lawrence used natural light to shoot almost every scene – quite a rarity in filmmaking. He did so to get the most natural performance out of his actors as possible. Lawrence is also known for only doing one or two takes per scene, a daunting prospect even for the likes of experienced actors Byrne and Linney.**

CARAVANS AND MOTORHOMES

Kosciuszko Mountain Retreat

Secluded retreat set among the beautiful snow gums, just a short drive to Perisher Valley. Cabins and camping accommodation also available. *1400 Kosciuszko Rd, Sawpit Creek; (02) 6456 2224; www.kositreat.com.au*

Khancoban Lakeside Caravan Resort

Located on the central-western border of the park, with tremendous fishing and boating nearby, and camping and cabin accommodation as well. *1362 Alpine Way, Khancoban; (02) 6076 9488; www.klcr.com.au*

CAMPING

There are over 35 different camping spots littered throughout Kosciuszko National Park, some with loads of facilities while others are more self-sufficient. Camping at Thredbo Diggings is very popular, while the Old Geehi Hut camping area beside the Swampy Plain River is the best spot for fishing and water activities. Check with the Snowy Region Visitor Centre for more information about campsites or visit the New South Wales National Parks website. *www.environment.nsw.gov.au/ NationalParks*

WHERE TO EAT

Terrace Restaurant

This award-winning establishment at the Denman Hotel in Thredbo was voted 'Australia's best alpine dining'. You're guaranteed an elegant dining experience; try the tasting menu (degustation) with matched wines. *Digging Tce, Thredbo; (02) 6457 6222; www.thedenman.com.au*

Cuisine on Lake Crackenback

Up-scale restaurant at Lake Crackenback Resort, which offers fresh fish and other creative dishes using local produce. Try a famous mountain cocktail at the Cuisine Bar before you dine. *1650 Alpine Way, Crackenback; (02) 6451 3000; www.lakecrackenback.com.au*

OTHER LOCATIONS

Dalgety New South Wales

A historic town on the banks of the Snowy River, Dalgety is located 34 kilometres south-east of Jindabyne. In 1903, the town was gazetted for Australia's capital city, but it was passed over because Sydney complained of its closer proximity to Melbourne. (Canberra was later chosen as the nation's capital city.) The stone and green-painted Beloka Church in Dalgety was used for the scene when Claire visits the minister.

Outside Cooma New South Wales

Cooma is the largest town in the Snowy Mountains and home to the Snowy Mountains Hydro-Electric Scheme, the largest civil engineering project undertaken in Australia. A property south-west of the town on the Monaro Plain was used for Gregory's house.

The plain was the location used at the beginning of the film for the tense car chase between Gregory and Susan. The plains can be identified by the large boulders and wispy brown rolling hills.

Q & A **Jane Needham, local resident of Jindabyne**

Jane Needham is a Jindabyne local. One day, out of the blue, she was approached by producers who wanted to use her house as a major shooting location in the film. Jane also works at Lake Crackenback Resort, where much of the cast and crew lodged during production.

Q: What was your role in the production of *Jindabyne*?

A: They used our house as the location for the Kane family home. I was sitting at home one day and there was a knock on the door. I answered and this young fellow was standing there and asked if we would be willing to have our home used in a movie. We moved out for three months. The production found us a unit in town.

Q: Did you get a chance to visit on set while they were shooting scenes in your house?

A: They invited us to come and watch one movie scene – when they have the barbecue on the front lawn. That was quite interesting.

Q: So they painted the interior of the house for the movie?

A: Yes, one day they rang up and said that the colours of the house don't photograph too well. They asked, 'Do you mind if we paint the house? We'll paint it back.' The deal was that they'd fix the house back as it was when they were done. In the end, I told them to just leave it. The new colour made it felt like a holiday. **The production crew were really fantastic; they left the house in immaculate condition. Even the pictures were put back exactly where they had been when they started.**

Q: What was it like when you watched the movie and saw your house for the first time on screen?

A: We have a small movie theatre here in Jindabyne and a lot of us saw it there. It was so weird – I don't think I actually paid that much attention to the story. We were all going, 'Oh look, there's such and such'. People were saying stuff like, 'I used to sit around that dining room table' or 'I had many a barbecue on that front lawn'. **It was quite weird to see our town up on screen like that.**

Q: What was the buzz like around town during the three months of shooting?

A: It was really fun! People were putting their names down to be extras and that sort of thing … it really brought a lot of interest and life into Jindabyne. It was March, April, May and at that time it's usually very quiet (apart from Easter). It lifted the economy enormously. **I'd say there were over a hundred production people here for that three-month period.** It was lovely to see all the stars. Us locals would just sit and have a coffee with them, they were all very nice.

Q: What was it like working at the Crackenback Resort while the production was in town.

A: A lot of the stars stayed there and the director, cinematographer … the higher-ups. They were delightful and fairly low key. We just treated them the same as anybody else.

Q: Did you have much interaction with actors like Laura Linney and Gabriel Byrne?

A: I didn't really see them at the resort because they'd be gone all day and I'd be gone by the time they got back.

They actually arrived early one morning at the house as we were moving out. The place looked like a bomb had hit it because we were in the process of moving out and they were four hours early. I asked if anyone would like tea or coffee and Laura Linney said, 'I'll help, come on, I'll help you Jane.' So she helped make the tea and coffee. She was very low-key, a very nice person. When we went to see the filming on the front lawn that day, we were walking along the road and we heard this person yelling out, 'Jane, Bill. Hi!' And it was Laura, even though she'd only met us once.

AND ANOTHER THING ...

NO ACTORS? NO WORRIES

Here are some of Australia's most well-known animated movies.

Happy Feet (2006) – George Miller's charming computer-animated romp about emperor penguins is the highest worldwide grossing Australian movie of all time (US $379 million). It won the 2007 Academy Award for Best Animated Film. *Happy Feet 2* is due to be released in late 2011.

Harvie Krumpet (2003) – This 22-minute claymation short garnered an Academy Award for Melbourne filmmaker Adam Elliot. It's about a Polish man with Tourette Syndrome living in Spotswood, Melbourne. It took 15 months to shoot – that's around one month of shooting for every one minute and 28 seconds of footage. Elliot released a feature-length claymation film, *Mary and Max*, in 2009.

Dot and the Kangaroo (1977) – A children's classic about a precocious girl named Dot who gets lost in the Australian bush and is befriended by a kangaroo. The film was a mix of animation and live action with the Blue Mountains and Jenolan Caves in New South Wales acting as the backdrop.

$9.99 (2008) – An Australian co-production with Israel, this 78-minute claymation feature follows a group of Sydneysiders living in an apartment complex as they search for the meaning of life. The film premiered at the Toronto Film Festival and used the voices of Geoffrey Rush, Anthony La Paglia, Claudia Karvan, Samuel Johnson and Barry Otto. Written by acclaimed Israeli author Etgar Keret.

Ferngully: The Last Rainforest (1992) – An enchanting tale about a group of fairies trying to save their magical rainforest from destruction by loggers. Famous voices include Robin Williams, Tim Curry and Christian Slater. Produced by Peter Faiman, who directed *Crocodile Dundee*. Many have found the themes and story of the animated tale very similar to the blockbuster *Avatar* (2009).

Kenny (2006)

> It takes a certain kind of person to do what I do. No-one's ever impressed; no-one's ever fascinated. If you're a fireman, all the kids will want to jump on the back of the truck and follow you to a fire. There's going to be no kids willing to do that with me. So I don't do it to impress people – it's a job, it's my trade and I actually think I'm pretty good at it.
> – *Kenny*

Kenny (Shane Jacobson) and his son (Jesse Jacobson) on the job at the Melbourne Cup

Director: Clayton Jacobson
Writers: Clayton Jacobson, Shane Jacobson
Producers: Clayton Jacobson, Rohan Timlock
Cast includes: Shane Jacobson, Eve Von Bibra, Ronald Jacobson, Ian Dryden, Chris Davis, Jesse Jacobson

ABOUT THE FILM

In 2006, the Aussie movie-going public had absolutely no intention of falling in love with a portly port-a-loo delivery man. But we just couldn't help it. He was just so damn affable – with never a bad word for anyone and (almost) infinite patience, he's been dubbed 'the knight in shining overalls'.

The septic mockumentary *Kenny* surrounds the aptly named Kenny Smyth (Shane Jacobson), a larger-than-life Aussie bloke and foreman at Splashdown, a portable toilet rental company in Melbourne.

Kenny's job is to go where no man, woman or child ever wants to go as he supplies temporary bathroom facilities to a variety of public events, including the Melbourne Cup, St Kilda Festival and the Avalon International Air Show. Along the way, he deals with the ugliest of the ugly punters and both the metaphorical and literal mess they leave behind. On top of this, our gentle protagonist must deal with a heartless ex-wife, semi-incompetent staff and his stubborn grouch of a father (Ronald Jacobson).

The underdog comedy was the highest grossing, locally made live-action film released in 2006. It received a rash of critical plaudits from local and international media. The film was so effortless and seemingly unaffected that many viewers actually thought it was a documentary.

There's no doubt that a lot of the film's success was due to Shane Jacobson and his brilliantly heartfelt, warm and natural performance – quite a remarkable feat

Kenny talks to a client about his toileting requirements

Busy shoppers on Chapel Street in South Yarra

Spring Racing Carnival at Flemington Racecourse

considering it was his first role in a feature film. The role earned him a Best Actor AFI Award. Other members of the Jacobson clan were vital to the film's success including talented director and co-writer Clayton Jacobson (Shane's brother), as well as Ronald (Shane and Clayton's father), who was spot-on as the crotchety patriarch.

LOCATIONS

Melbourne Victoria

Proclaimed as Australia's cultural capital, Melbourne has virtually everything you could ever possibly want from a major metropolitan city: towering CBD buildings, neo-Gothic banks and cathedrals, a green belt of parks and gardens, galleries, theatres and the best sporting stadiums in the country. (Don't even try and argue that last one, Sydney.)

Melbourne is a sophisticated culinary hub, with some of the country's best restaurants, not to mention our lauded baristas serving up espresso coffee at cosy cafes in nooks and crannies all over the place. It also constantly ranks high in worldwide surveys of the most liveable cities and it's easy to see why.

Melbourne was the chief shooting location for *Kenny*. The city has also been a desirable destination for dozens of other film and TV productions. The last few years have seen many international crews descend on Melbourne to shoot the films *Ghost Rider* (2007), *Charlotte's Web* (2006), *Where the Wild Things are* (2009) and *The Killer Elite* (2011).

VISITOR INFO

Melbourne Visitor Information Centre

Federation Square, cnr Flinders and Swanston sts; (03) 9658 9658; www.visitmelbourne.com or www.thatsmelbourne.com.au

THINGS TO SEE AND DO

Johnston Street, Fitzroy

This bohemian drag – known as the Spanish Quarter – in Melbourne's inner-north was the location used for the street festival early in the film. Like all the public scenes shot in *Kenny*, the filming actually took place during the real Hispanic Fiesta, which is held annually in November. Swathes of festival-goers probably don't even realise they are in the movie! The festival is a celebration of all things Hispanic and Latin American, with spirited Latin music, sweaty salsa dancing and copious amounts of food stalls offering mouth-watering paella and meat in many forms. Nearby Brunswick Street has some of the city's funkiest cafes, bars and

Funny part is, parents look at me and say, 'That's not much of a job, is it?' And I say, 'Well you had kids. You spent the first two years handling their shit and you weren't getting paid for that.' They shit green – the only things that should be green are pears, apples and Martians.
– Kenny

shopping and a visit here is high on the agenda for most visitors to Melbourne.

St Kilda

This suburb in Melbourne's inner-south is a relaxing bayside destination close to the CBD. It offers a strange mix of affluence and seediness; you can enjoy a brisk afternoon seaside stroll on the Esplanade and a few moments later find yourself in the red light district on Grey Street being given the evil eye – or the come on – by a street worker.

St Kilda was used for two major sets of scenes in the film. The first was the Gay Pride march, which takes place along Fitzroy Street, a lively drinking and eating strip, when Kenny joins the parade for a few metres to say g'day to an old mate. The scenes were shot during Midsumma Festival, an annual gay and lesbian festival held in January and February.

The second set of scenes was at the St Kilda Festival, which is held every year in February and attracts about half a million visitors. The festival is a helluva big weekend with incredible live music on a number of stages, entertainment and food stalls all along the beach foreshore, the Esplanade and nearby Acland Street. If you're not a fan of crowds, avoid it like the plague.

The nearby Art Deco Palais Theatre on Lower Esplanade is one of the city's great live music venues. It also hosts the opening night of the St Kilda Film Festival, a showcase of Australia's top 100 short films. *Kenny* actually started as a short film, titled *Kenny – Self*

Proclaimed Scatologist, which screened at the festival in 2004. It won Best Comedy and the Audience Choice Award at the festival that year.

Chapel Street

There is a proportion of Melburnians who think fashion is matching their jeans with their footy scarf. But there are many others for whom fashion is life. And their spiritual home is Chapel Street. The long stretch from South Yarra to Windsor is packed with boutique clothing, shoes and accessories shops.

Chapel Street was used for a couple of exterior shots in the film. The scene when Kenny stops at the local fish and chip shop was filmed at the Windsor end of Chapel Street. This area is less about fashion and more about the nightlife; some of the trendier bars around Windsor include La La Land, Back Bar, Hooha and The Railway Hotel. Chapel Street is also a destination for eating, with countless cool cafes and restaurants.

Flemington Racecourse

This world-famous racecourse is home to the Melbourne Cup, commonly known as 'the race

Kenny and his crew prepare for battle at the Calder Park Raceway

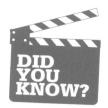

There are two scenes in the film in which a woman's face is pixilated: the scene involving Kenny's ex-wife and the woman who dropped her wedding ring in the toilet at the St Kilda Festival. This was not a privacy issue, but rather due to the fact that the same actress, Vicki Musso, played both roles. Pixilating her face was a way of not confusing the audience (plus it adds to the documentary feel).

that stops a nation'. Some of the final scenes of the film were shot on location at Flemington Racecourse on Melbourne Cup Day in 2004. The day will always be remembered for the immense downpour of rain (Melbourne weather at its most typical: unpredictable) and champion mare Makybe Diva winning the cup for a historic second year in a row. The Melbourne Cup takes place annually on the first Tuesday of November, as part of the week-long Melbourne Cup Carnival. For the majority of attendees, the actual horseracing takes a back seat to the fashion, schmoozing and boozing in marquees, and international A-list celebrities (much of the boozing having similar consequences to those depicted in the film). There are other race meets at Flemington throughout the year. The racecourse also holds craft markets once a month on a Sunday.

In 2010 the racetrack was used as a filming location for *The Cup*, a feature film telling the story of the emotionally-charged 2002 Melbourne Cup won by Media Puzzle. The film stars Stephen Curry as jockey Damien Oliver and UK actor Brendan Gleeson, who steps into the role of legendary Irish horse trainer Dermott Weld. *400 Epsom Rd, Flemington; (03) 9258 4666; www.vrc.net.au*

Bourke Street, Melbourne CBD

With its grid layout, criss-crossed with trundling trams and laneway culture, the Melbourne CBD has a style all its own. Bourke Street is one of the busiest streets in the city. It was the location for the scene when Kenny, finally fed up with being a treated like everyone else's punching bag, unleashes the contents of his port-a-loos into the car of an arrogant suit – surely one of Australian cinema's most joyous and triumphant moments, when the underdog bites back. The scene was shot outside a convenience store at 236 Bourke Street, which is currently a Target store.

Parallel to Bourke Street is Little Bourke Street, the axis on which Melbourne's Chinatown turns, which comes alive at night with scores of Asian eateries and funky hole-in-the-wall bars.

Further south is the Bourke Street Mall, a pedestrian and tram-only zone, the location of Myer and David Jones, Melbourne's largest department stores.

Old Treasury Building

The Old Treasury Building on Spring Street was the backdrop for a brief scene when Kenny has an altercation with an unnamed client. The colourful and vibrant flowers from the scene belong to the beautiful Treasury Gardens adjacent to the building. The building and gardens are on the edge of the CBD, a stone's throw away from the famous Melbourne Cricket Ground (or MCG, affectionately known as 'the gee'), which houses some fascinating exhibitions on sporting history. *Spring St (top of Collins St); (03) 9651 2233; www.oldtreasurybuilding.org.au*

Calder Park Raceway

This cathedral of Australian motor racing is located 25 kilometres north of Melbourne CBD in the suburb of Keilor. The raceway was the location for scenes near the end of the movie in

which Kenny and his Splashdown crew provide services for the motorsport event, culminating in one of their port-a-loos being set on fire by hammered hoons. This scene was scripted, but it's not very far from reality, as the punters' drinking and loutishness revs up even more than the drag cars.

Calder Park has hosted the Australian Grand Prix in the '80s, the first Australian NASCAR events, some of the country's premier touring-car events and concerts for artists such as Fleetwood Mac and Guns N' Roses. These days it mainly hosts off-street drag racing events. Sticking with the cathedral theme, the park also has a motoring-inspired church, where Kenny eats lunch in the film. *Calder Fwy, Keilor; (03) 9091 0800; www.calderpark.com.au*

Splashdown Corporate Bathroom Rentals

Although the film is fictional, Splashdown is a real bathroom rental company that played a huge role in getting *Kenny* made. Splashdown was a major sponsor and allowed the production to film at events they were catering loos for. The character of Kenny and his life story was inspired by Glenn Preusker, founder of Splashdown, who had a bit part in the film. The home base of Splashdown is in the industrial suburb of Brooklyn in Melbourne's north-west. All the scenes at Splashdown Headquarters were shot on location. *30–32 Buchanan Rd, Brooklyn; (03) 9314 6700; www.splashdown.com.au*

Lerderderg Gorge

Located in the Lederderg State Park, north-west of Melbourne and just outside Bacchus Marsh, the gorge was the spot where Kenny, brother Dave (Clayton Jacobson) and dad Billy (Ronald Jacobson) go camping. Lederderg State Park is over 20 000 hectares in size and there are some fascinating relics of goldmining to check out. It's also a popular spot for bushwalking, mountain

Kenny, Billy (Ronald Jacobson) and Dave (Clayton Jacobson) contemplate the sunset at Lerderderg Gorge

Kenny charms stewardess Jackie (von Bibra) during the flight

biking, four-wheel driving, camping, fishing and horseriding. *Access via Bacchus Marsh–Gisborne Rd from the east and Greendale–Trentham Rd from the north-west*

Melbourne Airport

For those on a flying visit to Melbourne, you can mark off your first *Kenny* filming location without even trying. The airport out at Tullamarine was used for an exterior night shot of Qantas planes at the international terminal. It was also used in the last scene when Kenny surprises Jackie (Von Bibra) as she leaves the airport. The scenes shot inside the plane were actually filmed inside a grounded Ansett aircraft in a hanger at the airport. This is the primary airport serving Melbourne and the second busiest in Australia. *Tullamarine Fwy; (08) 9297 1600; www.melbourneairport.com.au*

Kenny and son deal with an irrate patron at the Melbourne Cup

Maribyrnong Gym

All the scenes of Kenny at his boxing gym – doing his best Rocky impersonation – were shot at the Maribyrnong Youth Club. Ron Jacobson actually grew up in Maribyrnong and still trains regularly at the gym. Maribyrnong is 10 kilometres north-west of the CBD. *Hortense St, Maribyrnong; (03) 9317 8257*

Kenny's house

The interior and exterior shots of Kenny's house were shot in a small, two-bedroom flat in Middle Road in Maribyrnong.

Avalon Airport

Avalon is 55 kilometres south-west of Melbourne on the way to Geelong. This airport is well-known for hosting the annual Australian International Airshow in March. The scenes involving Kenny and his crew at the airfield were actually shot during the Airshow. *80 Beach Rd, Lara; (03) 5227 9100; www.airshow.net.au*

Australian Centre for the Moving Image

Known around the traps as ACMI, this uniquely designed building dedicated to the moving image is an absolute must-visit for film buffs. The 'Screen Worlds' permanent exhibition (free entry!) tells the fascinating history of Australian film, TV and other media with displays, videos, photographs and props. You can spend hours here checking out such original film memorabilia as Mick Dundee's hat, a glass sculpture from *Oscar and Lucinda* and a replica Interceptor from *Mad Max* as well as some Academy Award statuettes won by Melbourne locals Cate Blanchett and Adam Elliot. *Federation Sq, Flinders St, Melbourne; (03) 8663 2200; www.acmi.net.au*

WHERE TO STAY

Hotel Tolarno

An arty hotel on busy Fitzroy Street (formerly a gallery owned by delightful Melbourne art icon Mirka Mora), Hotel Tolarno is a style institution. Standard rooms to spacious executive and deluxe suites. Take advantage of the plethora of restaurants and bars nearby. It's a short stroll to Acland Street and St Kilda Beach, the latter a major filming location. *42 Fitzroy St, St Kilda; (03) 9537 0200; www.hoteltolarno.com.au*

Chapel Street Backpackers

Affordable hostel accommodation at the Windsor end of Chapel Street. Standard and deluxe dorms, and private twin and triple rooms with ensuite bathrooms. Opposite the Windsor Train Station and a five-minute walk to St Kilda junction. *22 Chapel St, Windsor; (03) 9533 6855; www.csbackpackers.com.au*

The Greenhouse Backpacker

An award-winning CBD-located backpackers joint, with single-sex and mixed dorms and private rooms. The rooftop garden with sunlounges and barbecue facilities is a treat in summer. It's a short walk to the Bourke Street filming location and Chinatown. *Level 6, 28 Flinders La; (03) 9639 6400; www.friendlygroup.com.au*

Tyrian Serviced Apartments

Stunning new serviced apartments on Johnston Street. Ultra modern one-, two- and three-bedroom apartments with fully-equipped kitchenette, European laundry and stylish lounge room. Be prepared to fork out a bit for this place. *91 Johnston St, Fitzroy; (03) 9415 1900; www.tyrian.com.au*

Quest Flemington

One-, two- and three-bedroom apartments within walking distance of Flemington Racecourse. Flat-screen TVs and wi-fi access. Book well in advance if you want to stay during the Melbourne Cup carnival. *600 Epsom Rd, Flemington; (03) 9371 2200; www.questflemington.com.au*

CARAVANS AND MOTORHOMES

Barwon Heads Caravan Park

Located outside of Melbourne in the sleepy seaside town of Barwon Heads, this caravan park was the site of Billy's small unit in the film. The park was also a filming location for the popular ABC TV show *Sea Change* in the '90s. It offers powered and unpowered caravan and camping sites, as well as cabins and beach houses (you can stay in Laura's home from the TV show). *Ewing Blyth Dr, Barwon Heads; (03) 5254 1115; www.barwoncoast.com.au/ barwon-heads-caravan-park/102*

Melbourne BIG4 Holiday Park

Ensuite powered sites, camping, cottages, cabins, units and villas. Games room with ping pong table and adventure playground for the kiddies. Conveniently located within short drives to the airport and the city (7 kilometres). *265 Elizabeth St, Coburg; (03) 9354 3533; www.melbournebig4.com.au*

Ashley Gardens BIG4 Holiday Village

Four-and-a-half-star holiday park accommodation with ensuite sites, powered camping, cabins, spa units and family villas. Located in the quiet suburb of Braybrook, a short drive to Calder Park. *129 Ashley St, Braybrook; (03) 9318 6866; www.aspenparks.com.au/ holiday-destinations/victoria/melbourne/ashley-gardens-big4-holiday-village/welcome.aspx*

WHERE TO EAT

The Espy Kitchen

In close proximity to two major *Kenny* locations in St Kilda, The Espy is a Melbourne's live-music institution. The Espy Kitchen serves up some brilliant and affordable meals, including seafood gumbo, lamb souvlaki and Moroccan-spiced tagine plus breakfasts on weekends. The music trivia TV show *Rockwiz* is filmed on location at the hotel and it has live music in three bars seven nights a week. *11 The Esplanade, St Kilda; (03) 9534 0211; www.espy.com.au*

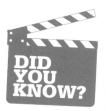

DID YOU KNOW? **While *Kenny* could have chosen a more glitzy Melbourne location for its world premiere, the lucky and appropriately named town of Poowong in South Gippsland was chosen for the film's first public screening.**

Kenny and son take a break from work

St Kilda's historic Astor Theatre

Thai Lime Lemongrass Restaurant

The location of the takeaway joint, formerly known as 'Fish N Chippers', which Kenny visits in the film is now occupied by a delightful Thai restaurant with excellent curries. Open for dinner. *97 Chapel St, Windsor; (03) 9521 2299*

Colmao Flamenco

Lively Spanish restaurant with great tapas, chorizo dishes and paella. Set menu and banquet options. Live Latin music and flamenco dancers on weekends in summer. *60 Johnston St, Fitzroy; (03) 9417 4131; www.colmaoflamenco.com*

Chinatown Dumpling Restaurant

A hidden gem in Chinatown with dirt-cheap, delicious and delightful dumplings – you must try the steamed pork and chive. Extremely busy during the dinner rush, with service to match. A stone's throw from Bourke Street. *Shop 3, 254 Swanston St; (03) 9663 3893*

Maribyrnong Boathouse

One of the best cafes in Melbourne has received a succession of awards for having the best pizza in the city. Casual and relaxed dining with marvellous views of the Maribyrnong River. Open for breakfast, lunch and dinner. Close to

Flemington Racecourse and Maribyrnong shooting locations. *7 The Boulevard, Moonee Ponds; (03) 9375 2456; www.theboat-house.com.au*

FILM FESTIVALS

Melbourne International Film Festival

Running for three weeks annually in July and August, MIFF (www.melbournefilmfestival.com.au) showcases some of the best films from all over the world with a diverse program of features, documentaries, animated and short films. Screenings happen all around the city at ACMI, Forum Theatre, Greater Union Cinemas on Russell Street and the RMIT Capitol Theatre. There are also industry talks and Q&A sessions with filmmakers.

Other major film festivals held during the year include the Melbourne International Animation Festival (www.miaf.net), Melbourne Underground Film Festival (www.muff.com.au) and the Melbourne Queer Film Festival (www.mqff.com.au).

CINEMAS

Astor Theatre

Old-time movie houses are harder and harder to come by these days. Located on Chapel Street – just a couple of hundred metres from

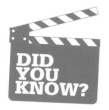

DID YOU KNOW?

Kenny the film spawned a TV series called *Kenny's World*, which aired on Network Ten in 2008. The show saw the return of our loveable toilet guru on an 'ex-poo-dition' travelling the globe checking out the dunnies in destinations including India, Egypt, Thailand and Indianapolis (USA) and discovering some very unique and different examples of toilet technology.

the filming location – this classic crusty film house has double features every night of the week from black-and-white to cult classics and new releases. The Astor is the only theatre in Melbourne that screens 70 millimetre films on a regular basis. *Cnr Chapel St and Dandenong Rd, St Kilda; (03) 9510 1414; www.astor-theatre.com*

St Kilda Openair Cinema

Balmy summer nights and films under the stars – does it get any better? From December to February, the top of the St Kilda Sea Baths screens a program of great new releases and the occasional classic thrown in the mix. Fully licensed with picnics welcome, the venue also hosts nightly indie bands and singer-songwriters. *St Kilda Sea Baths, 10–18 Jacka Blvd, St Kilda Beach; 1300 GET TIX; www.stkildaopenair.com.au*

Cinema Nova

Melbourne's premier art-house cinema has 15 screens, including Melbourne's first digital-only screen. Special events include Q&A sessions with local and international filmmakers, script readings and industry workshops. Its location on Lygon Street makes an espresso, gelato or pasta before or after the flick a necessity. *380 Lygon St, Carlton; (03) 9349 5201; www.cinemanova.com.au*

Rivoli Cinemas

Located in Melbourne's east, this stunning refurbished Art Deco/jazz moderne complex provides one of the best cinema experiences in all of Melbourne. Rooftop bar open on the weekends. *200 Camberwell Rd, East Hawthorn; (03) 9882 1221; www.villagecinemas.com.au/cinemas/rivoli-cinemas.htm*

OTHER LOCATIONS

Murchison Victoria

The small township of Murchison, just outside Shepparton on the banks of the Goulburn River is known as the 'River Bank Garden Town'. The town's historical highlights include the 1850s gold rush to the prisoner-of-war camps during World War II and the Murchison Meteor in 1969. Now the town is visited for its riverside proximity and local wine and cheese. The Murchison Cemetery on Cemetery Road was used as the location for the scene when Kenny visits his mother's grave.

Nashville USA

Kenny's first trip overseas takes him all the way to Nashville, Tennessee, to visit the International Pumper and Cleaner Expo – or, as Kenny affectionately calls it, 'Poo HQ'. The scenes were shot at the expo and his interaction with the various vendors and guests of the expo was, for the most part, non-scripted. Kenny also takes in some of the Nashville nightlife with Jackie and the Karaoke Cowboy before rushing home when his Dad falls ill.

Rockin' the suburbs – Melbourne

The suburbs of Melbourne have been the breeding ground for some of the greatest Australian films ever made. Here are some of them.

THE CASTLE (1997)

Voted in the top five Australian films of all time by AFI voters in 2008, the tale of the battling Kerrigan family was shot in various suburbs around Melbourne. The external scenes of the Kerrigan home were shot in Dagonet Street in Strathmore. Essendon and Melbourne airports were both used in scenes, while Brunswick, Toorak and the Melbourne CBD were also used as locations. There was no faking the High Court location, however, which was shot in Canberra.

MAD MAX (1979)

The dystopian George Miller cult-classic was made for around $300 000. It used a variety of locations around Melbourne – none more unusual than the University of Melbourne in Parkville, where the car park underneath the South Lawn was disguised as the interior of police headquarters. The exterior of the headquarters was shot at the Spotswood Pumping Station at Scienceworks Museum.

Other suburbs used for locations in the film were Port Melbourne, Williamstown, Sunbury and Kew.

ROMPER STOMPER (1992)

Geoffrey Wright's gritty drama about neo-Nazi skinheads (starring Russell Crowe) was set in Footscray and largely shot in the area. A bit of trickery was used in the opening scene of the film, when the skinheads attack a group of Asian teenagers at Footscray Train Station; this was actually shot at Richmond Railway Station. Footscray's neighbouring suburb of Newport was also used for filming, as was Point Addis Marine National Park in Anglesea.

NOISE (2007)

Nominated for the Grand Jury Prize at the 2007 Sundance Film Festival as well as numerous AFI Awards, this film, which flew under the radar when released in Australia, stars Brendan Cowell as a police constable suffering tinnitus and working on a murder investigation in the suburb of Sunshine. Sunshine was never actually used as a shooting location; the suburbs of Fawkner, Oakleigh and Preston were instead the major filming sites. Flinders Street and Burnley train stations were also used, as was the Sidney Myer Music Bowl.

CHOPPER (2000)

The movie that launched Eric Bana from sketch comedian (we all remember mullet-headed 'Poida' in the comedy skit show *Full Frontal*) to international movie star is the vehicle for arguably the best acting performance in an Australian film. Bana actually spent two days with Mark 'Chopper' Read prior to filming so he could get a better understanding of his character. Read was the one that suggested Bana play him after seeing him on the TV show *Full Frontal*. Pentridge Prison in Coburg was used for all the prison scenes. 'H Division', where much of the film was shot, was frequented by Read. The prison was closed down in 1997.

THE WOG BOY (2000)

This Greek-centric comedy was a monster hit at the Australian box office and even earned itself a release in the US. Its characters and themes followed on from the successful stage show *Wogs Out of Work* and its sequels, making fun of racism and both Aussie and immigrant culture. The 2010 sequel, *The King of Mykonos*, didn't achieve the success of the first film. Chapel Street was a major location for *The Wog Boy*; all the club scenes were shot at Chasers nightclub. The Yarraville village was another significant location, so much so that co-writer and actor Nick Giannopoulos was made a 'special ambassador' by the Yarraville Village Traders Association.

I LOVE YOU, TOO (2010)

Penned by comedian Peter Hellier, this romantic comedy about a commitment-phobe trying to win back the girl of his dreams stars Brendan Cowell, Yvonne Strahovski and Megan Gale and hits a multitude of hot spots.

The Grand Hyatt Hotel on Russell Street was used in a couple of scenes, as was the up-scale Spice Market bar next door. The Melbourne Sports and Aquatic Centre in Albert Park, BMW Edge and Transit Restaurant at Federation Square, Eve Nightclub in Southbank and the Williamstown Pier and Sailing Club were other locations used.

MALCOLM (1986)

The comedy about an introverted tram-builder named Frank (Colin Friels), who resorts to a life of crime with his ex-con roommate, is one of the favourite Melbourne-shot films. The suburb of Collingwood was used as a major location, with exterior shots of Malcolm's house filmed in Napoleon Street. Frank frequents The Leinster Arms Hotel, one of Melbourne's oldest pubs. CBD locations included the Commonwealth Bank on Collins Street (near the Queen Street intersection). South Melbourne, Kew and Preston were other locations used.

SPOTSWOOD (1992)

This light-hearted comedy stars Sir Anthony Hopkins as a productivity expert who manages the downsizing of an auto parts factory. The film was shot on location in Spotswood, with the Pumping Station at Scienceworks Museum used as a major set, as well as various other locations around Melbourne. The film also stars Russell Crowe, Toni Collette and Ben Mendelsohn and won three AFI Awards. It was released in the US with the title *The Efficiency Expert*.

Mad Max 2: The Road Warrior (1981)

A beaten-up Max (Gibson) looks out for Feral Kid (Minty)

> My life fades. The vision dims. All that remains are memories. I remember a time of chaos. Ruined dreams. This wasted land. But most of all, I remember The Road Warrior. The man we called 'Max'.
> – Narrator

Director: George Miller
Writers: George Miller, Terry Hayes, Brian Hannant
Producer: Byron Kennedy
Cast includes: Mel Gibson, Bruce Spence, Mike Preston, Max Phipps, Virginia Hey, Emil Minty

ABOUT THE FILM

The iconic Mad Max franchise is known the world over for its uncompromising action sequences and as the vehicle that catapulted Mel Gibson into the world of international superstardom. In light of Gibson's recent shenanigans, people may think that wasn't such a good thing. Maybe we shouldn't go there.

The second instalment in the series, *Mad Max 2: The Road Warrior*, takes place a few years after the first film, when we meet our lone hero Max (Gibson) wandering the arid, post-apocalyptic plains of the Australian outback.

In a wasteland where petrol is scarce, he stumbles upon a small group of settlers being terrorised by a vigilante band of raiders attired in bondage getup, hell-bent on commandeering the precious commodity. What follows is a fast-paced thrill ride, with a mind-blowing final action sequence that makes a Michael Bay production look like a Merchant Ivory film.

Mad Max 2 is a rare breed of sequel – on the action-meter, at least, it easily surpasses the original. No big surprise, since the $4-million budget was over a thousand per cent increase on the first Mad Max movie. Its huge box office success (it grossed nearly $30 million in the US) spawned a third instalment, *Mad Max: Beyond Thunderdome*. (Yep, that's the one with Tina Turner and her huge blonde hairdo.)

For years the rumour mill has been churning with whispers of a fourth film. Finally, it was confirmed that George Miller would return to Silverton and Broken Hill to shoot *Mad Max: Fury Road*, more than a quarter-century after

Max wanders the vast Australian plains with his best friend

the first. The film has been plagued by major delays, with flowers being the main culprit. Yes, you read that right: flowers. The area has received so much rain that the desert has been transformed into a green flower garden. Gibson will not return to reprise his leading role as Max. The film will star Tom Hardy as Max, Charlize Theron and Nicholas Hoult.

LOCATIONS

Silverton New South Wales

It's slightly odd to have a town in Australia where a film crew is likely to outnumber the people who actually live there. You'll be searching long and hard (and unsuccessfully) to find anywhere in Australia with such a tiny population (just over 50) that's as prolific as Silverton – or 'Hollywood of the Outback', as it's known around the traps.

Sizzling Silverton wasn't always as emaciated as it is today. In the 1880s, over 3000 people lived here. Alas, most soon flocked to nearby Broken Hill for its mining boom. Despite the lack of souls, Silverton is a popular tourist destination with several noteworthy and fascinating historical sights, as well as its own thriving art scene – you won't fail to notice some kooky creations around town. History and art aside, there's no doubting that Silverton's notability is largely due to its popularity for shooting films and commercials – the town has played gracious host to well over 20 different film and television productions over the last four decades. The town is located 26 kilometres north-west of Broken Hill right near the New South Wales/South Australia border.

VISITOR INFO

Silverton Visitor Information Centre

Beyond 39 Dips, 2 Layard St; (08) 8088 7566; www.silverton.org.au

THINGS TO SEE AND DO
Mundi Mundi Lookout

Five kilometres west of the main town is the Mundi Mundi Lookout. The lookout was the location for some major scenes, namely the spectacular tanker wreck at the end of the film. Only the crash was filmed here, though; the actual chase down the highway was filmed on Menindee Road outside of Broken Hill. Film folklore has it that the tanker crash stunt was deemed so dangerous that the stunt driver was ordered not to eat 12 hours beforehand, just in case something went wrong and he had to undergo emergency surgery.

Some locals believe that if you scavenge around the site long enough you might still find small remnants of the crash. The lookout was also the location for the opening chase scene involving Max and his black Interceptor (which has got to be the most famous Aussie car ever). *Mundi Mundi Rd*

Mundi Mundi Road

Locals have renamed the road 'Mad Max Way'. Stretches of the bitumen leading to and from Mundi Mundi Lookout were used in the opening and closing chase scenes. Certain sections of the road will look familiar: the hill looking up towards the dry face of Mundi Mundi Lookout. In the opening chase scene, this section was used when Max dodges the wreck in his Interceptor. While it may be tempting to kick your Toyota into fifth gear and hoon down the bitumen like Max, remember that this isn't an autobahn; speed limits apply, so drive safely.

The Pinnacles

By these three pimples of peaks just outside Broken Hill, about 20 kilometres south-west of Silverton, is the location of the 'The Compound'. The compound was at the base of the middle pinnacle. At the top of the middle pinnacle Max and his new buddy/prisoner the Gyro Captain (Spence) scope out the activity at the compound. Unfortunately, this is private property so access is prohibited without permission. However, you can still get great views of The Pinnacles from Adelaide Road, Mildura Road and the Broken Earth Restaurant in Broken Hill (on Federation Way).

Stephens Creek

About 25 kilometres east of Silverton is the desolate Stephens Creek. This tiny spot was used for the scene in which Max first encounters the Gyro Captain before he takes him prisoner. *Best accessed via Silverton Rd, through Broken Hill and then the Silver City Hwy*

Mad Max Museum

For Adrian Bennett, trading in the crisp weather of Yorkshire, England, for the harsh desert heat was only a small sacrifice to live a dream. Adrian's undying love for the post-apocalyptic action flick saw him, his wife Linda and his three sons move halfway across the world to Silverton to open this Mad Max–inspired house of memorabilia.

Inside Australia's only film-specific museum you'll find mannequins, costumes, over 500 photographs and two replicas of Max's Interceptor, one of which Adrian built himself in England and shipped over. There are also souvenirs for sale, including, of course, T-shirts and stubby holders.

Adrian and Linda also run the Silverton Hotel and Linda has offered a free pot to anyone that can stump her husband on Mad Max–related trivia. If that's not incentive enough to visit Silverton, what is? *9 Stirling St; (08) 8088 6128*

Silverton Hotel

There's absolutely no way you can make the trek all the way out to Silverton and not visit this pub. It's the heart and soul of the town and shares important ties with the film. The *Mad Max 2* production crew used the area next to the pub as their base camp for shooting, while the catering van parked itself in the beer garden of the hotel. I guess they just wanted to be near the beer. Most of the cast and crew used the beer garden for morning tea, lunch and afternoon tea.

The hotel interior is packed with movie memorabilia. For years a replica of Max's Interceptor sat parked out front, but a recent change in management saw the car flee with its owners, leaving only dust and tyre tracks in its wake. The hotel has been featured in many of the films shot in town, including *Wake in Fright* (1971) and *Dirty Deeds* (2002). *Layard St; (08) 8088 5313*

Art galleries

Silverton has three main art galleries: the Horizon Gallery (corner Burke Street), John Dynon Gallery (Stirling Street) and the Silverton Outback Art Gallery (Stirling Street). Each gallery has incredible works by very talented local artists. The Outback Gallery has affordable prints and souvenirs to purchase and decorated vintage Volkswagen bugs parked out front. Not sure why the bugs – it's hard to imagine Max driving around in one of those.

VW beetles outside the Outback Gallery

Camels take a breather outside the Silverton Hotel while their riders seek refreshment inside

If it's all the same to you … I'll drive that tanker.
– Max

Silverton Gaol Museum

Thousands of items – from old photographs to mining tools – vie for space in this old gaol and museum, giving visitors an insight into the history of the town. There's also some film memorabilia. *Burke St; (08) 8088 5317*

Silverton Historic Cemetery

This 42-acre historical site is a sobering reminder of Silverton's early years. Many of the residents met an early end from mining accidents, an all-too-common occurrence back in the day, while typhoid took too many of the children. *Belmont Rd*

Nelson's Opals

For over 30 years, this shop has been renowned for its wide range of opals, as well as minerals, souvenirs and artwork. Open seven days a week. *Burke St; (08) 8088 5318*

The Day Dream Mine

Located north-west of Silverton, about 20 kilometres outside Broken Hill, this historic abandoned mine was once a hub of activity before its closure in 1983. Visitors can take walking tours of the mine. *Apollyon Valley; (08) 8088 5682*

WHERE TO STAY

Silverton Hotel

Four inexpensive cabins equipped with ensuites. Light meals and plenty of cold beer on tap. *Layard St; (08) 8088 5313*

Blue Bush Country Cottage

In a peaceful setting alongside Black Hill Creek, this homey cottage sleeps four or five and the master bedroom is underground. *Silverton Rd; (08) 8088 4488*

WHERE TO EAT

Silverton Cafe

Built in the 1880s, this former house is today a lovely cafe, ideal for grabbing a quick bite between sightseeing. You'll actually start your sightseeing here, browsing the photos and memorabilia on display. Check out the main room of the house, which contains a collection of antique dolls – some made as early as 1869. May disturb Chucky-haters. Closed Mondays. *8 Stirling St; (08) 8088 6601*

CARAVANS AND MOTORHOMES

Penrose Park

Named after John Penrose, who was mayor of Silverton when the park was opened in 1937, this park has powered caravan and camping sites, bunkhouses sleeping eight and a large hall available to rent. Great picnic spots and all kinds of resident animals. *Penrose Park; 8088 5307*

Silverton War Memorial Youth Camp

Originally built in 1887 and used as a court house, the dormitory-style bunks sleep up to 52 people at a time. *Burke St; (08) 8088 6352*

TOURS

Heritage walking trail

A self-guided two-hour walk around Silverton's sights, taking in the Silverton Hotel, the Silverton Lookout and many other heritage buildings. Trail maps are available at the visitor centre or through the Silverton website. *2 Layard St; (08) 8088 7566; www.silverton.org.au*

Barrier Range Camel Safaris

While you're in town, why not buy a pet camel 'weed eater'. These 'ships of the desert' are also available for weddings, but you might just want to settle for a half-hour excursion or an overnight camping trip. *(08) 8088 5316; bookings at silvertoncamels@bigpond.com*

DID YOU KNOW?

Only two Interceptors were used in the filming of *Mad Max 2*. One was destroyed (on purpose) when it was pushed off the road and blown up in a scene. The other was sold to a junk yard, luckily purchased by a fan and restored. Now it's on display at the 'Cars of the Stars' museum in Keswick, England. The Interceptor is in good company – it sits alongside numerous Batmobiles, the Delorean from *Back to the Future* and Herbie the Love Bug.

AND ANOTHER THING ...

NATIONAL FILM AND SOUND ARCHIVE

Located in Canberra, the National Film and Sound Archive is a treasure trove of all things Aussie film. The archive houses the country's largest collection of preserved film material from the late 1800s to the present day, including sound recordings, videos, audio tapes, photographic stills, costumes, props and, of course, the films themselves.

The NFSA makes the collection available to the public through a variety of exhibitions (both permanent and travelling), screenings, live presentations and educational programs.

The permanent Exhibition Gallery is a must when visiting the NFSA; it's a fascinating interactive journey through over a century of Australian, film, TV, radio and recorded sound.

It's also hard to ignore the on-site shop (products also available for purchase online), which has some film goodies such as books, DVDs and giftware. You can even buy some old film canisters for a few bucks.

McCoy Circuit, Acton, ACT; (02) 6248 2000 or 1800 067 274; www.nfsa.gov.au

Hollywood of the outback – films shot in Silverton

From feature films to TV shows and commercials, the barren landscape of Silverton has provided the backdrop for many productions over the years. Here's a look at just a few of the well-known feature films and TV series shot in and around Silverton.

WAKE IN FRIGHT (1971)

Known as one of the great 'lost' films until it was digitally restored and released on DVD in 2009, this Aussie classic tells the story of an aggrieved school teacher who goes on a boozing bender in the small mining town of Bundanyabba (haven't we all been there?). The film was the first feature for Jack Thompson and the last for veteran actor Chips Rafferty, who died of a heart attack prior to the film's release. *Wake in Fright* premiered at the Cannes Film Festival and was nominated for the prestigious Palme d'Or. The Silverton Hotel was one of the main locations used in the film.

DIRTY DEEDS (2001)

This Aussie crime caper, set in the 1960s, sees organised crime from the US confront the local Aussie mafia as they jockey for a piece of the lucrative 'pokies' fortune. The film stars Bryan Brown, Sam Neill, Toni Collette, Sam Worthington, Kestie Morassi and larger-than-life American actor John Goodman. The film was shot in a variety of locations around Silverton as well as Broken Hill and locations throughout Sydney.

RAZORBACK (1984)

One of the first Australian horror films, the plot revolves around a small outback town being terrorised by a vicious, deadly wild boar ... think *Babe* meets *Jaws*. The Silverton Hotel featured prominently in the film, as well as other locations throughout the town. The cult classic was finally released on DVD in Australia in 2005 and scored an international release in 2009. The film stars John Howard, Gregory Harrison and Arkie Whiteley and was directed by Russel Mulcahy, who went on to direct *Highlander* (1986), *Swimming Upstream* (2003) and *Resident Evil: Extinction* (2007).

MISSION: IMPOSSIBLE II (2000)

Directed by John Woo, this action-adventure sequel stars Tom 'Mum's cooking a lamb roast' Cruise and was predominantly shot in and around Sydney. However, there were a few scenes shot in the Silverton and Broken

Hill area. *M:I II* was the highest grossing film of 2000, garnering almost US$550 million in worldwide box office takings. A third instalment of the franchise was released in 2006, while a fourth and final film is set to be released in December 2011.

HOSTAGE (1983)

This film, shot in the Silverton and Broken Hill area, is based on the true story of an Aussie teenage girl who finds out that her husband is an active member of the Nazi party. This US production was titled *The Christine Maresch Story* and used locations in Sydney and Germany. It stars Kerry Mack, Ralph Schicha and former *Home and Away* regular Judy Nunn.

A TOWN LIKE ALICE (1981)

Based on Nevil Shute's international best-selling novel, this hugely popular TV miniseries is a love story set after World War II (but with some prisoner-of-war flashbacks). Shot in a variety of locations around Silverton, the series starring Bryan Brown and Helen Morse was nominated for a Primetime Emmy and swept the Logies in 1982. The book had been adapted to a film in 1956 with Peter Finch and Virginia McKenna.

COMRADES (1986)

Shot partly in Silverton, as well as Broken Hill and the UK, *Comrades* is the story of the Tolpuddle Martyrs, six English labourers who are deported to Australia in the 1830s.

The brave group of men forms one of the first ever trade unions in an attempt to receive fair wages. The film is based on a true story and stars Vanessa Redgrave, Imelda Staunton and James Fox. The film was nominated for the prestigious Golden Bear Award at the Berlin International Film Festival in 1987.

The Man from Snowy River (1982)

If it was easy to get to know it, it would be not challenging. You've got to treat the mountains like a high-spirited horse; never take it for granted.

— *Jim*

Clancy (Thompson), Spur (Douglas) and Jim (Buchinson) swap stories around a campfire

Director: George Miller
Writers: John Dixon, Fred Cul Cullen
Producer: Geoff Burrowes
Cast includes: Tom Burlinson, Kirk Douglas, Sigrid Thornton, Jack Thompson, Lorraine Bayly

ABOUT THE FILM

Overseas tourists coming to this great land often have preconceived notions of what Australia is all about: rugged outback landscapes, broad accents and blokes in thongs and swagman hats swilling cans of Fosters. Sure we have a few of those types wandering around, but an oft-forgotten segment of classic Australiana is all about cattle musters, wild brumbies and the beautiful Victorian High Country. This was the setting for George Miller's 1982 re-imagining of

Banjo Paterson's famous 1890 poem *The Man from Snowy River.*

After the death of his father, young horseman Jim Craig (Burlinson) goes to work for wealthy cattle rancher Harrison (Douglas), a ruthless American (and estranged twin brother of his father's best friend). Jim promptly falls head over heels for Harrison's headstrong daughter, Jessica (Thornton), much to the chagrin of Daddy-dearest. A series of events culminates in an exciting wild horse chase through the steep and densely wooded terrain of the High Country, where 'any slip was death' (A.B. Paterson). The final riding scenes have you on the edge of your seat and put most Hollywood westerns to shame.

Watching the film almost 30 years later, it's gratifying to see how well *The Man from Snowy River* stands the test of time – from its engaging storyline to the spectacular horseriding scenes. It's the authenticity of this film that makes it so

Jim and Jessica (Thornton) ride through the stunning High Country

> It changes so suddenly.
> One moment it's
> paradise, the next it's
> trying to kill you.
>
> — *Jessica, on the High Country*

special. Bona fide High Country cattlemen were used in the film and almost all of Tom's riding scenes in the film starred the actor himself (after months of rigorous training).

The success of the film spawned a sequel in 1988, *The Man from Snowy River II* (released in the US as *Return to Snowy River*), as well as a TV series in 1993 starring Guy Pearce (with a few cameos from Hugh Jackman). *The Man from Snowy River* was nominated at the 1983 Golden Globe Awards for Best Foreign Film, yet it was inexplicably snubbed by the AFIs, not even receiving a nomination for Best Film.

LOCATIONS

MERRIJIG
VICTORIA

The small hamlet of Merrijig is one of Victoria's hidden gems. Nestled in the Delatite River valley, Merrijig is approximately 24 kilometres east of the larger, more populated Mansfield, the gateway to the Victorian snowfields.

According to the film's producer Geoff Burrowes, the town of Merrijig was chosen as the base of operations for *The Man from Snowy River* for numerous reasons, particularly the range of quality accessible

Horseman Jim gallops through the High Country

High Country features and the culture of the cattlemen in the area. The panoramic vistas and natural beauty that many locals describe as 'God's Country' was another obvious reason. Many locations in and around Merrijig, including spots in Alpine National Park, as well as Mansfield, were used as filming locations for both *The Man from Snowy River* and its sequel.

Around this area is the High Country wine region, famed for its shiraz, riesling and viognier, and cellar door outlets abound. For those who like to quaff amber ales just as much as vino, there are also microbreweries making boutique beers from crystal-clear mountain waters.

VISITOR INFO

Mansfield Visitor Centre

175 High St, Mansfield; (03) 5775 7000; www.mansfield-mtbuller.com.au

Merrijig Town Information

www.merrijig.com.au

THINGS TO SEE AND DO

Harrison's Homestead site

The bare paddock on a property on Buttercup Road (owned at the time by a local, Charlie Hearn) was the location of Harrison's Homestead. The homestead itself, the barn and all the outbuildings were built entirely from scratch for the production. Alas, all the sets were torn down after production so there's no chance of wandering the property and snapping photos of the rustic edifices (it's still private property, so such behaviour wouldn't be appreciated, anyway). While the kitchen, barn

and stockmen's huts were all built for interior shoots, the homestead was not. Hence all the homestead interior scenes were filmed at studios in Port Melbourne. These studios no longer exist, having been replaced with residential apartments. The Buttercup Road property was used again in *The Man from Snowy River II* – all the sets had to be built from scratch and subsequently torn down again. What a waste! *Buttercup Rd*

Falls Nest Spur

Horseriding near Merrijig

To the west of Mt Stirling, just near Falls Nest Spur, is a tiny logging track where Jim's father Henry (Terry Donovan) meets his maker, thanks to a rowdy pack of brumbies and a runaway tree log (not exactly a pleasant way to go). The scene begins with father and son cutting down a tall woollybutt tree (also known as alpine ash). The tree was prepped by local identity 'Bundles' Campagnolo, so Burlinson and Donovan could come in at the last minute and look like genuine mountain men on screen as they crosscut sawed the colossal tree. Timberrrrr!!! *Via Circuit Rd*

Pretty Valley

Around 7 kilometres east past Merrijig on Mt Buller Road, Pretty Valley was a location used for the exhilarating horse chase scenes at the tail end of the film. The vast expanses of Pretty Valley were perfect for the large stable of well-trained horses to gallop freely and re-enact an authentic stallion chase. The space has some sensational views of Mt Buller. The valley lies just opposite the Pinnacle Valley Resort. *Mt Buller Rd*

Howqua Hills

Perhaps the best place to channel your inner Banjo Paterson is the magnificent Howqua Hills. The long stream of water to the west of the hills (known as the Howqua River) was used as a location in the film's concluding horse chase scenes. The shallow crossing just above Sheepyard Flat is the exact spot where the horses run through the river (about 17 kilometres into the bush due west from Merrijig).

Sheepyard Flat got its name because, after the valley was settled, shepherds put their sheep on the flat land at night and took turns keeping the dingoes at bay.

The banks of the Howqua River are camping heaven, not to mention an ideal spot for angling

Rebuilt replica of Craig's Hut

(in trout season) and canoeing (depending on the water levels). The Howqua Hills area is located in the far west of Alpine National Park. *Access via Howqua Track, off Mt Buller Rd*

Mt Magdala

The ominous cliff face where Jessica ends up after travelling into the harsh wilds of the High Country was filmed at a place called Tommy Standup on Mt Magdala, in an area known as Hell's Window. The cliff has a genuine drop of thousands of feet so a stunt double was brought in for Sigrid for these scenes. Mt Magdala is around 50 kilometres south-west of Mansfield in Alpine National Park. *East of Mt Lovick and Lovick Hut, via Alpine Walking Track*

Craig's Hut

Aside from the snow-crusted slopes (and bars) in winter, the most popular tourist spot in all of the High Country is Craig's Hut, located 40 kilometres past Merrijig at Clear Hills (a long spur off Mt Stirling dropping into the King River). This famous hut was built for use as the home of Jim and Henry Craig (you probably already worked that one out) in the scenes at the beginning of the film. The site was chosen for its spectacular views of Mt Cobbler to the north.

Until 2006, when it was destroyed by bushfires, Craig's Hut was the only remaining set from the film. Volunteers built a replica of the hut shortly after, though it has came under scrutiny for not being authentic enough.

There's a camping area near the hut, as well as plenty of rich wilderness to explore by foot, mountain bike and four-wheel drive. Parts of Mt Stirling were used for the scenes when Jim searches for a lost and frightened Jessica. *Access via Clear Hills Track off Circuit Rd or by foot from Circuit Rd car park; the road is closed to vehicular traffic from early June and re-opens in late October (depending on when all the snow melts)*

Mansfield

The township of Mansfield sits at the foot of the Great Dividing Range, just west of Merrijig. The western side of the main town was used in the street scenes when Harrison arrives to collect his prized colt. The old town buildings required very little set dressing for the scene, though they had to cover the bitumen roads with sand for authenticity. The townscape has changed greatly since the early '80s and many of the original buildings seen in the film are no longer standing.

Parts of Mansfield were also used for the scenes when Jessica battles the brutal storm before Jim rides to the rescue.

Mansfield is the gateway to the Mt Buller ski fields, Victoria's largest and most popular ski and snowboarding resort. While the focus in winter is on snow, in the summer months Mansfield offers a plethora of other activities to enjoy, including bushwalking, horseriding, mountain biking, fishing and four-wheel driving.

The Bluff

East past Sheepyard Flat, through the Eight Mile Flat Campground along Eight Mile Spur is the way to reach the wide-open splendour of The Bluff, a 1725-metre-tall treeless summit. The Bluff has some of the best panoramas in Australia. The most popular way to access The Bluff is via the Bluff Trail, a moderate 27-kilometre-return trek completed on foot or horseback. The trek takes two days and is best done in summer or autumn. *Further information through Parks Victoria; 13 1963; www.parkweb. vic.gov.au*

Traditional pub in Mansfield

WHERE TO STAY

Buttercup Cottage and Private Apartment

Spacious cottage and self-contained apartment in the heart of the High Country. Curl up in front of the cosy fireplace with a bottle of local red or just enjoy the mountain views any which way you look. Throw a ball around for the resident cottage canines, Harriett and Molly, a constant source of cuteness. *271 Buttercup Rd, Merrijig; (03) 5777 5591; www.buttercup.com.au*

Merrijig Motor Inn Resort

Comfy motel-style single rooms with queen beds, as well as bunk and family rooms. Start the day with a hearty continental breakfast and a stroll along the Delatite River. *1915 Mt Buller Rd, Merrijig; (03) 5777 5702; www.merrijigmotorinn.com.au*

Pinnacle Valley Resort

An all-seasons Grand Mercure Resort with studio and one-bedroom apartments (and chalets for those with a bit of extra cash to splash) with all resort facilities. Short drive to Mt Buller and close to Pretty Valley. *1 Mimosa Dr, Merrijig; (03) 5777 5788; www.pvr.com.au*

Wappan Station

Get a taste of the rural life in this unique farmstay south-west of Mansfield near Lake Eildon. Get a gang of 20 together and stay in the shearers' quarters for a real High Country experience. Relax – you won't have to shear any of the 16 000 sheep to earn your keep. *904 Royaltown Rd, Maindample; (03) 5778 7786; www.wappanstation.com.au*

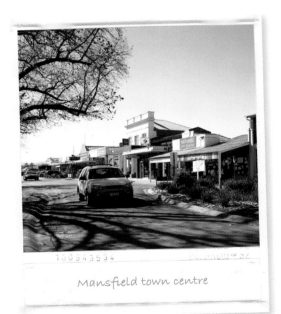
Mansfield town centre

CARAVANS AND MOTORHOMES

Mansfield Holiday Park

The closest caravan park to Mt Buller and a short drive to Lake Eildon. Cabin and camping accommodation also available here. It's a nice and cheap base to set up before attacking the slopes. *Mt Buller Rd, Mansfield; (03) 5775 1383; www.mansfieldholidaypark.com.au*

High Country Holiday Park

Friendly staff and a relaxed attitude is the name of the game at this holiday park, with cabins and spa cottages, as well as camping under the beautiful Victorian night sky – summer nights are magical. *1 Ultimo St, Mansfield; (03) 5775 2705; www.highcountryholidaypark.com.au*

CAMPING

Buttercup Creek Reserve

Large camping area with five sites beside Buttercup Creek just a few kilometres north-east of Merrijig. It's a great base from which to explore the surrounding areas by foot or mountain bike and there's awesome fishing to be had by the creek. *Access via Carter Rd and Buttercup Rd*

Craig's Hut camping area

Camping facilities at one of Australia's famous film locations. Beautiful scenic lookouts and hiking. *Access via Clear Hills Track off Circuit Rd or by foot from Circuit Rd car park*

Blue Range Camping Reserve

A small campsite north-east of the Mansfield township; a great spot for horseriding and four-wheel driving. *Access via Blue Range Creek off Walker Rd from Bridge Creek along Mansfield–Whitfield Rd*

Alpine National Park

There are many camping areas around the Mansfield area in this 646 000-hectare national park. Highlights include Lovicks Hut, Bluff Hut and the Upper Howqua camping area. *www.parkweb.vic.gov.au*

WHERE TO EAT

Hunt Club Hotel

Established in 1873, the Hunt Club is one of Australia's oldest pubs. Breathe in the history and enjoy a classic counter meal by the stone fireplaces and timber bar. *1870 Mt Buller Rd, Merrijig; (03) 5777 5508; www.huntclubhotel.com*

The Deck on High

A Thai-inspired venue where you can enjoy tapas on the outdoor rooftop or dishes like Korean barbecue plate or orange-glazed duck in a more formal setting. Also serves breakfast on the weekend and takeaway. For pre- or post-dinner libations, the piano bar or oriental room is the ticket. *13 Main St, Mansfield; (03) 5775 1144; www.thedeckonhigh.com.au*

Magnolia Gourmet Country House

Modern regional fare with seasonal dishes and local wines. Don't miss schnitzel night on Wednesdays, when they offer over 15 varieties of schnitz from 'the Russian' with beetroot and bacon to 'the Aussie' with bacon, egg and gravy (they taste better than they sound). A large selection of local wines from Mansfield to the Yarra Valley. Open Tuesday to Saturday. *190 Mt Buller Rd, Mansfield; (03) 5779 1444; www.magnoliamansfield.com.au*

TOURS

Lovick's High Country Adventures

Mt Buller's snowy peaks

Since 1965, the Lovick family has run some of the best adventure tours in regional Victoria. Run by Charlie and his wife Glenda, Lovick's Adventures offers weekend or longer ten- and twelve-day horse treks through the magnificent snow gum forests and High Country plains. Many of these rides take in locations of the film – from Craig's Hut to the Howqua Hills.

Charlie knows a thing or two about the film – he was the Master of Horse for *The Man from Snowy River* and its sequel. As well as being in the movies as a rider, he was the one that taught Tom Burlinson how to ride. (See the Q&A on pages 146–7 for a chat with Charlie about his involvement in the film.) In fact, Tom Burlinson has even tagged along on a Lovick's tour, so you might get lucky and ride with Jim Craig himself!

Treks cater for beginners to advanced riders. They offer a special five-day tour in December, Push the Bush, where you experience the thrill of herding cattle and a variety of accommodation options. Definitely not to be missed. *Davies Rd, Merrijig; (03) 5777 5510; www.lovicks.com.au*

Did you know?

Tom Burlinson has admitted that some of the riding of his character, Jim, was carried out by a stuntman. But in the famous scene where Jim careens down the dangerously steep hill it was, in fact, Tom in the saddle.

Watsons Mountain Country Trail Rides

Offers a five-day 'Man from Snowy River Ride' tour, which takes in many locations from the film. On day four, you tie up your horses for lunch at the Riverhouse Hideout, near the Goulburn River, where you can view memorabilia from the film. *Three Chain Rd, Mansfield; (03) 5777 3552; www.watsonstrailrides.com.au*

Stirling Experience

The five-day Crosscut Walk is an amazing journey that takes in Craig's Hut, The Bluff, Mt Speculation, Mt Magdala, Mt Howitt and the Cross Cut Saw. Meals by the campfire and stunning sunsets guaranteed. Stirling Experience also has summer and winter accommodation, ski equipment hire and other tours of the area, including four-wheel-drive expeditions. *Telephone Box Junction, Stirling Rd, Mt Stirling; (03) 5777 6441; www.stirling.au.com*

OTHER LOCATIONS

EUROA VICTORIA

Euroa is located between Seymour and Benalla, just north-west of Mansfield. A spot outside the town was used as the location of Spur's Hut, home of the legless and impoverished Spur, Jim's friend with the heart of gold. The hut was a set built for the film and no longer stands. They also filmed outside of Euroa for the scene where the train arrives in town, bringing with it Harrison's prized colt.

Horseriding on Mt Buller

AND ANOTHER THING ...

FILM JARGON – WHAT ON EARTH IS A BEST BOY?

Gaffer – Not just a kind of tape used by drug-addled roadies and for feeble attempts to try and patch up your leaking lilo, a gaffer is the head of the electrical department on a film, mainly in charge of lighting. And they use all kinds of tape on the job!

Key grip – Hang on tight, don't drop that verrrrrry expensive camera equipment! While key grips aren't really standing around holding cameras all day; their job is to do with holding cameras – usually setting up dollies, tracks and cranes to hold the camera and enable smooth movement. On large films they might use up to 25 grips.

Best boy – Sounds like favouritism? You bet. Before the days of film, if someone wanted to borrow your most experienced apprentice for a job, they'd ask for your 'best boy'. In film they are assistants, either to the gaffer or the grip.

Dolly – Not as cute and girly as it sounds, film dollies are like trollies, often run on tracks like trains and with arms like cranes. They have to be nice and strong to keep a 350-kilogram camera steady. If you're in charge of it, you're the dolly grip.

Focus puller – The production assistant might disagree (schlepping back and forth in a vain attempt to get the director's coffee order right), but it's generally accepted that the focus puller has the hardest job on set. Their job is to maintain the sharpness of the image, working with the cinematographer and using a variety of different camera lenses to achieve this.

Foley – Whenever you hear a horse galloping on screen, just think of a guy in a room hitting coconut shells on the ground. A vital part of the sound mixing process is foley recording, which is the reproduction of everyday sounds (doors closing, footsteps) using a variety of props. Foley artists will hole-up in a room and record themselves crackling cellophane, chomping on an apple and splashing water to get the desired effect. Named after Jack Foley, who started the process in 1927 at Universal Studios.

Apple box – These wooden boxes are used by the grip department to prop up lights, furniture, workbenches and steps. Even the talent sometimes require an apple box to look taller in a particular scene, such as when a shorter Magda Szubanski is acting opposite James Cromwell (6 feet, 7 inches) in *Babe*.

Location recce – A term location scouts use which basically refers to a location visit. Location recces (short for reconnaissance) take place in pre-production and generally involve the location manager, director and cinematographer. Depending on the film, some productions will involve dozens of location recces over many months.

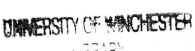

Q & A Charlie Lovick, the Master of Horse on *The Man from Snowy River*

Along with his father Jack and brother John, fifth-generation cattleman Charlie Lovick was one of the vital players in helping *The Man from Snowy River* get made. Aside from being the Master of Horse on the film (with his contribution being honoured by a super-prominent position in the film's credits), Charlie provided insider knowledge of the mountains and had a role in the film as a rider.

Q: *How did you first get involved in* The Man from Snowy River *film?*

A: My forebears were pioneers who moved to the area in 1860 and we've been here ever since. Traditionally we've been mountain cattlemen and horsemen – that was the passion that developed after the goldmining days brought them here. Years ago we combined the cattle and the horses and tourism. We used to take people up to the High Country to muster and drive our cattle.

One night we were sitting around a campfire in the High Country with some young turks from Melbourne, having a few beers. They thought it would be fantastic to make a feature film to bring the area to the awareness of the Australian public. **My old man said, 'Well if you ever do that, it'd be great to do *The Man from Snowy River*.'** They said that sounds like a great idea. So they sat around, drank more beer and decided that they'd form a company and write a script. If they ever did make the movie, they asked if we'd be prepared to do all the horse work and help with locations and expertise.

'No worries!' We all had a bit of a giggle, we thought it was just pie in the sky. Lo and behold, six months later they rang us up and said they had formed a company, had a script written, got the money and we were it.

Q: *What did the Master of Horse role involve?*

A: The production company had little expertise in movie-making; they'd been in TV for years, but had never done a feature film. To make it authentic, they knew the movie had to show real people on real horses, which was us blokes. **I became the interface between the production company and all the local yokels that my father and I had invited to ride.** It was invitation-only; you only got to ride in that movie if you passed muster. **All the riding in those scenes looked fantastic, because it was the real deal. They were full-on mountain horsemen.** I was the bloke explaining to the horsemen what they had to do.

Every time we rode to do a shot, it was basically full-on warfare – **no-one from Mansfield was gonna let anyone from Omeo beat them down the hill and vice-versa!**

I took young Tom Burlinson under my wing, we had a rapport. Because it was my horse they were using, I was the one that educated Tom to ride. He was a non-rider when he got there. I was the bloke they were asking about shots, what was authentic and what wasn't. That's how it came to be that I was the man in charge of the horse work.

The horse work is authentic. It was important to educate Tom up to a standard where he could actually sell himself as a horseman. He excelled at that.

At that time lots of people thought the Red Centre was our outback. **But the High Country has more history and heritage than anywhere**

else in Australia. We wanted to bring that out, too. I thought we did it pretty bloody well in the end.

Q: *You were in both movies. What was it like being in front of the camera?*

A: In the full-on horse scenes, there wasn't a worry in the world. That's our area of expertise. But when we got in front of the camera and had to do bit of a scene, of course we went to water [laughs]. We got tongue-tied, we didn't know which way to look. It was hilarious to look at the rushes. But we did learn as we went along; it was a hell of a learning curve.

We hoped that it was going to be a great movie, but we had no idea it was going to be received so well. **Each day when we saw the rushes we knew we had something ... something that was different than anything else we had ever seen.**

Q: *What impressions really stand out when you think about both films?*

A: I'm very proud of the way that Tom Burlinson came through and became such a consummate horseman. He'd ask me what I thought about some of the very spectacular and dangerous scenes, 'Charlie, can I do that?' and I'd say, 'Without doubt Tom, you can.' I got emotional when it all got put together. There's nobody that can pick anything wrong with that young man's horse handling and his riding style. He put so much time and effort into it, and that allowed us to have those downhill scenes. In his more sedate riding scenes, he is poetry in motion with the horse and that sells to everybody.

Geoff Burrowes, the producer, is now my brother-in-law – he married my little sister between the first and second movies.

There's a lot of camaraderie in the High Country, but there's a lot of competition as well. That movie gave all of us an opportunity to ride together and get to know each other. Those friendships have never ever been lost. **It's brought towns together from one side of the divide to the other.**

I never get sick of watching the movie. I don't get embarrassed by it because it really does stand the test of time. And it really depicts a genuine way of life out there.

Q: *I heard that back in 2009 there was a reunion of all the 'crack' riders from the film.*

A: It was sensational. Tom and Sigrid and Gus Mercurio and a few others came down and I got as many of the old crack riders as I could together. We just had a good catch up, and a few beers, and got to know each other again. The response from the crowds to these old blokes riding around on horses was great. They didn't realise the esteem they were held in by the general public. They were national heroes and didn't realise it.

Q: *What is it about the Victorian High Country that you love so much?*

A: It gets into your bloodstream. There's a combination of challenge, freedom and achievement. When you get out there and the elements are with you one day and against you the next, that's when **the partnership between you and your animal come to the fore**. It's an experience you won't find anywhere else. Chuck in the early morning sunrises and sunsets, the misty lakes and the big storms, [and] you yearn to get back there all the time.

From humble beginnings

Everyone has to start somewhere! Here are a few of our favourite Aussie A-list actors and their first on-screen roles.

ROSE BYRNE (1979–)

Byrne got her start on the soap *Echo Point*, a short-lived series that aired from June to December 1995. The soap revolved around the intertwining lives of a group of people living in a bayside community. Rose played the innocent dreamer Belinda O'Connor, a 15-year-old pigtailed schoolgirl. The series also gave career starts to Martin Henderson and Ryan Kwanten.

HUGO WEAVING (1960–)

Weaving made his big screen debut in the 1981 feature ... *Maybe This Time*, a drama about a university research assistant going through a mid-life crisis. Weaving had a minor role as 'Student 2'. The film was nominated for six AFI Awards. Weaving came to prominence three years later for playing English cricket captain Douglas Jardine in the acclaimed TV miniseries *BodyLine*.

TONI COLLETTE (1972–)

Collette made her screen debut on an episode of the long-running TV show *A Country Practice*. Collette played the character of Tracy in an episode titled 'The Sting: Part One' which aired in January 1990. The episode saw beloved Wandin Valley plumber Bob suffer a life-threatening bee sting.

JACK THOMPSON (1940–)

Screen legend Jack Thompson also got his start in television. His debut was in the 1968 afternoon soap *Motel*. The half-hour program was adapted from the British serial *Crossroads* and was set at the Greenfield Motel (on the highway between Sydney and Canberra) run by the Gillian family. Jack played the role of Bill Burke. The series lasted 132 episodes.

NICOLE KIDMAN (1967–)

Kidman's first movie role came in *Bush Christmas*, the 1983 drama about the Thompson family struggling to keep their farm from foreclosure. Kidman played the role of eldest daughter Helen. Nic's follow-up film, also released in 1983, was the classically corny *BMX Bandits*. Her first TV appearance was promoting *BMX Bandits* on the hit show *Young Talent Time*.

GEOFFREY RUSH (1951–)

Rush's role in the 1981 movie *Hoodwink*, the story of a sly bank robber who pretends to be blind, was his first feature film. He played the small part of a detective alongside Judy Davis, Michael Caton and Colin Friels. Rush's formative acting years were dedicated to the stage, so his film and TV credits weren't extensive before *Shine*.

RUSSELL CROWE (1964–)

Crowe wasn't even eight years old before he got his first big break on the small screen. He played the role of an orphan boy in an episode of the TV series *Spyforce*. The series, which ran from 1971 to 1973 on the Nine Network, starred Jack Thompson and was about a group of Australian Intelligence officers during World War II. Over the next couple of decades Crowe would appear in TV shows such as *The Flying Doctors*, *Neighbours* and an episode of the Greek-flavoured comedy *Acropolis Now* (in an episode titled 'Teenage Mutant Ninja Greeks'). It wasn't until 1990 that Crowe appeared in his first film, *Prisoners of the Sun*.

CATE BLANCHETT (1969–)

After graduating from NIDA in 1992, it wasn't long before Blanchett got her first break in an episode of *Police Rescue* in 1993. She also appeared in the *Police Rescue* telemovie a year later. Her first recurring TV role came on the ABC miniseries *Heartland* in 1995, a show about a small coastal town that is rocked by the mysterious death of an Aboriginal girl. The eight-part series also starred Ernie Dingo. Her first feature film role was the 1997 Bruce Beresford–directed *Paradise Road*, about a group of women imprisoned on the island of Sumatra during World War II. The film starred Glenn Close and Frances McDormand.

HUGH JACKMAN (1968–)

Though we first saw Jackman on an episode of *Law of the Land* in 1994, it was his role in the short-lived TV series *Correlli* (1995) that is of more significance – that was the prison drama where Hugh was cast opposite Deborah-Lee Furness, who he married. A year later he would appear in a few episodes of *Snowy River: The McGregor Saga*. His first feature film was the 1999 romantic comedy *Paperback Hero* with Claudia Karvan. Hugh also recorded a song on the film's soundtrack.

MEL GIBSON (1956–)

Gibson got his first big break on the classic Aussie TV show *The Sullivans*, where he played the character of Ray Henderson. *The Sullivans* featured many future stars back in the day, including Sam Neill, Kylie Minogue, Kerry Armstrong, Michael Caton and Gary Sweet. A year later, Gibson made his feature film debut, although it was an uncredited role as a baseball player in the American production *I Never Promised You a Rose Garden* (1977). *Summer City* (1977) was his first Australian feature and two years later he cracked it big with his starring role in *Mad Max*.

BRYAN BROWN (1947–)

Brown had his screen debut as the lead role in Stephen Wallace's *The Love Letters from Teralba Road* (1978), a 50-minute drama about a violent man who tries to win his girlfriend back with a series of romantic letters. The next few years would be a dream run for Brown, who featured in *The Chant of Jimmie Blacksmith* (1978), *Newsfront* (1978), *The Odd Angry Shot* (1979) and *Breaker Morant* (1980). Brown would go onto a successful international career, becoming familiar to US audiences with his role in the US miniseries *The Thorn Birds* (1983).

RACHEL GRIFFITHS (1968–)

Griffiths got her acting training in a community theatre group. Her screen debut was a tiny role in an episode of the sketch comedy show *Fast Forward* in 1992. She also had a recurring role playing various characters in another sketch comedy series, *Jimeoin*, in 1994. Griffiths also starred in the short-lived ABC show *Secrets*, about four university graduates recruited by a spy agency. The film that put Rachel on the acting map, *Muriel's Wedding*, was her feature film debut.

ERIC BANA (1968–)

Bana is known for getting his start on the comedy sketch show *Full Frontal* during the mid '90s. While he is best-known for the uber-ocker character Poida, Bana also had a variety of other hilarious recurring characters. These included a spoof of popular current affairs host Ray Martin (complete with helmet-like plastic hairdo) and Eddy, the crusty European immigrant who always used the phrase 'it's a complete shemozzle'. Eric's success on *Full Frontal* led to his own sketch comedy series in 1997 called *The Eric Bana Show Live*. Eric's first feature role came in *The Castle* (1997) as Con, the kickboxing husband of Tracey Kerrigan (Sophie Lee).

SAM WORTHINGTON (1976–)

It's been a monstrous couple of years for Worthington. Big-budget blockbusters such as *Terminator: Salvation* (2009) and *Clash of the Titans* (2010) brought him to the world's attention. There's also that little James Cameron movie *Avatar* (2009), which became the highest grossing film of all time, taking in almost US$3 billion worldwide. Worthington's first feature was the 2000 Aussie tap-dancing-blokes flick *Bootmen*, opposite Adam Garcia. Wortho also did several guest TV appearances, with roles on episodes of *Water Rats* and *Blue Heelers* the same year. He was actually born in England, but moved to Perth when he was two months old.

JUDY DAVIS (1955–)

Before Davis burst onto the scene as Sybilla Melvyn in Gillian Armstrong's 1979 drama *My Brilliant Career*, she made her feature film debut in the 1977 production *High Rolling in a Hot Corvette*. This comedy tells the story of two carnival workers who take a holiday in the hopes of sex, drugs and wild times. In 1985, Davis earned an Academy Award nomination for her role in *A Passage to India*. While acting in many TV movies, Davis bypassed roles in TV shows, until 2007 when she starred in *The Starter Wife*, which earned her an Emmy Award.

NAOMI WATTS (1968–)

Another UK-born Aussie convert, Watts' big-screen debut came as a 18 year old in the 1986 period romance *For Love Alone*, co-starring with Sam Neill and Hugo Weaving. The film's plotline centres on a young woman who falls in love with a teacher in the 1930s. Naomi Watts played the role of Leo's girlfriend; the character of Leo was played by John Polson, now an accomplished Hollywood director (*Swimfan*, 2002, *Hide and Seek*, 2005) and the man who started Tropfest.

Watts had minor TV parts in *Home and Away* (1988), *Hey Dad* (1990) and *Brides of Christ* (1991). She appeared in the sequel to *The Year My Voice Broke* (1987), called *Flirting*, opposite Nicole Kidman, Thandie Newton and Noah Taylor.

ABBIE CORNISH (1982–)

A star on the rise, Cornish got her first big break on the ABC TV show *Wildside* in 1999, a drama about a group of police officers in inner Sydney. Cornish appeared in nine episodes of the show and her performance earned her an AFI Award for Best Young Actor. A few years earlier, at the age of 15, Cornish made the finals of a modelling competition through *Dolly Magazine*, which kicked off to her career in front of the camera. Her first big-screen break came in *The Monkey's Mask* (2000), a crime thriller also starring Susie Porter, Marton Csokas and Brendan Cowell that didn't receive great reviews. Cornish really made an impact in the 2004 film *Somersault*, winning the AFI Award for Best Actress.

BILL HUNTER (1940–)

Screen legend Bill Hunter's credits date all the way back to 1957, when he appeared as an uncredited extra in the film adaptation of *The Shiralee* starring Peter Finch and Rosemary Harris. His next role, also uncredited, was as a swimmer's double in the international production *On the Beach*, which starred Gregory Peck and Ava Gardner. Credited roles started in the mid '60s, when Hunter appeared in TV shows such as *Doctor Who*

and *Skippy*. The Mick Jagger vehicle *Ned Kelly* in 1970 was Hunter's first credited film role, for playing an officer. He has appeared in 53 films since, his latest being *The Cup* (2011), portraying legendary horse trainer Bart Cummings.

GUY PEARCE (1967–)

Pearce was a fully fledged soap star before he made a splash on the silver screen. Pearce played the role of Mike Young for 421 episodes on the hit soap *Neighbours* from 1986 to 1989. He made the jump to *Home and Away* a couple of years later. His first major film role came in the 1990 drama *Heaven Tonight*, while his first Hollywood film was the critically acclaimed *LA Confidential* (1997), which won two Academy Awards. Pearce was born in the UK and grew up in Geelong, Victoria.

MIA WASIKOWSKA (1989–)

Young starlet on the rise, Wasikowska first appeared on our TV screens in a two-episode stint on the medical drama *All Saints*. This led to a role in the 2006 AFI award-winning film *Suburban Mayhem* opposite Emily Barclay. Her big break came when she was cast in 2008 in the US as a suicidal teen gymnast in the HBO TV series *In Treatment*. Her outstanding work on the drama, which led to the title role in Tim Burton's *Alice in Wonderland* (2010), saw her chosen to for title role in another Jane Austen adaptation, *Jane Eyre* (2011).

Muriel's Wedding (1994)

> You're terrible, Muriel.
> – Joanie

Muriel's dad, Bill (Hunter), in the burnt-out backyard of their Porpoise Spit home

Director: P.J. Hogan
Writer: P.J. Hogan
Producers: Lynda House, Jocelyn Moorhouse
Cast includes: Toni Collette, Rachel Griffiths, Bill Hunter, Jeanie Drynan, Sophie Lee, Matt Day, Daniel Lapaine

ABOUT THE FILM

The early to mid-'90s was a blessed time for the Aussie film industry. It started with Paul Mercurio in his tank top and the constant 'Bogo Pogo' references in Baz Luhrmann's hilarious dancesport parody *Strictly Ballroom*. Then we had the campy *Adventures of Priscilla, Queen of the Desert*, which became a cultural phenomenon both here and overseas. Then there was *The Castle*, the heart-warming underdog-versus-High Court fable about the Kerrigan family and their quest to keep their beloved suburban home. In amongst all this, Australia met a girl by the name of Muriel, a chubby, loveable loser who preferred being called 'Mariel' and had a fondness for trying on wedding dresses.

Directed by P.J. Hogan (as opposed to the other famous Hogan), *Muriel's Wedding* tells the story of said slacker, Muriel Heslop (Collette), a socially awkward young woman unhappily living with her family in the fictional town of Porpoise Spit. When she is dropped by her vacuous so-called 'friends', Muriel reunites with old high school pal Rhonda (Griffiths). This friendship with her vivacious chum drastically changes the trajectory of her life and launches her into a world of phony weddings, ABBA singalongs and sexual misadventures.

The film was a critical darling and box-office hit. Though it's considered a comedy, most of the audience could also relate to the family drama and self-esteem issues at the movie's heart. The film earned Toni Collette a Golden Globe nomination for Best Actress in a Musical or Comedy, and both Toni and Rachel's performances caught the attention of international audiences, launching their now flourishing Hollywood careers. Hogan's career also shot off like a rocket after the film; he went on to direct *My Best Friend's Wedding* (1997), *Peter Pan* (2003) and *Confessions of a Shopaholic* (2009).

Muriel (Collette) on her special day

Gold Coast Queensland

The Gold Coast is Australian tourism's treasure chest, a coastal playground with some of the world's most magnificent sun-drenched beaches, thriving nightlife and lush hinterland hideouts. Over ten million visitors a year agree. This fun-in-the-sun wonderland was used for two major locations in the film: Muriel's fictitious home town of Porpoise Spit, (which is, in fact, Coolangatta) and Hibiscus Island, which was shot on location at Sea World Resort in Southport on the north end of the Gold Coast (a place known as The Spit, not to be confused with Porpoise Spit).

In between these locations is Surfers Paradise, the lively hub of the Gold Coast. Further inland is the suburb of Oxenford, home to Warner Bros. Movie Studio where many international productions have been filmed. It has certainly suffered from overdevelopment through the years and has definite pockets of tacky, but the wonderful climate and natural beauty has won over many and Surfers lives on as an Australian favourite.

Hamilton Island, situated in the heart of the Whitsunday Islands near the Great Barrier Reef, was also used briefly for exterior shots to depict the fictitious town of Porpoise Spit.

VISITOR INFO

Coolangatta Information and Booking Centre

Shop 22, Showcase on the Beach, Griffith St; (07) 5569 3380; www.verygoldcoast.com.au

Surfers Paradise Visitor Information Centre

2 Cavill Ave; (07) 5538 4419 or 1300 309 440; www.surfersparadise.com

THINGS TO SEE AND DO

Coolangatta

City slickers beware: even a short visit to Coolangatta might induce serious thoughts of an abrupt sea change. The southernmost suburb of the Gold Coast, this laid-back beach town boasts some of the most glorious beaches in all of Australia. The town was used as the location of Porpoise Spit. There's one particular aerial shot that captures Griffith Street, one of Coolangatta's busier streets.

The location for the Heslop family home was actually shot in Sydney. Coolangatta was also the setting for the 1984 classic *Coolangatta Gold* starring Colin Friels. With its relaxed charm, surfable beaches and great cafes, Coolangatta is a calmer alternative for those shying away from the more packed Surfers Paradise.

Sea World Resort and Water Park

This enormously popular marine wildlife park was the location for Hibiscus Island, the holiday destination that a desperate Muriel follows her friends to after they drop her like a hot potato. Here Muriel reunites with Rhonda and they perform the classic ABBA song, *Waterloo*, attired in daggy '70s getup at the resort's talent night.

Sea World is one of the world's premier marine parks, with daily dolphin and seal shows, other performances (such as Sesame Street or pirates), displays including sharks and rays, thrilling rides and luxurious accommodation. *Sea World Dr, Main Beach; (07) 5588 2205 or 13 3386; seaworldresort.myfun.com.au*

Surfers Paradise

Though not featured in the film, Surfers Paradise is where the beach-based tourism push all began and a visit to the Gold Coast ain't complete without seeing its hub. Lined with high-rise apartments and breathtaking beaches, this epicentre is a charming blend of relaxed sun-worshipping and bustling nightlife.

Stroll through Cavill Avenue Mall where you can enjoy an alfresco brunch or hit Orchid Avenue at night for some pumping nightclubs. Parts of Surfers Paradise were used as locations for the film *Gettin' Square* (2003) and the short-lived TV series *The Strip* (2008). Surfers is only a short drive (or a long walk) from Coolangatta and Southport at each end of the Gold Coast .

Note for anyone over the age of 20: avoid Surfers Paradise like the plague during Schoolies Week (around the end of November). This is the time when hordes of rambunctious, recently graduated high-schoolers swarm here for a week of mayhem.

Warner Bros. Movie World

The famous catchcry 'Hollywood on the Gold Coast' pretty much sums up this fantastic theme adventure park about 20 kilometres north of Surfers Paradise. The young ones will have a ball interacting with Bugs Bunny and Tweety, who roam the park with their fellow Looney Tunes pals; they're more than willing to pose for photos (or give hugs if you ask nicely). Older teens and adults will be exhilarated by the thrill rides, such as the Superman Returns Rollercoaster and the Batman-themed 4.5G Force Vertical Launch. Certainly not for the faint of heart!

Within the environs of the park and, regrettably, off limits to the public are the working film studios. Films that were partly shot at the studios include *Scooby Doo* (2002), *Peter Pan* (2003), *House of Wax* (2005), *Fool's Gold* (2008), *Daybreakers* (2009) and *The Chronicle of Narnia: The Voyage of the Dawn Treader* (2010). *Pacific Mwy, Oxenford; (07) 5573 3999 or 13 3386; movieworld.myfun.com.au*

Gold Coast beaches stretch for miles

Muriel gleefully holds her prize – the wedding bouquet

The truth? I tell the truth too. Nicole's having an affair with Chook. Muriel saw them f--king in the laundry on your wedding day. Stick your drink up your arse, Tania. I'd rather swallow razor blades than drink with you. Oh, by the way, I'm not alone. I'm with Muriel.
– *Rhonda*

Muriel and Rhonda (Griffiths) in their ABBA getup

Muriel scowls at what Bill has to say

Australian Outback Spectacular

Strap yourself in for an action-packed, no-holds-barred tribute to the Australian bush. This bold theatrical production recreates legendary bush stories (in the vein of *The Man from Snowy River* and the Light Horse Brigade of World War I). You're guaranteed some of the best stunt horseriding you'll ever see, backed by a 52-piece orchestra and accompanied by a traditional three-course Aussie barbecue dinner of steak, damper and pavlova. Bewdy! *Pacific Mwy, Oxenford; 13 3386 or (07) 5573 3999; outbackspectacular.myfun.com.au*

WHERE TO STAY

Komune Resort

Sayonara smelly bunk beds and grotty shared showers; this is the new breed of hostel. This ultra-modern, fully pimped-out accommodation offers deluxe shared apartments (including a 'no dudes allowed' girls-only sanctuary), as well as private lodgings with all the trimmings. Chillax by the inviting rooftop pool with other young travellers while enjoying an in-house pizza. *146 Marine Pde, Coolangatta; (07) 5536 6764; www.komuneresorts/goldcoast*

Sleeping Inn

The new choice for backpackers in Surfers Paradise. Apartment-style hostel resort with cheap shared dorms and private rooms. Fun stuff includes nightly activities, a games room, pool table and a free bus service to the local cinema. *26 Peninsula Dr, Surfers Paradise; (07) 5592 4455; www.sleepinginn.com.au*

Sea World Resort

Adjacent to Sea World, choose from 405 rooms, four restaurants and two bar areas, as well as the Waterplay area (year-round) and Water Park (seasonal) for the kids and the young at heart. Check out their jet boat, jet ski and parasail packages. *Sea World Dr, Main Beach; 13 3386 or (07) 5588 0000; seaworldresort.myfun.com.au*

CARAVANS AND MOTORHOMES

Kirra Beach Tourist Park

Wake up to the crashing of the waves and the salty ocean breeze at this spacious caravan park right on Kirra Beach near Coolangatta. Powered and unpowered sites, camping and villa accommodation. *Charlotte St, Kirra; (07) 5667 2740; www.goldcoasttouristparks.com.au/park/kirra-beach*

Southport Tourist Park

Minutes from Surfers Paradise and Sea World, this park has powered caravan sites, budget rooms, villas, units and even a five-bedroom house. *6 Frank St, Gold Coast Hwy, Southport; (07) 5531 2281; www.southporttouristpark.com.au*

WHERE TO EAT

Crave, The Coolangatta Hotel

The 'Cooly' was named Hotel of the Year by the Australian Hotels Association in 2009, so you might want to book. Grab a crisp lager and a meal from the diverse menu, which includes seafood crepes, lamb shank pie and their special seafood basket. After your meal you can take in a gig; they often have big-name bands playing in the band room and lesser-known acts and DJs in the main bar. *Cnr Marine Pde and Warner St; (07) 5589 6888; www.thecoolyhotel.com.au*

The Waterfall Cafe

Casual poolside dining at Sea World Resort. All the classics: steak sandwiches, burgers and fish and chips. If you're after something different, the resort has three other restaurants – the Shoreline loves buffets, Japanese at Hatsuhana, and light meals and happy hours in the Lobby Lounge. *Sea World Dr, Main Beach; 13 3386 or (07) 5588 2222; seaworldresort.myfun.com.au*

Chateau Beachside Boardwalk Cafe

You gotta try the famous Surfers Paradise buffet breakfast, a Gold Coast stalwart. Best value for money under $15; eat enough and you'll last till happy hour! *Cnr The Esplanade and Elkhorn Ave, Surfers Paradise; (07) 5538 1022*

CINEMA

Australia Fair Cinemas

Located in the huge Australia Fair Shopping Complex in Southport (adjacent to Sea World). There are eight regular cinemas and two Gold Class cinemas showing the latest new releases. *Level 1, Australia Fair Shopping Centre, Southport; (07) 5571 2666; www.eventcinemas.com.au*

DID YOU KNOW? **To fully get into the character of Muriel Heslop, Toni Collette stacked on 18 kilograms for the role. She worked carefully with a dietician to achieve the result. Ten years later she did it again, putting on 11 kilograms for her role in Richard Curtis' 2005 film *In Her Shoes*. That film also required her to lose all the weight during the shoot.**

A sign greets beachgoers in Surfers Paradise

Sydney New South Wales

You remember the movie *Independence Day*? You know, the cheesy blockbuster released in 1996 with Will Smith punching aliens and President Bill Pullman flying a fighter jet to ward off an alien ship. Throughout the film we see the foreboding alien crafts looming over the world's most iconic cityscapes and landmarks: the Empire State Building in New York, the great pyramids of Egypt, the White House in Washington DC, the Eiffel Tower in Paris and, yes, the Sydney Opera House. This inimitably designed structure, along with the imposing steel arch of the Harbour Bridge, are the postcard snapshots that come to mind when people think of Australia. As much as Melburnians may protest, Sydney is Australia's signature city.

For decades, Sydney has been a hotbed of local film and television productions. Sydney's diverse and aesthetically distinctive locales, drastically different from one suburb to the next, make it a location scout's dream.

One of the first films shot in Sydney was *The Kid Stakes*, a silent comedy directed by Tal Ordell, shot in Woolloomooloo in 1927. Since then, the city and surrounding suburbs have been locations for countless films (see pages 163–5 for profiles of a few of them).

The opening of Fox Studios in 1998 brought a slew of huge international productions to town, including *The Matrix* (1999), *Star Wars II: Attack of the Clones* (2002) and *Superman Returns* (2006).

Muriel's Wedding was shot in several locations around the city, including Darlinghurst, Parramatta and Narrabeen.

In December 2010, the city of Sydney became only the second city in the world to be named a 'City of Film' by UNESCO (the United Nations Educational, Scientific and Cultural Organization). The title was given in recognition of Sydney's long history of filmmaking and infrastructure.

The excited bride in her limo

St Mark's Church, the location of the illustrious wedding

When I lived in Porpoise Spit, I used to sit in my room for hours and listen to ABBA songs. But since I've met you and moved to Sydney, I haven't listened to one ABBA song. That's because my life is as good as an ABBA song. It's as good as 'Dancing Queen'.
— *Muriel*

VISITOR INFO

Sydney Visitors Centre

Cnr Argyle and Playfair sts, The Rocks and 33 Wheat Rd, Darling Harbour; (02) 9240 8788 or 1800 067 676; www.sydney.com

THINGS TO SEE AND DO

St Mark's Church

Designed by Edmund Blacket in 1852, this neo-Gothic house of worship was the location for Muriel's (or should we say Marial's) phony marriage to South African swimmer David Van Arckle (Lapaine). The church is in the suburb of Darling Point, just over 3 kilometres west of Sydney's CBD. The interior and exterior of the church were used in the film. Notably, it was also the place where Elton John and his then partner Renate Blauel married on Valentine's Day in 1984. *53 Darling Point Rd, Darling Point; (02) 9363 3657; www.stmarks-darlingpoint.com.au*

Kinselas Hotel

If only the walls could talk, they would moan over memories of bad perms, acid-wash denim and Olivia Newton John–style hijinks. During the '80s and '90s, Kinselas was the club of choice for ragers in Sydney.

Kinselas was used as the nightspot where Muriel and Brice (Day) go on their first date as Rhonda rages on the dancefloor with a couple of random hunks. The days of disco are indeed dead as Kinselas has been turned into an up-scale bar. *383 Bourke St, Darlinghurst; (02) 9331 3100; www.kinselas.com.au*

Oxford Street

With nightspot names like Rainbow Room, Midnight Shift and Slide Bar, plus the fact that cute girls in short skirts aren't given a second look, you're correct in assuming Oxford Street is Sydney's queer zone. This ab-fab stretch of road

just south-east of the Sydney CBD contributed two locations in the film. One was Videorama, the video shop where Muriel works when she first moves to Sydney. The shop was located at 135 Oxford Street, but has long been closed. The dry cleaner where Rhonda works across the street has also closed. Every March, Oxford Street is the main drag for Sydney's world-famous Gay and Lesbian Mardi Gras.

House of Jean Fox

This bridal shop was used in the scene when Muriel first tries on a wedding dress, leading her on a frenetic path checking out wedding gowns all across Sydney. The shoot took place at the House of Jean Fox on Macquarie Street in Parramatta in Sydney's west. The shop relocated to nearby Argyle Street and has moved to a third location on Victoria Street in North Parramatta. Macquarie Street is a bridezilla's paradise (and a groom's worst nightmare), with Park Avenue Bridal, Visions in White and Bridal Secrets all wonderlands of white chiffon and silk mikado. *Macquarie St, Parramatta*

Narrabeen

'… *Santa Cruz and Trestles, Australia's Narrabeen*' – in 1963 the Beach Boys sang the praises of this beachside suburb, 23 kilometres north of the CBD. Most people would be surprised to know that the exterior and interior shots of the Heslop house were actually shot in the Sydney suburb of Narrabeen. The relaxed coastal vibe of the suburb made it easy to recreate a property in the fictional Porpoise Spit. The suburb has some magnificent beaches. Either that or the Beach Boys are liars.

National Institute of Dramatic Arts (NIDA)

This acclaimed Australian national theatre, film and television school's alumni includes Cate

The disgruntled Tania (Lee) is not impressed by the talent show

Blanchett, Baz Luhrmann, Hugo Weaving and Mel Gibson. Head down to the theatre spaces and watch performances by the students – one day you'll be able to say, 'Oh I saw so-and-so back when they were just starting out.' The large interior lobby of the NIDA also has some great memorabilia, including production posters, performance costumes and sculptures. *215 Anzac Pde, Kensington; (02) 9697 7600; www.nida.edu.au*

Fox Studios Australia

Opened in May 1998, Fox Studios is Australia's busiest film studio. Consisting of eight sound stages (obviously not open to the public), the movie wonderland has hosted numerous productions, including *Dark City* (1998), The Matrix trilogy (1999, 2003), *Moulin Rouge* (2001), *Star Wars Episode II: Attack of the Clones* (2002) and *Episode III* (2005), *Superman Returns* (2006) and *Australia* (2008), just to name a few. It's also the home base for a slew of production companies and film-related businesses.

Fox Studios also has a lively entertainment quarter, which has an abundance of bars, restaurants, cinemas, bowling, laser skirmish and even rock climbing. There are also markets every Wednesday, Saturday and Sunday. Fox Studios is located in Moore Park in Sydney's inner south-east and is only a few minutes' drive from Oxford Street and Kensington. *Driver Ave, Moore Park; (02) 8117 6700; www.eqmoorepark. com.au and www.foxstudiosaustralia.com*

WHERE TO STAY

Westend Backpackers

Located on Pitt Street, close to Oxford Street and a couple of filming locations, this funky hostel has dorms, double and triple rooms with private bathrooms plus a pool table, complimentary airport transfers and free pasta and rice every night. *412 Pitt St, Sydney; (02) 9211 4588 or 1800 013 186; www.westendbackpackers.com*

Cambridge Hotel

Award-winning mid-range hotel, a short walk to Oxford Street and Kinselas. It's eco-friendly with funky modern rooms to suit all comers and pretty affordable premium and deluxe spa rooms, too. Cafe 212 on Riley and cocktail bar on site to get you started. *212 Riley St, Sydney East; (02) 9212 1111; www.cambridgehotel.com.au*

Mint Fiori Apartments

Comfy and very affordable apartments, with indoor swimming pool, gym and 24 hour convenience store downstairs. Close to Macquarie Street, Westfield Shopping Centre and ANZ Stadium – these days Parramatta ain't so bad. *13–15 Hassall St, Parramatta; (02) 9635 0235; www.staymint.com*

Vibe Hotel Rushcutters

A short walk to St Marks Church, site of Muriel's faux wedding, this mod-retro hotel overlooks the sailboats and bright green parklands of

Rushcutters Bay, a hop, skip and a jump to Double Bay boutiques or 'Paddo' markets. The rooftop pool is just what the doctor ordered during the sticky summer months. *100 Bayswater Rd, Rushcutters Bay; (02) 8353 8988; www.vibehotels.com.au*

CARAVANS AND MOTORHOMES

BIG4 Lakeside Holiday Park Narrabeen

Pretend you've dropped into Porpoise Spit at this highly rated caravan and camping facility, which also has four-star self-contained accommodation. It's bordered by the Narrabeen Lake and close to the divine northern beaches. *Lake Park Rd, North Narrabeen; (02) 9913 7845; www.sydneylakeside.com.au.*

WHERE TO EAT

Grotta Capri Restaurant

This Italian restaurant was used for the interior of Breakers nightspot in Porpoise Spit, where Muriel's gal pals drop her because of her nerdy and frumpy ways. The decor is seriously special – dim blue lights, glowing walls of fish tanks and bulky coral dangle from the ceiling. Try their signature 'Grotta Mob', a veritable feast of hot and cold seafood including lobster, barbecued king prawns, smoked salmon and grilled octopus. The restaurant was also a location for the films *Son of the Mask* (2005) and *The Night We Called it a Day* (2003), as well as the TV series *Underbelly: A Tale Of Two Cities*. *97–101 Anzac Pde, Kensington; (02) 9662 7111; www.grottacapri.com.au*

Oxford Hotel

A gay-friendly hotel right across the street from the former Videorama; hoe into some steaks and parmas at the LA warehouse–styled main bar. If you're in need of a late-night snack in gentleman's club surrounds, hit the Supper Club. The Polo Lounge on the second level, inspired by New York's Upper West side gentlemen's clubs, is ideal for a quiet scotch on the rocks. *134 Oxford St, Paddington; (02) 9331 3467; www.theoxfordhotel.com.au*

El Jannah

Said to be the best charcoal chicken in Sydney, complemented by bellissimo homemade garlic sauce; chips and salad are vital accompaniments. Located in Granville, just south of Parramatta. *4–6 South St, Granville; (02) 9637 0977; www.eljannah.com.au*

Driftwood Cafe

Doubling up as a homewares store, this popular hangout has all-day breakfast as well as burgers, salads and tapas for lunch. Metres from Narrabeen Beach. *Shop 8, 18 Ocean St, Narrabeen; (02) 9970 8911; www.driftwoodcafe.com.au*

FILM FESTIVALS

Sydney Film Festival

Running for two weeks annually in June, SFF (sff.org.au) screens films from over 40 countries, as well as some of the best local productions (from features to animated shorts). There are also Q & A sessions and talks by industry folk. Screening venues include the State Theatre, the Art Gallery of New South Wales and the Sydney Opera House.

The Grotta Capri Restaurant feels like a deep, dark ocean cave

It's a lovely life at Manly Beach in Sydney

does screen the occasional commercial flick. Wine and espresso bar on site. *17 Oxford St, Paddington; (02) 9360 6099; www.palacecinemas.com.au/cinemas/verona*

Event Cinemas Parramatta

Located in the Westfield Shopping Complex, this large cinema complex shows new releases on 11 screens, including one Vmax screen. *Level 4, 159–175 Church St, Parramatta; (02) 9407 2777; www.eventcinemas.com.au*

TOURS

Sydney Movie Tours

Aussie movie buffs will wet their pants just reading the brochure. You can choose from a variety of movie tours, including the half-day tours around the salubrious locations for films such as *Muriel's Wedding*, *Two Hands*, *Australia*, *The Adventures of Priscilla, Queen of the Desert* and *Looking for Alibrandi*. They also offer a general city walking tour, specialised *The Matrix* and *Superman Returns* walking tours and events for corporate dos and hens/bucks turns. *(02) 9537 4566 or 1300 302 640; www.sydneymovietours.com.au*

Other major festivals include the Sydney Underground Film Festival (September, www.suff.com.au) and the Fantastic Planet Sydney Science Fiction and Fantasy Film Festival (www.fantasticplanetfilmfestival.com).

Tropfest

It started life modestly in a Kings Cross cafe in 1993, but Tropfest has grown to become the world's largest short film festival. The films are simultaneously screened in Sydney and Melbourne in February, with the awards handed out at Sydney's Domain Botanic Gardens. *www.tropfest.com*

CINEMAS

Palace Verona

Located on Oxford Street, the Verona specialises in art-house films, although it

DID YOU KNOW? **Legend has it that director P.J. Hogan flew to Europe to meet with the band ABBA after they denied his request to use their music in the film. After much sincere convincing and a promise of a percentage of profits from the film, they relented and the rest is daggy film soundtrack history.**

Rockin' the suburbs – Sydney

The suburbs of Sydney have been used as locations for some of our most memorable movies. Here are some of the more well-known local movies shot in and around the harbour city.

THEY'RE A WEIRD MOB (1966)

Based on the popular novel by John O'Grady, this is the story of a fish-out-of-water Italian immigrant Nino (Walter Chiari) who moves to Sydney for a job. The comedy was hugely successful upon its release and was one of our local film industry's defining films. There aren't many places in Sydney that this film didn't cover, from Bondi Beach to Manly Beach, Circular Quay and Neutral Bay. The beach party scenes were shot on Clark Island, just off Darling Point, while the location for the house that Nino built was in the suburb of Greenacre in Sydney's south-west.

LANTANA (2001)

The first film to win the top six categories at the AFI Awards, including all the acting awards and best film and best director, *Lantana* is considered by many to be the finest production to ever come out of the industry. The film used Balmain and The Rocks as major locations, and the suburbs of Narrabeen and Pittwater were also used for filming.

BMX BANDITS (1983)

The unforgettable image of a 15-year-old Nicole Kidman two-wheeling around the streets of Sydney, fleeing bank robbers in a tight pink T-shirt, is indelibly imprinted on many an Aussie's mind's eye. Incredibly, the film was nominated for four AFI Awards and it had a release in the US, where it was retitled *Short Wave*. *BMX Bandits* was shot all over Sydney; probably the most memorable location was the Manly Waterworks, which was used in the scenes for the waterslide escape. Manly Oval was also used. The scenes in the shopping centre were shot at Warringah Mall in Brookvale. The suburbs of Kingsgrove, Penrith and Balgowlah were also locations.

LITTLE FISH (2003)

This was Cate Blanchett's first film shot in Australia since *Oscar and Lucinda* in 1997. Directed by Rowan Woods, this story of a reformed drug addict won five AFI Awards, including Best Film. The film used many central-Sydney locations, including the CBD and Haymarket. Many scenes were shot in Cabramatta in Sydney's south-west, including the scenes shot in the video shop. Bankstown, Fairfield, Bexley North and Sylvania Waters were also locations used.

LOOKING FOR ALIBRANDI (2000)

This coming-of-age film starring Pia Miranda, Anthony LaPaglia and Kick Gurry won Best

Film at the 2000 AFI Awards. It had a heavy Sydney presence, with shooting taking place all over the city and surrounding 'burbs. Alibrandi's suburban home was on Cardigan Street in Glebe, while Alibrandi's school was played by Kingcoppal-Rose Bay School of Sacred Heart in Rose Bay. The tomato festival scene was shot on the streets of Five Dock in Sydney's inner-west. Leichhardt, Marrickville, Manly, Cremorne and Bellevue Hill were other locations used.

DON'S PARTY (1976)

Election nights aren't the same without a viewing of this enduring Aussie classic. Adapted from a play by David Williamson and directed by Bruce Beresford, the film is still as fresh and witty as it was when released 40 odd years ago. The play was set in Melbourne, but for the movie the house is supposed to be on Sydney's north shore. In reality, the film was shot in a house in Windham Place in the suburb of Westleigh in Sydney's north-west. The film was shot over four and a half weeks.

COSI (1996)

This charmer centres on a young amateur theatre director who takes a job teaching drama to the patients in a hospital's mental ward. The film stars Ben Mendelsohn, Barry Otto, Colin Friels and David Wenham and it reunited Toni Collette and Rachel Griffiths for the first time since *Muriel's Wedding*. Much of the film was shot on location at Rozelle Hospital, just west of the Sydney CBD. Balmain and Bondi Beach were other locations used.

ERSKINEVILLE KINGS (1999)

The film was Hugh Jackman's last local role and only his second feature film before being cast as Wolverine in the X-Men franchise. This dramatic film saw Jackman play the role of Wace, a damaged soul who reunites with his brother after the death of their father. The film was shot in Erskineville and the adjoining suburbs of Newtown and Enmore. The King Hotel, the main location of the pub, was actually the Hollywood Hotel in Surry Hills.

PUBERTY BLUES (1981)

For a taste of chauvinist Aussie blokes at their best, just before feminism fought back, revisit Bruce Beresford's coming-of-age drama based on the popular novel by Kathy Lette and Gabrielle Carey. It's all about growing up on Sydney's south shore – boy crushes, peer pressure, experimentation, chauvinism, surfing and hassles with parents. Both the book and the film were set on the beaches of Cronulla, which is where the majority of the film was shot. To placate the nervous film censorship board, the age of the girls in the film was changed to 16, although the book's protagonists were actually only 13.

THE SQUARE (2008)

Directed by former stuntman Nash Edgerton, brother of actor Joel Edgerton (who co-wrote and produced the film), this noir-influenced thriller about an adulterous man caught up in a web of organised crime was nominated for eight AFI Awards. It also won the Film Critics Circle of Australia award for Best Screenplay. The film used Sydney's south, with the suburbs of Cronulla, Caringbah and Sutherland being the main locations.

NEWSFRONT (1978)

Written and directed by Phillip Noyce and starring Bill Hunter, Bryan Brown and Wendy Hughes, *Newsfront* follows the lives of two movie newsreel reporters who risk their lives to get the all-important footage. Various locations around Sydney were used for filming, including the Narrabeen Lake for the scenes involving the Newcastle floods. Other locations used include the State Theatre in George Street, Walsh Bay and Surry Hills.

THE SUM OF US (1994)

Jack Thompson and Russell Crowe play father and son in this light but tender drama about a grieving widower looking for love and his relationship with his homosexual son. The film was shot in a variety of places in the harbour city, including Darling Harbour (the scene of the marriage proposal) and the peninsula suburb of Balmain just west of the Sydney CBD. The film was nominated for six AFI Awards and David Stevens won Best Screenplay – the film was based on a play written by Stevens that ran off-Broadway in New York in 1990.

CANDY (2006)

This story of two young bohemians in love – a poet and an artist – who get sucked into the abyss of heroin addiction was nominated for eight AFI Awards, taking home one award for Best Adapted Screenplay. It was based on the novel of the same name by Luke Davies and starred Heath Ledger and Abbie Cornish.

The film was mostly shot in Sydney; one of the more recognisable locations is Luna Park in Milsons Point, with scenes filmed on the Rotor ride. The amusement park has been the backdrop for a few film and TV productions, including the 2000 family comedy *Our Lips are Sealed* starring Mary-Kate and Ashley Olsen.

CLUBLAND (2007)

This heart-warming coming-of-age drama centres on young Tim (Khan Chittenden), who must contend with his overbearing comedienne mother (played brilliantly by British actress Brenda Blethlyn). The film utilised many location throughout Sydney, including Marrickville, West Ryde, Bankstown and Cronulla. Blethlyn actually co-wrote much of the stand-up material she performed in the film. Young actress Emma Booth won the Best Supporting Actress AFI Award for her role as Tim's love interest, Jill. It was released as *Introducing the Dwights* in the US.

HEATWAVE (1982)

One of the earlier films from director Phillip Noyce, *Heatwave* is set one sweltering summer in a housing development in Sydney. The film is about an idealistic architect (Richard Moir) who's in charge of designing a new housing project – until he has a change of heart when meets the spokeswoman opposed to the development (Judy Davis). Also starring Bill Hunter and Chris Haywood, the film was shot in Kings Cross and Newtown. Noyce shot most of his earlier films in Sydney, including *Newsfront* (1978; see separate entry) and the opening scenes of *Dead Calm* (1989).

Oscar and Lucinda (1997)

Lucinda (Blanchett) and Oscar (Fiennes) in an unguarded moment

In order that I exist, two gamblers, one obsessive, the other compulsive, must meet.

— *Narrator*

Director: Gillian Armstrong
Writer: Laura Jones
Producers: Robin Dalton, Timothy White
Cast includes: Cate Blanchett, Ralph Fiennes, Ciaran Hinds, Tom Wilkinson, Richard Roxburgh, Geoffrey Rush

ABOUT THE FILM

Based on the Miles Franklin and Booker Prize–winning novel by acclaimed writer Peter Carey, *Oscar and Lucinda* is a sombre yet romantic tale of gambling and unrequited desire. The story takes place in the mid-1800s in Sydney and chronicles the relationship between two misfit gamblers. Oscar Hopkins (Fiennes) is a deeply religious priest who flees to Australia from rural England to escape his gambling ways.

It's not long before Oscar encounters the eccentric Lucinda Leplastrier (Blanchett), a wealthy heiress and glass factory owner who has a penchant for penny poker and other games of chance. Told from the perspective of Oscar's great grandson (the inimitable voice of Geoffrey Rush as the narrator), the film explores the love between these two outcast soulmates while exploring many deep issues, such as religious morality and colonialism.

Oscar and Lucinda received mixed reviews upon release, doing modest numbers at the Aussie and international box offices. The film showcases the talents of Geoffrey Simpson, whose stunning cinematography captured the majestic beauty of the coastal United Kingdom and the rugged charm of the New South Wales landscape. Costume designer Janet Patterson received an Academy Award nomination for her

One of the film's promo shots

> The Australian sun
> will scorch your
> congregation as though
> they are in hell itself.
>
> — *Mr Ahearn*

The calming waters of Walsh Bay

extraordinary Victorian-era costume creations, while renowned production designer Luciana Arrighi's creation of the glorious glass church is itself a work of art.

Under Armstrong's direction, all the elements of the film mesh together beautifully. The film is probably best remembered, however, as being the feature film breakout role for Blanchett – a relative unknown at the time – who plays Lucinda with a marvellous depth and complexity. Just a year later, Blanchett played the title role of *Elizabeth*, a part that earned her an Academy Award nomination. She went on to win the 2005 Best Supporting Actress Oscar for her role in Martin Scorcese's *The Aviator*.

LOCATIONS

SYDNEY NEW SOUTH WALES

Aside from its landmark architecture, beautiful harbours, national parks and resplendent beaches, what makes Sydney one of the most unique cities in the world is just how different it can be from one spot to the next. There is literally a new discovery to be made every single day, whether you've been holidaying in the city for a week or lived here for 20 years. It's this fresh quality that has made Sydney the film capital of Australia – and why the city was the perfect location for shooting much of *Oscar and Lucinda*. The production utilised a dozen locations in and around the city. These locations included Millers Point and Cockatoo Island to the north, Vaucluse in the east and Newtown in the south. Outlying suburbs to the city's north were also used to recreate the New South Wales bushland.

VISITOR INFO

Sydney Visitor Centre

Cnr Argyle and Playfair sts, The Rocks and 33 Wheat Rd, Darling Harbour; (02) 9240 8788 or 1800 067 676; www.sydney.com

THINGS TO SEE AND DO

Cockatoo Island

Bang in the middle of Sydney Harbour, Cockatoo Island was the location for the exterior shots of Prince Rupert's Glassworks factory, which quickly comes under the ownership of go-getter Lucinda when she arrives in Sydney. The building used as the Glassworks is the old power station, which was built in 1918 and provided electricity to the entire island until it was connected to the Electric Light and Power Supply Corporation in Balmain in 1938. Cockatoo Island used to contain the largest shipbuilding yard in Australia and was also used to house prisoners.

Today, it's a popular tourist destination just a short skip on a ferry or water taxi from Circular Quay. Guided, self-guided and audio tours of the island take in attractions such as the convict barracks and military guardhouse, the industrial precinct and the Sutherland and Fitzroy docks, which were a hive of activity during wartime.

Cockatoo Island was also used as a filming location for *X-Men Origins: Wolverine* (2009) starring Hugh Jackman. *Sydney ferries run daily from Circular Quay to Cockatoo Island; access visitor information from Muster Station, just near the arrivals wharf; (02) 8969 2100; www.cockatooisland.gov.au*

Walsh Bay

This area just past The Rocks was the filming location for the seaport where Lucinda first sets foot in Sydney. The bay might be unrecognisable – the filmmakers decided to digitally insert the old IXL Jam Factory building into the shot to give the scene more of a period feel. This factory (now an art hotel) is located in Hobart, Tasmania. Hobart was actually the first location choice for this scene, but was rejected for fiscal reasons.

Walsh Bay is one of Sydney's creative and culinary hubs and consequently has an excellent selection of eateries. On the creative side, it's the home of the Sydney Theatre Company, the Sydney Theatre and the Sydney Dance Company. Various spots around Walsh Bay host the Biennale of Sydney arts festival and the annual Sydney Writers Festival.

Enjoy the self-guided heritage walk and sculpture walk – you'll be treated to some very interesting pieces, including the bizarre *Still Life with Stone and Car*, in which a large granite boulder is meshed into the back of a mangled Ford Festiva. Looks like a scene out of *Deep Impact. Detailed guides of heritage and sculpture walks available on the Walsh Bay website: www.walshbaysydney.com.au*

Millers Point

Just a hop, skip and a jump north of Walsh Bay was the location used for the Chinese opium den where Oscar and Lucinda run into each other on a late-night gambling binge. This dimly lit house of iniquity, the scene of smoky oriental games of chance, was created at the former Grazcos wool store on Windmill Street. The wool store is now owned by a private business, so it's not advisable to stride through the doors, order a

Mai Tai and declare to all and sundry that you're 'feeling lucky'.

The old wool store can also be seen in the background when Oscar leaves to rapturous applause as he begins his journey from Sydney to Bellingen. The building right next to the wool store in the direction of the city was used for some of the interior Glasswork factory scenes. Millers Point has undergone an enormous transformation over the last 20 years and now thrives on good food and culture. *Bond Store 2, 28 Windmill St, Millers Point*

Elizabeth Bay House

Oh Sydney, you've done it again! Where else in the world can you be walking grimy streets lined with strip clubs and adult bookshops, turn a couple of corners and you're breathing in the rich past of a 200-year- old colonial mansion? Owned by the Historic Houses Trust, this homestead, just a few blocks east of Kings Cross, was the location for Lucinda's luxury residence when she first arrives in Sydney.

Old Grazco's Wool Store in Millers Point

This location is also used for the Sydney residence of Mr Haslett (Hinds) and the restaurant where Oscar and Lucinda dine while they formulate the plan to ship the glass church to Bellingen. Wander through the interior of the beautifully preserved property and gardens and then step down to the underground cellar to view a video of the house's history. Helpful curators are usually willing to treat you to an on-the-spot history lesson. *7 Onslow Ave, Elizabeth Bay; (02) 9356 3022; www.hht.net.au/museums/ebh; open Friday to Sunday (daily in January)*

Vaucluse House

Built in 1803 by Sir Henry Brown Hayes, this Gothic-revival structure was the filming location for the scene in which Lucinda plays a spot of cards with Jimmy D'Abbs (Barry Otto) and some other upper-class Sydneysiders. The house and grounds, also owned by the Historic Houses Trust, occupy 23 hectares of well-kept gardens. The house is wonderfully preserved and parts are open to visitors – you can walk through the old drawing room, butler's pantry and little tea room. The house also runs a variety of events, from knitting displays to children's story time, jazz in the garden and morning teas. *Wentworth Rd, Vaucluse; (02) 9388 7922; www.hht.net.au/museums/vaucluse_house; open Friday to Sunday (daily in January)*

Strickland House

This famous manor, also used as a location in the movie *Australia*, was used for a short scene in the film in which a Bishop bets a room full of people, including an antsy Oscar, that he can execute the old 'remove the table cloth from underneath the dinner set' trick. Aside from a few stray plates, he actually pulls it off! *52 Vaucluse Rd, Vaucluse; (02) 9337 5999*

Elizabeth Farm

Said to be the oldest homestead in Australia, this farm in Rosehill in Sydney's west was the location of the house to which Lucinda brings Oscar shortly after his move to Sydney. This is the spot where they have some fun scrubbing floors (apparently that can be fun) and share a rather restrained kiss.

Built in 1793, the homestead is best known as being the birthplace of the Australian wool industry – Brit John Macarthur imported some Spanish Merino sheep in 1797 and by 1801 he was the largest sheep rearer in the colony.

Also owned by the Historic Houses Trust, parts of the homestead are open to visitors. The sensory audio tour of the cotton palm and giant bamboo areas of the surrounding gardens is a must. *70 Alice St, Rosehill; (02) 9635 9488; www.hht.net.au/visiting/museums/elizabeth_farm; open Friday to Sunday (daily in January)*

Old Government House

Sitting on 260 acres of Parramatta parklands, Old Government House is indeed that – in fact, it's said to be Australia's oldest public building.

The well-preserved interior of this mature property, fitted with a stunning hand-crafted crystal chandelier, was used as Oscar's residence when he arrives in Sydney. The house runs ghoulish ghost tours once a month and normal tours, both by appointment. *Parramatta Park, Pitt St, Parramatta; (02) 9635 8149; www.oldgovernmenthouse.com.au*

Camperdown Cemetery at St Stephens Anglican Church

St Stephens Anglican Church

Located in the diverse suburb of Newtown in Sydney's inner-west, this place of worship was the location where Lucinda shares a moment with Oscar in the church. The faded church is a Newtown landmark and has been running religious Sunday services since 1849.

The church is surrounded by the Camperdown Cemetery, Sydney's most famous historic cemetery. Camperdown was Sydney's main general cemetery in the mid-1800s and has been the final resting place for many important Australian colonial figures. It was also used as a location for *The Adventures of Priscilla, Queen of the Desert*. Standard warnings apply: may be haunted by ghastly ghouls. The ghost in residence here is said to be Bathsheba, the former second matron of the Sydney General Hospital. Medication time! *189 Church St, Newtown; (02) 9557 2043; www.ststephens.org.au*

Ingleside

The semi-rural suburb 30 kilometres north of Sydney's CBD was used for the scenes involving the convoy of men, including Oscar and Mr Jeffries, transporting the glass church to Bellingen. The horrific scene in which Mr Jeffries orders the execution of Aboriginal natives was filmed here. The suburb is mostly comprised of semi-rural properties and thus it wasn't hard to portray the New South Wales countryside.

Deep Creek Reserve

This bushland reserve in Elanora Heights (close to Ingleside) was the location for the interior and exterior scenes at the local pub. Mr Jeffries is killed here after a bit of argy bargy with Oscar. The watering hole was built for the production and destroyed after filming. The reserve is 39 hectares in size and home to an interesting array of native birds, animals and wildflowers. *Located between Wakehurst Parkway and Narrabeen Lagoon (in the south), Deep Creek (on the west) and Woorara Ave (in the north)*

Gunyah Beach

The short scene when Lucinda confronts a troubled Oscar on the beach was shot here at Broken Bay, north of Elanora Heights, just south of Brooklyn and west of Palm Beach. The beach and bay is a great spot for swimming, watersports and fishing.

WHERE TO STAY

Holiday House and Apartments at Cockatoo Island

Need a weekend break? These two charming Federation houses, with apartment and duplex living, are waiting for you, screaming 'location, location, location'! The amenities include cooking facilities and a barbecue, and you're surrounded by beautiful gardens and unforgettable clifftop harbour views. *(02) 8898 9774; www.cockatooisland.gov.au/camping/houses.html*

Billabong Gardens

Budget backpacker accommodation in upbeat and diverse Newtown, you can choose from clean dorm rooms or private rooms. Dip in the pool, surf your day away with dirt cheap wi-fi and chill in the spacious lounge with other backpackers. A stone's throw from St Stephens Anglican Church and only a two-minute drive to the Enmore Theatre. King Street's batch of funky cafes and restaurants are frequented by students and musos – Billabong welcomes bands gigging or recording nearby! *5 Egan St, Newtown; (02) 9550 3236; www.billabonggardens.com.au*

Sydney Harbour YHA

Hugely popular and highly rated, brand-spanking-new hostel a few hundred metres from Circular Quay. Clean and comfy shared and private rooms, with rooftop views of the Opera House and Harbour Bridge. It's just a few minutes' walk to film locations at Walsh Bay and Millers Point. *110 Cumberland St, Millers Point; (02) 8272 0900; www.yha.com.au*

Quest Apartments Rosehill

Ironically located next to Sydney's famous Rosehill Garden Racecourse (more gambling!), Quest offers very affordable apartments from studios to two-bedders. Literally a one-minute walk to the Elizabeth Farm filming location and close to Parramatta's Old Government House. *8 Hope St, Rosehill; (02) 9687 7711; www.questrosehill.com.au*

Watsons Bay Hotel

One kilometre north of Vaucluse, this luxury hotel offers a variety of accommodation options overlooking the serene bay. Enjoy a drink in the enticing beer garden. *1 Military Rd, Watson's Bay; (02) 9337 5444; www.watsonsbayhotel.com.au*

CARAVANS AND MOTORHOMES

BIG4 Lakeside Holiday Park Narrabeen

Highly rated caravan and camping facility, also with self-contained accommodation, bordered by the Narrabeen Lake and close to surf on the northern beaches and Ingleside. *Lake Park Rd, North Narrabeen; (02) 9913 7845; www.sydneylakeside.com.au*

Terrey Hills Motel and Caravan Park

Powered sites and ensuite cabins a few kilometres west of the Deep Creek Reserve. Nearby bushlands are a great place for birdwatching, bushwalking and fishing. *319 Mona Vale Rd, Terrey Hills; (02) 9450 1781; www.terreyhills.com.au*

CAMPING

Cockatoo Island

This spot is gold! Unpowered campsites right on the water's edge. Camping packages available, which include site and tent hire, mattresses, chairs and lantern. Kitchen facilities and solar-powered showers. *(02) 8898 9774 or email camp@cockatooisland.gov.au for bookings*

WHERE TO EAT

Green Gourmet

An animal-friendly, Asian-inspired vegetarian and vegan joint with delicious yum cha on weekends. You may never go back to meat. *115–117 King St, Newtown; (02) 9519 5330; www. greengourmet.com.au*

A bay near Vaucluse House

Vauxhall Inn

Prepare to go 'all-in' at the Vauxhall, one of Sydney's premier full-time poker rooms, close to Old Government House and Elizabeth Farm shooting locations. Try their $9 weekday lunch specials, be it beef burger, steak sandwich or fettuccine bosciola. *Cnr Parramatta and Woodville rds, Granville; (02) 9637 2288; www.vauxhallinn.com.au*

Hickson Road Bistro

Drop in for a bite pre or post your theatre date – hey, why not both! This casual eatery is right next to the Sydney Theatre and offers a variety of modern international dishes. *20 Hickson Rd, Walsh Bay; (02) 9250 1990; www.culinaryedge. com.au/page/hickson_road_bistro.html*

Millennium

Ask anyone who knows the Sydney pizza scene and they'll point to Millennium in Vaucluse. Not the cheapest pizza on the block – but with 27 different types available, it's hard to go wrong. Eat-in and takeaway available. *693 Old South Head Rd, Vaucluse; (02) 9388 8033*

> Where is the sin? We bet. It is all in Pascal you know, we bet there is a God, we bet our life on it. We calculate the odds, the return, that we shall sit with the saints in paradise.
>
> — *Oscar*

Did you know?

The mid-coast of New South Wales was also the filming area for another significant Australian film, Fred Schepisi's *The Chant of Jimmie Blacksmith*. Released in 1978, the film was a defining movie in Australian cinema history. The film was shot in Bellingen, Kempsey, Scone, Armidale, Gulgong, Dorrigo National Park and Bellbrook. A property at Millbank, near Kempsey, was the location for the horrific killing scene where Jimmie (Tommy Lewis) finally snaps and butchers the unsuspecting family.

The Canteen Cafe

A licensed cafe on Cockatoo Island, which offers a range of sandwiches, cakes, salads and hot meals. Get your food and bevvies to go and enjoy them at one of the island's many scattered picnic spots. *Located past the main entry archway on the left, as you step off the ferry at Parramatta Wharf*

CINEMAS

Dendy Newtown

One of the funkiest cinemas in town with trendy decor and cosy boutique theatres screening art-house films and documentaries. Tight-arse Tuesdays and free parking behind the cinema. *261 King St, Newtown; (02) 9550 5699; www.dendy.com.au*

Dendy Cinema Opera Quay

One of Sydney's most prominent cinema venues, this fully licensed film house (i.e. you can take your tipple with you into the cinema) sits on the promenade overlooking Sydney Harbour and screens a great selection of art-house and commercial films. *Shop 9, 2 East Circular Quay, Circular Quay; (02) 9247 3800; www.dendy.com.au*

NORTH COAST
NEW SOUTH WALES

From Grafton at the bottom to Tweed Heads on the border, the tropical region of northern New South Wales is an idyllic area filled with stunning coastlines, crashing beaches and wide rivers and lakes. The area attracts tourists in the summer like flies on ... er, manure – particularly Byron Bay with its great weather and relaxed coastal vibe.

To the west of Grafton was a hot spot for locations used to shoot *Oscar and Lucinda*, including the small towns of Jackadgery and Cangai as well as the Clarence and Mann rivers. The town of Grafton is worth a visit, with amazing 19th-century buildings set amid a mist of mauve jacaranda trees.

VISITOR INFO

Clarence River Visitor Information Centre

Pacific Hwy, South Grafton; (02) 6642 4677; www.clarencetourism.com

THINGS TO SEE AND DO

Jackadgery

Overlooking the beautiful Mann River, the old mining town of Jackadgery was used to replicate the town of Bellingen in the film. (The real Bellingen lies just south-west of Coffs Harbour.) Bellingen was passed over as a shooting location because it's too built up to replicate rural New South Wales in the era of the film. The Bellingen River, which runs through Bellingen, was also not suitable to shoot the floating glass church sequences.

Most of the sets in Jackadgery were built from scratch. The Mann River was used in the scenes of the floating Glass Church. It was the only river the production crew scouted in the state that had the width and depth to allow for the difficult sequences to be properly executed.

Dangar Falls in Dorrigo National Park, northern NSW

To this day, Jackadgery still attracts a handful of optimistic prospectors who pan for gold and fossick for gemstones. The countryside is quite spectacular, while the Mann River is an ideal spot for fishing, canoeing, swimming and bushwalking. *Gwydir Hwy, 47 km west of Grafton*

Cangai

Around 10 kilometres north-west of Jackadgery is the wee town of Cangai, nestled in between Grange State Forest and Gibraltar Range National Park. This rural spot was used as the exterior setting of Miriam Chadwick's (Josephine Byrnes) country home. Cangai is a great base from which to explore Gibraltar Range National Park, a World Heritage–listed park with preserved rainforests and giant granite boulders. *Off Gwydir Hwy*

Clarence River

At the junction of the Clarence River and the Orara River was the location for the scene with Oscar and Percy (Bille Brown), after Oscar kills Mr Jeffries (Roxburgh) outside the bush pub. The Orara River meets the Clarence River just north of Ramornie, about 20 kilometres west of Grafton. The Clarence River is almost 400 kilometres long; it runs all the way from

Did you know?

While holidaying in Egypt when she was 18, Cate Blanchett was asked to be an extra in a crowd scene for a boxing film called *Kaboria*. Her experience on the set was not a pleasant one – she walked out after being yelled at by the director.

Grafton up to Iluka. Fisherfolk gather near Grafton for the abundance of eel-tailed catfish and snub-nosed garfish.

The interior of a farm house in Ramornie was used for the scene when Miriam takes advantage of Oscar after his arduous trip into town. *Ramornie is accessed via Gwydir Hwy*

Signature purple jacaranda trees in Grafton

Grafton

This well-tended garden city has 24 parks, many displaying the signature jacaranda trees that the town is known for. Enjoy the National Trust–classified buildings, galleries and numerous local art and craft shops. Grafton is a great place to base yourself while exploring the surrounding film locations on the New South Wales north coast.

Bellingen

'Bello' was the original location of the story; the novel's author, Peter Carey, was living in Bellingen when he wrote *Oscar and Lucinda*. However, the town was just too built up in 1996 to recreate old-time rural New South Wales for the film.

Bellingen is 120 kilometres south of Grafton, just through Coffs Harbour. It's an utterly charming country town, lined with beautiful old buildings and faded weatherboard facades. Bellingen has many attractions, including a heritage walk and the bat colony at Bellingen Island. There's also the Global Carnival (held annually in October), a music festival with a diverse range of stylings – all the way from electro to folk and classical.

Byron Bay

Byron Bay is beachside bliss. (Trying saying that ten times fast!) On the easternmost mainland point of Australia, it's 170 kilometres north-east of Grafton. This tourist town attracts a diverse mix of celebrities (Hoges and Linda used to live here), international backpackers, hippies and surfers, particularly during the warmer months. They come for all the sun-drenched beaches and huge range of eateries and watering holes and stay for the breezy way of life (and perhaps a massage or two). Apart from the summer holidays, the population also swells significantly during Easter for the East Coast Blues and Roots Festival. *www.visitbyronbay.com*

WHERE TO STAY

Wave Hill Station

Slap on the overalls and get farming, Aussie style! This beautiful 5000-hectare cattle farm offers farmstay accommodation giving guests the opportunity to try their hand at the daily farm activities, including fencing, cattle work and horse muster (for proficient riders). If that doesn't knacker you, activities on offer include horseriding, canoe and kayak hire, tennis, swimming, fishing and adventure packages. Accommodation includes the Homestead, 'Dingo Dam' cottage, caravan and camping options. Around 18 kilometres north-east of Cangai via Grafton. *Carnham Rd, Fineflower; (02) 6647 2145; www.wavehillfarmstay.com.au*

Motor Inn Hilldrop

Dirt-cheap country-style motel around 30 kilometres west of Jackadgery (just outside of Grafton). Its 12 ensuite units with modern amenities offer real bang for your buck. *706 Gwydir Hwy, South Grafton; (02) 6644 9220; www.hilldrop.com.au*

Fitzroy Motor Inn

Great-value motel accommodation located on Fitzroy Street in the heart of Grafton with three-and-a-half-star queen and family rooms and larger groups can stay in the four-bedroom Federation house. Swimming pool and barbecue area on site. *27 Fitzroy St, Grafton; (02) 6619 5121; www.fitzroymotel.com.au*

Looking towards the lighthouse at Byron Bay

CARAVANS AND MOTORHOMES

Mann River Caravan Park

This Jackadgery park has caravan and camping facilities, along with modest cabin accommodation. *Gwydir Hwy, Jackadgery; (02) 6647 4662*

The Gateway Village

This excellent park offers powered and ensuite sites, cabins and wireless internet just 3.5 kilometres north of Grafton town centre. *598 Summerland Way, Grafton; (02) 6642 4225; www.thegatewayvillage.com.au*

CAMPING

Nymboida National Park

Not far from Ramornie (west of Grafton), sites for self-sufficient campers who plan to do a spot of extreme whitewater canoeing or rafting, swimming or fishing in the Nymboida and Mann rivers. Nymboida River campground is the most popular and easiest to access camping area. *Ramornie Forest Rd via Gwydir Hwy or Old Glen Innes Rd*

Washpool National Park

Just north of Cangai, this area has some spectacular walking tracks, with plenty of bush camping areas including Bellbird and Coombadjha. *Access via signposts on the Gwydir Hwy, just past Jackadgery*

WHERE TO EAT

Cafe at Mann River Caravan Park

Enjoy the crowd-pleasing 'Mountain Burger' or some of Jackadgery's homemade ice-creams at the caravan park's attached cafe and general store. *Gwydir Hwy, Jackadgery; (02) 6647 4662*

Did you know?

Actor Ralph Fiennes constantly had producer Robin Dalton on edge. Fiennes had a propensity for going on long ocean swims when the production was on location in New South Wales. Although Fiennes is a strong swimmer, Dalton couldn't help worry that she would lose her lead actor and friend to the rough seas. On one occasion, when Ralph refused to come in from the choppy surf, Robin had to wade through the water fully dressed and yell at him until he obliged.

Zack's on Bent Street

Award-winning restaurant in Grafton (at the Bent St Motor Inn) specialising in the best Aussie cuisine has to offer, including a delicious selection of desserts and sorbets. *62 Bent St, South Grafton; (02) 6643 4500; www.bentstreetmotorinn.com.au*

Roches Family Hotel

Just a block from the Clarence River, this popular Grafton bistro boasts the world's longest one-piece wooden dining table. Great value, with lunch specials under $6. *85 Victoria St, Grafton; (02) 6642 2866*

OTHER LOCATIONS

PAYNES CROSSING
HUNTER VALLEY, NEW SOUTH WALES

This rural area in Hunter Valley wine country was the location of Lucinda's family home at the beginning of the film. A spot just near the homestead was also used for the scene of Lucinda floating in the lake early in the film.

CORNWALL ENGLAND

This area at the southernmost point of England, was used for all the locations set and shot in England. Boscastle, Bossiney, Crackington Haven, Morwenstow, Port Isaac and Trebarwith Strand were all Cornwall areas used in the film.

AND ANOTHER THING ...

THE APPLE ISLE – FILMS SHOT IN TASSIE

You wouldn't say that Tasmania is a thriving film and television hub. The tiny island state has been home to approximately 30 feature films over the years, a few of them relatively obscure and unknown. But that's not to say that Tassie hasn't had a lasting impact on the film industry.

The first feature film reportedly shot in Tasmania was the 1927 adventure/romance *For the Term of His Natural Life*. Based on the famous Marcus Clarke novel, the film is about a wrongfully accused convict who is sent to a penal colony in Van Diemen's Land. The film, which stars hugely popular American silent film actor Jane Novak, was largely shot in and around Sydney. However, Port Arthur in Tasmania's south-east was used for some of the filming.

Probably the most famous film shot in Tasmania was the 1987 flick *The Tale of Ruby Rose*, which centres on a young woman who takes a journey across the wild and vicious Tassie wilderness to find her family. The film, which was shot in the central highlands of the state, was nominated for three AFI Awards including Best Film and Best Director for Roger Scholes (it won Best Score).

Over the last few years Tasmania has grown in popularity as a filming location. *Dying Breed* (2008) a cannibalistic horror flick was set and shot on the Pieman River, while *Van Diemen's Land* (2009), a story about the infamous convict Alexander Pearce, utilised Lake Binney, Pine Tier Lagoon and Wild Rivers National Park as filming locations. Even Eric Bana made it down to Tassie for his car doco *Love the Beast* (2009).

The latest major feature film to be shot in Tasmania is *The Hunter*, about a mercenary sent to hunt the last Tasmanian tiger. It is based on the novel by Julian Leigh and stars Academy Award–nominated actor Willem Dafoe.

Tasmania was also the location for the shooting of the 1999 TV documentary series *Walking with Dinosaurs*. Produced by the BBC and winner of three Emmy Awards, the series used real locations along with CGI (computer-generated imagery) effects to bring the lost world of dinosaurs back to life. The production also used locations in Chile, New Zealand, the Bahamas, California and New Caledonia.

Q & A Peter Lawless, location manager for *Oscar and Lucinda*

Peter Lawless is one of Australia's most experienced location managers. His credits include *Babe*, *Oscar and Lucinda*, *Mighty Morphin Power Rangers: The Movie* (1995), *Red Planet* (2000), *Mao's Last Dancer* (2009) and all three Matrix films. He started out as a caterer on *Gallipoli*, before Peter Weir offered him a small role in the film as an ANZAC.

Q: *How and why did you decide on Robertson for* Babe?

A: It had to look like England and there aren't many places like England. We could have gone with Dorrigo, or half a dozen other places in Victoria and South Australia. But they wanted it in New South Wales, so the closest English environment near Sydney was Robertson.

Q: *What memorable experiences did you have while scouting* Babe?

A: The farm was actually found by Phil Hearnshaw, the first AD [assistant director]. I did everything but the farm. I had to find somewhere for the end sequence for the film (when Babe does the sheep-trial in front of the crowd). I scouted Sydney, Berrima, Kangaroo Valley, Bowral ... all over the place looking for this end sequence. I was kind of looking for an oval or an English field with a picket fence. There was one at Chevalier College, which was the most suitable. I presented lots of sites and that was the one that was chosen.

Then someone told me about this place called Ranelagh House. We had been talking about the place at dinner and the history of it and how it used to have English gardens, tennis and bowls. On a hunch I went down and had a look. It was this old, ramshackle, two- or three-storey country accommodation. Nothing was left of the garden, but there was still an atmosphere there. I walked out the back and stood on the hill and looked down at this field with all these cows. It looked like it must have been a cricket pitch or something. **I thought that this was where we could put this oval because of the English trees, the fantastic vista and the light bursting through the clouds – the beam of God, you know? It had the horizon and the foreground was fantastic. All we needed to do was build a grandstand and a picket fence and it was the perfect setting.**

So I rang [production designer] Roger Ford and told him I had found somewhere better. I told him that it didn't have a picket fence, it didn't have a grandstand, but that it was much better. Roger came down and had a look and said, 'I think you're right.' So he rang George [Miller] and George had to come back from Sydney. It is by far one of my favourite location finds, partly because of the process, but also because it looks so perfect.

Q: *Did you have any idea how big the film was going to be?*

A: From the very first night's rushes, we knew we had a good film. When Andrew Lesnie [the cinematographer] screened a shot of Babe walking from point A to point B on cue we all looked at it and thought that this was going to work. It looked beautiful! The pig wrangler's name was Karl-Lewis Miller; he was from the US. The pig walked up the path, stood at the door and looked up at the door, and then opened the handle. Every day from then on was a joyful day because we were working on something that looked good and was going to be fantastic.

Q: *When does your role as a location manager on a production start and end?*

A: I start really early, I'm one of the earliest people on. I can be on even before a director or a production designer. There's usually a director, but not always a production designer. I do work all the way through the production, though the fun bits for me are the finding of the locations, the creative process of putting the elements together and being part of the decision-making process. After that, I quickly slide down the ladder of importance.

Q: *There were plenty of locations for* Oscar and Lucinda. *How was that?*

A: It was fantastic. **You couldn't hope for a better project because it had period elements, which is always a pleasure, and it had the city and the country.** I love the bush, I love getting out in the bush.

We were going to film in Hobart for period Sydney, which was a good call, and we went very close to doing that, but had to pull out at the end because of the cost. I don't think the film suffers much for it, but Hobart at that time would have been fantastic. It was a really good double for the period. I was a bit heartbroken that we didn't go there, but it's understandable.

Q: *Were there any challenges? What about finding the location for the river?*

A: Fortunately, I had done a lot of canoeing and whitewater rafting up on the Clarence and the Mann rivers, so I knew the territory. When I suggested that area, I went and looked at it and thought it would work. But what about all the other rivers in New South Wales? So **I spent five days in a helicopter looking at every river in New South Wales, from the Victorian border right up to and over the border into Queensland. We looked and we looked, we landed, we got out and looked.** We flew around trying to find all the elements: deep enough and big enough to float a barge with a church on it.

It also had to be uncivilised. Below the fresh water line is where the rivers are wide, but that's where there's lots of civilisation, i.e. power lines. To get away from the civilisation you have to go further upstream, which means you're into narrower, shallower rivers. The only rivers that offered that were the Macleay River and the Clarence and the Mann. **I think I spent about $25 000 on helicopters looking around for the right river!**

We all went and looked at the Macleay River with Gillian and it looked fantastic. We went to have lunch at the pub on the way out, the Taylor's Arms Hotel. We'd ordered our meal and one of the locals came up and said, 'So you like our rivers, do you?' We said, 'Yeah, we love it.' And he said, 'Yeah, we love it, it's fantastic. It's the fastest-rising and quickest flooding river in Australia.' Gillian's jaw just dropped. We didn't even finish our meal. That was it for the Macleay.

So we went back to what I had found originally, a particular bit of the Mann River. I had been taken there by a fisherman. We were driving and driving, going up and down in this four-wheel drive, bumping along. I said to him, 'This is a long way, mate. I don't think we'll go this far, the crew hates travelling.' **He said, 'Do you want to see it or not? It's what you want!' So I shut up and we got there and it was fantastic, it was exactly what we wanted.** But we had to put a road in, which cost us $50 000.

Another problem was that there were these big boulders in the river 6 feet down. We had to figure out how to get rid of these huge rocks under the water. They drilled them and put chains on them and got dozers to pull them out of the river. It took three days just to do that.

Then when we were filming, the river starting dropping. We were losing our height. So I had to get permission to dam the river. We got the State Emergency Services people in and put 16 000 sandbags across the river to raise the river height a metre and a half to bring it back up again. The river level came back up and we kept filming. Then we got a phone call from the SES people saying that there's a 4-metre flood coming down the river and that we had to get rid of our sandbags! We had to get out there and remove 16 000 sandbags within two hours! The river came down and it flooded through. We had to just leave the two barges, one with the camera gear on it and the other with the church on it (the grips did get the crane off). Then we couldn't film there for three days because it was so muddy. We had to go do other filming and come back later. Then the river started dropping again and we had to put the 16 000 sandbags back in the river!

Q: *What has been your biggest challenge in film?*

A: My biggest challenge was for *The Matrix.* The Wachowski brothers asked me to take them up to one of the tallest buildings in Sydney. I took them and we were out on the roof, standing there looking around and they said, 'Well … which building could we land a helicopter on?' You need a flat roof with not too many antennas and air-conditioning units and it had to be one of the tall ones. **So I looked around and I said, 'You can probably land a helicopter on that one over there.' They said, 'Alright Lawless, set it up then.'**

That was the start of a very challenging process, getting permission to build a helipad on top of a building. There have been a number of really wealthy people who have tried to get approval for a helipad in Sydney, like Kerry Packer, but they'd all been knocked back. I had to talk a building into letting us build a helipad on the top. It was the building at 201 Kent Street (AON Tower).

Then I had to get permission to land a helicopter. There were also other things … They wanted to fly the helicopter up the streets, halfway up the buildings. Then they wanted to fly them across the city with somebody hanging on a rope underneath. Then they wanted Keanu Reeves to climb out of a window of a 40-storey building and walk on the ledge. **They wanted to do all this crazy stuff and I had to get Sydney to agree to it.**

Q: *What was it like working on The Matrix sequels? Was it different after all the hype from the first one?*

A: I personally found it very different. The first film was so adventurous, from my perspective, because it was all on location. **When Keanu Reeves is walking on the ledge 40 floors above the city streets, he is walking on a real ledge 40 floors above the ground – not in a studio walking on a ledge.** I had to find a building where we could take the glass out of the window so we could get a camera and a crane out so we could shoot walking on the ledge outside. And all the helicopter stuff and jumping out of windows, it was all real. The second and third movies … I was grateful to have the work, but it was nowhere near as interesting for me.

Q: *Of all the films you've worked on, what have been your favourite locations?*

A: I've done a couple of films in the Red Centre. I've worked in the Kimberley, Coober Pedy and Alice Springs. Also down in the Flinders Ranges. I kind of like the outback. It's such a relief to get away from all the hurdles you have to jump and the strictures you have to go through in the city. **To finally be out somewhere where your soul is boundless with the horizon. The job is a lot easier because there's space out there.** Having breakfast in the desert is fantastic, the day goes from chill to heat. **You're really alive when you're working in the outback.**

A plaque in Walsh Bay commemorates a scene from The Matrix

The Allianz Centre – where Neo and Trinity rescue Morpheus

Martin Place, where the woman in red walks past

Picnic at Hanging Rock (1975)

This we do for pleasure, so that we may shortly be at the mercy of venomous snakes and poisonous ants. How foolish can human creatures be.

— *Mrs McCraw*

Albert (Jarratt) and Michael (Guard) discuss life over a bottle of wine

Director: Peter Weir
Writer: Cliff Green
Producers: Hal McElroy, Jim McElroy
Cast includes: Rachel Roberts, Helen Morse, Dominic Guard, Jeff Jarratt, Anne Lambert, Margaret Nelson, Jackie Weaver

ABOUT THE FILM

Some films – most films, actually – have a certain shelf life before they start to look dated. *Picnic at Hanging Rock*, however, doesn't fit that bill. Although it was made over three and a half decades ago, the film still stands its ground as a brilliant highlight of Australian cinema. Based on Joan Lindsay's haunting novel, the story begins on St Valentine's Day 1900, when a group of precocious teens from an exclusive finishing school sojourn to Hanging Rock Recreation Reserve for a an innocent picnic.

Clad in ethereal white flowing dresses, a few of the more curious young lasses go exploring around the mysterious rock. And they never return. A taut, spellbinding mystery unravels, teeming with tense ambiguity and hypnotically stunning scenery. The hauntingly beautiful soundtrack brings all the elements of this cinematic masterpiece together.

Picnic at Hanging Rock was among the first Australian feature films to reach international audiences and it received critical acclaim in the US and the UK. Peter Stack of the *San Francisco Chronicle* described the film as 'one of the most hauntingly beautiful mysteries ever created on film'. All this time later that still very much rings true.

The girls of Appleyard Cottage before tragedy struck

Miranda (Lambert, front) and friends laze about
at the foot of the rock

With this film, Peter Weir burst onto the scene as one of our best young directors. Russell Boyd, whose deft skill behind the camera, nabbed a BAFTA (British Academy of Film and Television Arts) for his cinematography.

The film also gave every teenage boy in Australia a new pinup girl – Anne Lambert, who scored the role of angelic blonde Miranda after a series of contemporary soapie roles and the famous 'Fancy Nancy' Fanta soft drink ad.

Keeping the spirit alive, *Picnic at Hanging Rock* is screened every year on Valentine's Day at the Hanging Rock Recreation Reserve.

LOCATIONS

HANGING ROCK RECREATION RESERVE
VICTORIA

The famous cliffs known as Hanging Rock are located around 80 kilometres north of Melbourne, just a hop, skip and a jump from Woodend. Originally named Mt Diogenes in 1836, Hanging Rock was purchased by the state government in 1886. Even before the release of the film, the big boulders were a hugely popular tourist spot, thanks largely to the unique volcanic rock formations (or mamelon – French for nipple, which kinda gives you a hint about the shape), which were formed from a

Hanging Rock as seen from the base

particular type of stiff lava over six million years ago. Thousands of years of rainwater have also contributed to their distinctive shape.

Over 70 000 people visit the reserve each year. According to Park Ranger Guido Bigolin, Hanging Rock attracts a vast array of different visitors, including almost all of the film's cast over the years. Director Peter Weir has reportedly come back a couple of times since he shot on location here.

By all accounts, Joan Lindsay's novel is completely fictitious. Well, almost all – some of the more imaginative theorists believe that the events depicted in the novel (and subsequently in the film) are loosely based on events that occurred in Lindsay's life.

Of course it's no surprise that a significant percentage of the thousands of people who wander through the imposing volcanic rocks claim to have paranormal experiences. From tourists seeing ghostly images in their Hanging Rock photos to the bounty hunters who pocketed a piece of the rock as a souvenir only to mail it back because it brought them bad luck, the area continues to make a mysterious impression.

VISITOR INFO

Hanging Rock Recreation Reserve
South Rock Rd (via Calder Hwy); (03) 5427 0295; www.visitmacedonranges.com/natural-attractions/hanging-rock

Woodend Visitor Information Centre
High St, Woodend; (03) 5427 2033; www.visitmacedonranges.com

The rocks all round – Mt Macedon itself – must be all of 350 million years old. Siliceous lava, forced up from deep down below. Soda trachytes extruded in a highly viscous state, building the steep-sided mamelons we see in Hanging Rock. And quite young geologically speaking. Barely a million years.

— Miss McCraw

THINGS TO SEE AND DO

Explore the rock

Don't be scared … it's just a movie! The best way to explore this rocky attraction is on the Hanging Rock Summit Walk. Noted as a 'moderate' grade walking track, it's 1800 metres to the summit, with a return trip taking about 50 minutes if moving at a leisurely pace. The trek can be a little strenuous for some, as it's slightly steep and some of the paths closer to the summit are a little uneven. The walk gives visitors the opportunity to explore all the nooks and crannies of this unique natural formation. Needless to say, the panoramic views in between the boulders at the top of the hill are absolutely beautiful.

Most of the filming locations are situated around the base of the rock, as it was a logistical nightmare for the film crew to lug cameras and lighting gear all the way to the top. The scenes in which the schoolgirls laze about eating cake were shot on the south-eastern side at the start of the summit walk. This area is marked as 'Queen Mary's Profile' and 'Morgan Blood's Waterfall' (named for Mad Dan Morgan, a bushranger thought to have hid out up here). Follow the stairs up and you will encounter other locations from the film where the girls in white explore before tragedy strikes.

While exploring Hanging Rock you will also see over 100 varieties of indigenous plants, a vast array of birdlife and koalas, kangaroos and wallabies. The reserve also offers guided night walking tours of the rock during the summer months. *Per-car entry fees to the park apply*

Hanging Rock Discovery Centre

Learn all about the history of the rock, from detailed geological facts to hands-on interpretive displays. There are also displays about the film, including some info on director Peter Weir and author Joan Lindsay. *Located at the base of Hanging Rock, opposite Hanging Rock Picnic Cafe*

Picnicking

What trip to Hanging Rock would be complete without a picnic? Cram your esky with sangers and lamingtons and loaf about in the exact same spot as the schoolgirls did. There are coin-operated barbies located throughout the park if you're more inclined for some sizzling snags and steaks. Every February, Hanging Rock hosts *The Age* Harvest Picnic, a celebration of Victorian food and wine with cooking demonstrations, live music and children's activities. *www.harvestpicnic.com.au*

Hanging Rock Racecourse

Watch the gee-gees gallop around at one of Victoria's most popular country race tracks, which has been hosting meetings for over

From the top of the rock you can see for miles

120 years. The racing club has two major meetings: on New Year's Day and Australia Day. Located within Hanging Rock Recreation Reserve. *(03) 5422 1866; www.countryracing. com.au/clubs/hangingrock*

Activities

There are four tennis courts and two sports ovals available for hire at the reserve. There's also some good fishing in the dam, which is located in the centre of Hanging Rock Racecourse.

WHERE TO STAY

Hanging Rock Cottage

Stunning bed and breakfast only 300 metres from Hanging Rock. Fortify yourself with a relaxed lunch on the patio, breathing in that fresh country air, after you attack the rock. The *Picnic at Hanging Rock* DVD in every room is a nice touch. *30 Maxted Dr; (03) 5427 0581; www.hangingrockcottage.com.au*

Holgate Brewhouse

Ever had fantasies of living in a brewery? 'Real beer, no bull' is their slogan, with a nod to the bulls' heads on the Holgate family coat of arms. This boutique brewery offers stylish and modern rooms with ensuites just a few steps away from the bar taps. They have brewery, winery and spa tour packages available with your room and it's only a five-minute drive to Hanging Rock. *79 High St, Woodend; (03) 5427 2510; www.holgatebrewhouse.com*

Campaspe Country House

Sophisticated 1920s English-style manor with modern comforts, first-class rooms and an

intimate French-influenced restaurant on site. *29 Goldies La, Woodend; (03) 5427 2273; www. campasphouse.com.au*

WHERE TO EAT

Hanging Rock Picnic Cafe

Fuel up with an alfresco Devonshire tea before you tackle the climb; this cafe is perfectly situated at the base of the rock. There's an attached gift shop where you can purchase souvenirs from the movie, including DVDs and a collector's book. *Located at the base of Hanging Rock; (03) 5427 0295*

Schatzi's Cafe and Restaurant

At this award-winning Austrian-themed restaurant, they also do some classic Australian fare and a very filling big breakfast. *Shop 1, 104 High St, Woodend; (03) 5427 4447*

Bourkie's Bakehouse

Do you like vanilla slices? What a stupid question, everyone likes 'snot blocks', don't they? Bourkie's is famous for their sweet custardy treats, placing first in the Great Australian Vanilla Slice Triumph in 2003 and 2004. Add one of their award-winning meat pies and you've got a balanced meal! *115 High St, Woodend; (03) 5427 2486; www.bourkies.com.au*

Albert finds a torn piece of clothing in his search for the girls

Except for those people down there, we might be the only living creatures in the whole world.

– Edith

The afternoon sun strikes Martindale Hall

Miranda's bedroom is little-changed since the film shoot

MARTINDALE HALL
SOUTH AUSTRALIA

This Georgian-style two-storey National Trust–listed mansion is one of the South Australia's most famous buildings. Standing on the 11 000-acre Martindale Station, the mansion was built in 1879 for the substantial sum of £30 000 by Edmund Bowman. Bowman was a wealthy young pastoralist who lived the princely life of a well-to-do bachelor until he was forced to sell the house in 1891 during the depression.

In a grand romantic gesture, the place was bought by William Tennant Mortlock as a wedding present for his bride-to-be. It remained in the Mortlock family until 1950. A minor renovation in 2002 helped return the mansion to almost mint condition.

Martindale Hall played an enormous role in *Picnic at Hanging Rock*, acting as Appleyard

Did you know?

In the film, all the schoolgirls' watches stop at noon when they are at Hanging Rock. According to executive producer Patricia Lovell, some of the crew's watches eerily began to play up while shooting at the rock – some running slower than usual and some stopping altogether.

College, the girls' finishing school. Almost all exterior and interior college scenes in the film were shot at Martindale Hall. The only exception was Mrs Appleyard's study, for which a precise replica set was built at the South Australian Film Corporation studio in Adelaide. Martindale Hall is located a couple of kilometres south of the main town of Mintaro in the Clare Valley wine-growing region.

VISITOR INFO

Martindale Hall

Manoora–Mintaro Rd, Mintaro; (08) 8843 9088; www.martindalehall.com

THINGS TO SEE AND DO

Martindale Hall Museum

During the day, Martindale Hall is a museum open to visitors wanting a fascinating glimpse into early Australian-European life. Every single room in this house is distinctive – from the smoking room, adorned with antique guns, spears and trophies, to the billiards room, lined with bookcases stacked with old, leather-bound books. The books' musky redolence alone will transport you back in time. Glide up the elegantly carpeted staircase to see The White Room, Miranda's bedroom in the film. There's also a gallery exhibiting a number of portrait paintings. *Open weekdays 11am–4pm and weekends 12–4pm (special 'High Tea' events held by appointment)*

Incident at Martindale

These brilliant whodunnit nights are hugely popular with guests at Martindale – or anyone in the mood for a night of Agatha Christie-esque crime capers. Gather ten or 12 friends and enjoy this mystery hosted by Inspector Percival Plodd over dinner. You'll feel like you're stuck in a game of Cluedo – Professor Plum, in the study, with a candlestick? The crime is solved by dessert and guests can retreat for a game of billiards or enjoy a snifter of port while perusing a book in the library. By appointment.

The Mintaro Maze

A labyrinth out of *Alice's Adventures in Wonderland*, with over 800 well-manicured conifers making up this man-sized maze. Twist and turn your way through the puzzle or play a game of giant chess or noughts and crosses. Gift shop on site. Open Monday to Thursday and every day on public holidays and school holidays. Located a couple kilometres north of Martindale Hall. *Jacka Rd, Mintaro; (08) 8843 9012; www.mintaromaze.com.au*

WHERE TO STAY

Martindale Hall

'Original' is the operative word to describe these lodgings; much of the furnishings in the guest rooms dates back to the early and mid-1900s. From the drawing room to the billiards room and library, all the way to evening meals served by a butler and maid, you really do feel like you've stepped out of a time machine. There are ten rooms on offer, some of which were used as locations in the film. *Manoora–Mintaro Rd, Mintaro; (08) 8843 9088; www.martindalehall.com*

STRATHALBYN
SOUTH AUSTRALIA

Settled by Scots in the 1830s, Strathalbyn is a wee gem hidden on the Fleurieu Peninsula just south of Adelaide. The heritage town is renowned for its historic streetscapes and country charm and lays claim to being the unofficial antiques capital of South Australia.

A little trickery went on in the filming of *Picnic at Hanging Rock* – Strathalbyn was used as the small Victorian town of Woodend for the film. In 1974, Woodend was already too modernised to be used as a turn-of-century country town. After much location scouting Strathalbyn was locked in. With a little bit of clever set design, it easily replicated 1900s Woodend. Many Strathalbyn locals were used as extras in the film.

High Street shops in Strathalbyn

VISITOR INFORMATION

Strathalbyn Tourist Information Centre
Old railway station, South Tce; (08) 8536 3212; www.visitalexandrina.sa.gov.au

THINGS TO SEE AND DO

Albyn Terrace

The self-guided heritage walk takes in over 30 heritage buildings. Albyn Terrace is the street used in the scenes when Mrs McCraw and the schoolgirls travel to and from Hanging Rock via horse and cart. Some of the buildings seen in the film are still standing today. *Self-guided walk maps available from the visitor centre*

Antiques on High Street

Check out the wares in High Street's sensational antique shops. One of the town's main thoroughfares, it has the Antique Bazaar of Strathalbyn, Bowerbird Antiques and

Did you know?

Of all the young actresses cast to play schoolgirls in the movie, Anne Lambert (who played Miranda) was the only one with any real acting experience. Peter Weir wanted some 'innocent faces' in the roles and cast most of the girls from rural South Australian towns.

Collectables and The Pickled Walnut within a stone's throw of each other. What's old is new again. *High St, between Chapel and Grey sts*

National Trust Museum

This museum in the former police station and courthouse depicts the town's history using old farm machinery, a blacksmith's shop, and old photographs and newspaper clippings. Fascinating pioneer and wartime exhibits. *1 Rankine St; (08) 8536 2656; www.strathmuseum.org.au*

Station Master's Gallery

A gallery in the old railway station, which also houses the visitor centre, where you can take in local and touring art exhibitions Wednesday through Sunday. *Old railway station, South Tce; (08) 8536 3212*

WHERE TO STAY

Victoria Hotel

This old bluestone, built in 1865, blended seamlessly into the backdrop of scenes in the film shot on Albyn Terrace. Well-priced modern spa rooms with queen beds. Cheap meals downstairs in the pub or try the recently renovated bistro. *16 Albyn Tce; (08) 8536 2022; www.victoriahotelstrathalbyn.com.au*

Watervilla House Bed and Breakfast

A stone's throw from Albyn Terrace, this heritage-listed B&B is surrounded by perfectly manicured gardens. Choose from the Oak, Kitchen, Courtyard and Verandah rooms, you can't go wrong with any of them. *2 Mill St; (08) 8536 4099; www.watervillahouse.com*

WHERE TO EAT

Appleseed Cafe

There's no better place in town for a quick focaccia, warm quiche or a mucho tasty baked tater. If that's not enough to get you in the door, their all-day brekkie will. *30 High St; (08) 8536 8195*

Jack's High Street Bakery

A relaxed bakehouse serving up some of the best coffee in town with biscuits, cakes and light meals also on offer. *24 High St; (08) 8536 4147*

OTHER LOCATIONS

Stirling, South Australia

A building at the Marbury School, around 16 kilometres south-east of the Adelaide CBD in Stirling in the Adelaide Hills, was used as the home of Colonel Fitzhubert (Peter Collingwood) and his wife (Olga Dickie) in the film. This is where the character of Irma (Karen Robson) goes to convalesce after her ordeal at the rock.

Did you know?

Legendary Aussie screenwriter and playwright David Williamson was originally chosen to adapt the novel for the screen, but was unavailable. He recommended TV writer Cliff Green for the job (*Homicide* and *Matlock Police*).

Q & A Russell Boyd, cinematographer for *Picnic at Hanging Rock*

Continued from pages 84–5.

Russell Boyd has been the director of photography on some of the greatest Australian films including *Picnic at Hanging Rock, Gallipoli* and *Crocodile Dundee*. He has collaborated with director Peter Weir on many other feature films, including *Master and Commander: The Far Side of the World*, for which he won an Academy Award in 2003. He recently worked on another Peter Weir film, *The Way Back*, about seven courageous prisoners who escape a Siberian labour camp in 1940. The film was shot in Bulgaria, India and Morocco.

Q: *How did you first get into cinematography?*

A: As a teenager I wanted to become a press photographer. My mother found me a job at Cinesound in Melbourne – they used to do theatrical news. That was in 1961, just when television was really steaming ahead and theatrical news was dying out. They also used to do commercials at Cinesound. **I came to Sydney to do some documentaries and then I worked as a cameraman at Supreme Films in Sydney doing a lot of commercials. Eventually I got into doing features.**

Q: *When did you first get your feature film break?*

A: I had a done a few weekend films with director Michael Thornhill. Eventually he got a feature film together to direct, called *Between Wars,* and asked me to shoot it for him. It was a really good break.

Q: *As a cinematographer, how much input do you have in the scouting of locations?*

A: Quite a bit. On a feature film we usually get what is called 'non-consecutive prep' – sometimes you do stuff weeks and weeks ahead. Usually that involves going to a select few locations for different scenes. **If there's a good reason why I think one location is better than the others, I'll speak up about it then. Sometimes they listen to me and sometimes they don't,** but usually they show the cinematographer respect. It's got a lot to do with logistics, whether we can get the equipment in there, so the practical side comes into it as well. Mostly I look at light and camera angles.

Q: *Picnic at Hanging Rock was your first collaboration with Peter Weir, a director you have gone on to work with many times over. How did that partnership come about?*

A: I had just done *The Man from Hong Kong* with Brian Trenchard-Smith, and Hal McElroy was the first AD [assistant director] on it. I think he recommended me. Hal introduced us on the way to the airport to go to South Australia to check out the locations for *Picnic*. **I hadn't really sat down with Pete and talked about the film at all until we were actually picking out locations.**

Q: *Did you find any of the locations challenging to shoot?*

A: I'll tell you about two of the challenges. For the scene where the girls go up to the top of the rock and they have the St Valentine's Day cake, there's a big, big pan around. It's a lovely shot. John Seale, the camera operator, helped me design it with Pete; the three of us collaborated on it. But I figured out when we were up on the rock that the only time of day that the light would actually come in and the trees would be nicely backlit was midday. At that time the light would only last for an hour and drop behind the rock itself. I said to Pete and Hal, who was one of the producers, 'I think we're going to have to shoot this scene over a few days because we're only going to have the light for an hour and a half each day where it's going to be perfect. The rest of the time it's going to be no good.' **They looked at me like I was mad because they'd never worked with me before.** We had a terrific first AD in Mark Egerton, and so he scratched his head and said, 'I think I can figure this out so we can do it over a number of days.' **I was very pleased with the result because the light is so critical in that scene – in fact, in all of *Picnic at Hanging Rock*, the light was critical.**

One of the other problems we had was a mechanical thing. In those days, lighting equipment was fairly heavy and to get any lights up on the rock at all, we were going to have to have to take a couple of generators up. The day before we started shooting they hired a helicopter to lower the generators in because it was almost impossible to get them up there otherwise. On one of the runs one of the generators actually got dropped and it was rendered useless, so we had to struggle through with just the one generator in a very specific area. So I had to light the rest of it from the very top of the rock with reflector boards and bounce light.

Peter said many, many years ago – probably on *Picnic* actually – that the art of directing is turning a compromise into a bonus. I think that applies to cinematographers as well.

Q: *I've heard about eerie things happening on set, did you feel this mystery in the air?*

A: Nah, I think that might have been a bit of media folklore. I don't think my watch stopped. I would doubt its validity to be honest, but I'm a bit of a sceptic.

Q: *Did you have an inkling during production that the movie was going to be something really special?*

A: Once I started working with Peter I knew that he was very special. I look at the film from time to time because I'm giving a talk or lecture about it. And I'm simply amazed at Peter's direction. I think it was only his second feature-length film and we shot it in a hurry. So I'm always amazed at all the subtleties that he managed to get into it in that short amount of time.

I don't think we realised it was going to be a masterpiece or an icon. I don't think we realised that until we actually saw it. It's one of the benchmark classic early Australian films, along with Bruce Beresford's films, Gillian Armstrong's, Fred Schepisi's and the list goes on. It was a great time to be working in the business.

Q: *You won a BAFTA Award for the film, did that help with your career?*

A: It certainly did in Australia. Not so much internationally, because the film didn't get such a wide audience over there. But it did help me get my foot in the door in Hollywood; a few directors I ended up working with were aware of *Picnic* and had seen it. I think it was more after *Gallipoli* that the ball started rolling for me over there.

Producers, writers, editors and more!

Here's a look at a few of the people who have shaped the Australian film industry from behind the scenes.

JAN CHAPMAN, PRODUCER (1950–)

Newcastle-born, Chapman is a prolific producer, behind films such as The Last Days of Chez Nous (1992), *The Piano* (1993), *Holy Smoke* (1999), *Lantana* (2001) and *Bright Star* (2010). Chapman started at the ABC in the '80s. *Two Girls* (1986) was her first major collaboration with director Jane Campion (nominated for an Oscar for *The Piano)*, who she has worked with many times. Chapman received the Order of Australia in 2004 for her contribution to the local film industry.

JILL BILCOCK, EDITOR (1948–)

Bilcock has been nominated for nine AFI Awards. She cut and spliced together such Aussie classics as *Strictly Ballroom* (1992), *Muriel's Wedding* (1994) and *Japanese Story* (2003). Melbourne born and bred, Bilcock's international film credits include *Romeo and Juliet* (1996), *Elizabeth* (1998),

Road to Perdition (2002) and *The Young Victoria* (2009). Bilcock was nominated for an Academy Award in 2002 for *Moulin Rouge!* and has received four BAFTA nominations.

DAVID WILLIAMSON, WRITER (1942–)

Screenwriting royalty, Williamson was behind *Don's Party* (1976), *The Club* (1980), *Gallipoli* (1981) and *Phar Lap* (1983). With over 30 produced plays under his belt, he is undoubtedly the most successful stage scribe this country has ever produced. Seven of his plays have been adapted for the screen, including *Don's Party*, *The Club*, *The Removalists* (1975), *Travelling North* (1987) and *Emerald City* (1988). His latest screenwriting venture, *Zebras*, about a young soccer team in South Africa, will be directed by Bruce Beresford.

MATT CARROLL, PRODUCER (1944–)

Matt has been responsible for some of the most groundbreaking films in Aussie cinema history, including *Sunday Too Far Away* (1975), *Storm Boy* (1976), *Breaker Morant* (1980) and *The Club* (1980). His first feature was *Shirley Thompson vs The Alien* (1972), about a group of extraterrestrials who plan to invade Australia. Carroll has also worked on a number of television productions.

WORKING DOG, PRODUCTION COMPANY (1994–)

Working Dog is the creative collective behind Aussie comedy classics *The Castle* (1997)

and *The Dish* (2000). The team of Rob Sitch, Santo Cilauro, Tom Gleisner, Jane Kennedy and Michael Hirsh got their start on the side-splitting ABC comedy series *The D Generation* and *The Late Show*. Their first Working Dog production was the critically acclaimed mockumentary series *Frontline*. Working Dog is also behind several popular TV shows. Their latest feature film is *25* (2011), a comedy starring Rachael Taylor and Josh Lawson, shot in Melbourne.

RICHARD FRANCIS-BRUCE, EDITOR (1948–)

Francis-Bruce's bio on the IMDB website is impressive to say the least. His early Aussie films include *Mad Max: Beyond Thunderdome* (1985) and *Dead Calm* (1990). In Hollywood he really hit his stride, editing *Lorenzo's Oil* (1992), *The Shawshank Redemption* (1994), *Se7en* (1995), *The Rock* (1996), *Air Force One* (1997) and *The Green Mile* (1999) in the '90s! Francis-Bruce's golden run from 1994 to 1997 saw him nominated for three Oscars, though he went home empty-handed on all three occasions.

STUART BEATTIE, WRITER (1972–)

Beattie's first feature was the family-friendly *Joey* (1997) about a young boy who tries to save a baby kangaroo. Darker work made him hot international property a few years later: *Collateral* (2004), *Derailed* (2005) and *30 Days of Night* (2007). Beattie also co-wrote the three Pirates of the Caribbean films

and worked with Baz Luhrmann on *Australia*. For *Tomorrow, When the War Began* (2010), he adapted the screenplay from the John Marsden novel and then directed it. Beattie's upcoming projects include Pirates of the Caribbean and Tomorrow, When the War Began sequels and a screen adaptation of the popular video game Halo.

IAN JONES, CINEMATOGRAPHER (1954–)

From working as a clapper loader, focus puller and steadicam operator on some early Aussie productions – including *The Man from Snowy River* (1982) and *Mad Max: Beyond Thunderdome* (1985) – Jones developed into a fully fledged cinematographer, with his first feature of note being Rolf de Heer's film *Bad Boy Bubby* (1993). Jones has almost 50 diverse film credits to his name, from shooting *Police Academy: Mission to Moscow* (1994), to his AFI Award–winning turn behind the lens for *Ten Canoes* (2006).

ARTHUR CAMBRIDGE, COLOUR GRADER (1936–)

Colour graders are responsible for enhancing and altering the colours you see on screen. Cambridge has worked on close to 90 films as a colour grader or timer in a career spanning 25 years to date: just think of any Australian film made between about 1979 and 2003 and he most likely worked on it. Cambridge was honoured with the Byron Kennedy Award at the 1998 AFI Awards for his contribution to Australian film.

Rabbit-proof Fence (2002)

See that bird? That's the spirit bird. He will always look after you.

— *Maud*

Gracie (Monaghan), Daisy (Sansbury) and Molly (Sampi) huddle to stay warm

Director: Phillip Noyce
Writer: Christine Olsen
Producers: Phillip Noyce, Christine Olsen, John Winter
Cast includes: Everlyn Sampi, Tianna Sansbury, Laura Monaghan, David Gulpilil, Kenneth Branagh

ABOUT THE FILM

Based on a memoir by Doris Pilkington Garimara, *Rabbit-proof Fence* is set in Western Australia in 1931. It follows the lives of three young Aboriginal girls – sisters Molly (Sampi) and Daisy (Sansbury) and their cousin Gracie (Monaghan). They are taken away from their mother and sent to a camp in Moore River under the directive of AO Neville (Branagh), the man heading the White Australia policy.

Longing for their family and the comforts of home, it's not long before the resourceful girls flee the camp in search of the rabbit-proof fence, a barrier hundreds of miles long they know will lead them back to their home in Jigalong. Their epic journey is shadowed by Moodoo (Gulpilil), an Aboriginal tracker, while they also have to contend with the coppers, hunger pangs and the unforgiving desert terrain.

As expected, *Rabbit-proof Fence* created much controversy upon its release in 2002, reigniting the debate about the Stolen Generation. The term 'Stolen Generation' refers to children of Aboriginal and Torres Strait Islander descent who, from the late 1800s to the late 1960s (the timeline varies depending on the source – another contentious element of the debate), were snatched from their families under government directives in an attempt to better assimilate

Molly carries the exhausted Daisy along the rabbit-proof fence

RABBIT PROOF FENCE
The longest fence in the world
[total length: 2,021 miles/3,256.5km]

them into 'white' society. These children were placed with institutions and white families to achieve this. In 2008, a newly elected prime minister Kevin Rudd said sorry to Indigenous Australians for crimes perpetrated against them, particularly the Stolen Generation.

While the history is grim, this is a carefully crafted film. Its success rode on the back of the brave performances of the three young Indigenous actors. Their looks of desolation and longing say more than any scripted words could ever say. Casting these girls took a long and exhausting search by director Noyce, who spent months visiting Indigenous communities looking for the right actors.

Noyce does a remarkable job leading the troops, while acclaimed cinematographer Christopher Doyle – who also shot *In the Mood for Love* (2000) and *Hero* (2002) – captures the magnificence of the Australian desert with that perfect balance of hazard and beauty. The film won three AFI Awards, including Best Film, and legendary UK muso Peter Gabriel was nominated for a Golden Globe for his moving score.

If only they would understand what we are trying to do for them.

– *AO Neville*

LOCATIONS

ONKAPARINGA RIVER NATIONAL PARK
SOUTH AUSTRALIA

Only 32 kilometres south of Adelaide, the 1544-hectare Onkaparinga River National Park straddles the second largest river in South Australia. The river's rocky course stretches from Clarendon on the north-east to Old Noarlunga in the west. Visitors and locals flock to the park to tackle some of South Australia's most impressive and challenging walking tracks. Apart from working up a nice sweat and burning a few calories, you'll have a chance to see the beautiful species of wildflowers and native kangaroos, echidnas and other bird and reptile wildlife that frequent the area.

The park was a major filming location for *Rabbit-proof Fence*; it was used to recreate the Moore River settlement, the Aboriginal internment camp that Molly, Daisy and Gracie are sent to after being torn away from their home and their mother.

VISITOR INFO

Onkaparinga River National Park and Recreation Reserve

(08) 8204 1910; www.environment.sa.gov.au/ parks/sanpr/onkaparinganp/index.html

THINGS TO SEE AND DO

Location of the Moore River settlement

The main use of Onkaparinga National Park for filming was the re-creation of the Moore River Native Settlement. The real settlement, which is now defunct, was located west of the town of Mogumber in Western Australia around 135 kilometres north of Perth. The settlement was built in 1918. Among its many uses, one was to function as a boarding house for many Aboriginal children during the era of the Stolen Generation.

The south-west section of the park, just off the Sundews Track, was the exact spot used for the construction and shooting of the Moore River settlement.

The entire set was built from scratch based on old photos from the period, as well as visits to the real location by Noyce and his crew. It was the first time any national park in Australia had allowed a movie production to construct a set of that magnitude. The construction of the seven buildings, including the church, took around six weeks, a task made all the more difficult by several days of inclement weather – Murphy's Law states that film crews always bring rain when they don't want it! The set was razed at the conclusion of filming.

Walking trails

Onkaparinga National Park has a variety of bushwalking trails, from easy strolls to more challenging treks. The Wetlands Walk is a comfortable 4.5-kilometre signposted walk designed to give walkers exposure to the fascinating flora and fauna of the wetlands. The Echidna Walk is a moderate trek traversing through pink gum, grey box and sheoak bushland. Those that can handle some steep inclines should try the Sundews River Hike, which descends via the Sundew Lookout to the bottom of the gorge. *Brochure of walking trails available at www.environment.sa.gov.au/parks/pdfs/BROCHURE_ONKAPARINGA.PDF*

Cycling

Cycling is permitted in Onkaparinga River Recreation Park on signed pathways around the estuary. The tracks can suit all cyclists, from casual Sunday two-wheelers to lycra-clad Tour de France enthusiasts. Even penny farthings are welcome, though you must wear knickerbockers and a top hat to ride one! The trails are part of the McLaren Vale to Marino Bikeway. The closest bike hire is in McLaren Vale at Oxygen Cycles, just a few kilometres south of the park. *Oxygen Cycles, 143 Main Rd, McLaren Vale; (08) 8323 7345; oxygencycles.blogspot.com*

Canoeing on the Onkaparinga River

Rock climbing

Take a deep breath, don't look down and tackle some of the fantastic rock climbing and abseiling areas in the south-east area of the park, near the Chapel Hill Road entrance at Gate 10. Rock hounds must provide all their own equipment and report climbing activities to the Belair District Office prior to climbing. *Belair District Office (08) 8278 5477*

Outdoor activities

There are plenty of other activities to enjoy in the park – particularly fishing, which is permitted in the waters of the estuary in the recreation park. The estuary is also popular for canoeing and kayaking (bring your own craft).

Pack a hamper and enjoy a picnic at Chapel Hill or Perrys Bend.

Like most undeveloped areas, you may come across snakes sunning themselves on trails – particularly in the warmer months when they're more active. They're generally shy creatures, so if you stay out of their way, they will most likely stay out of yours.

WHERE TO STAY

Chapel Hill Winery Retreat

Located on Chapel Hill Road, right at the foot of Onkaparinga River Recreation Park,

Did you know?

The casting of the three young actresses to play Molly, Gracie and Daisy was a long process for director Phillip Noyce and casting director Christine King. They conducted over 1200 interviews in numerous Indigenous communities before locking in the final three girls. None of them had any acting experience prior to shooting.

this secluded retreat has ten rooms with eco-friendly rainwater showers and spectacular views of the vines. It's good to be green. *1 Chapel Hill Rd, McLaren Vale; (08) 8323 9182; www.theretreatatchapelhillwinery.com.au*

Mick O'Shea's Irish Pub

Free-flowing Guinness is just the ticket at this hugely popular Irish pub, which also offers Tudor-style motel accommodation (from standard to family rooms). Mick's is located in Hackham, just north-east of the park, to be sure, to be sure. *Main South Rd, Hackham; (08) 8384 6944; www.mickosheas.com.au*

CARAVANS AND MOTORHOMES

McLaren Vale Lakeside Caravan Park

Powered and unpowered sites with luxury ensuites and modern cabin accommodation, two tennis courts, a playground for the kids, and cycling and walking tracks. *Field St, McLaren Vale; (08) 8323 9255; www.mclarenvale.net*

Moana Beach Tourist Park

Caravan accommodation in Moana Beach, one of South Australia's most popular patrolled beaches, which is just west of the park. Accommodation options range from powered sites to holiday units and executive cottages. *44 Nashwauk Cres, Moana; (08) 8327 0677; www.moanabeachtouristpark.com.au*

WHERE TO EAT

d'Arry's Verandah Restaurant

Award-winning restaurant and one of the most esteemed rural eateries in all of South Australia.

Enjoy views of the Willunga escarpment and St Vincents Gulf as you enjoy a sumptuous lunch or dinner. Located at d'Arenberg Winery. A little indulgence goes a long way. *Osborn Rd, McLaren Vale; (08) 8329 4848; www.darrysverandah.com.au*

Blessed Cheese

Doubling as a cheese shop and provedore, as well as a licensed cafe, this haven of dairy serves up some of the best coffee in McLaren Vale and tasty breakfast to boot. *150 Main Rd, McLaren Vale; (08) 8323 7958; www.blessedcheese.com.au*

Musk lorikeet in Belair National Park

BELAIR NATIONAL PARK SOUTH AUSTRALIA

This 835-hectare park only 13 kilometres from the Adelaide CBD has the distinction of being the oldest national park in South Australia. The park lies on the west of the Adelaide Hills and offers a natural landscape of beautiful eucalyptus forests and bright native flora and fauna. Activities on offer in the park include a tour of Old Government House, bushwalking and even a hit of tennis. The park was used as a location for a couple of scenes in the film: the girls sleep here their first night on the run and tracker Moodoo follows them in the rain here.

VISITOR INFO

Belair National Park

(08) 8278 5477; www.environment.sa.gov.au/parks/sanpr/belair/visit.html

THINGS TO SEE AND DO

Film locations

Filming took place in two spots within the park. The scene when the girls spend their first night on the run, under the large tree, was shot in the north-west section of the park just off Sir Edwin Avenue. Access to this spot is just left past Playford Lake, when you enter the park from Upper Sturt Road.

The other shooting location took place in the far north-east of the park, for the scene when tracker Moodoo follows the girls in the rain. It's located at the end of Queens Jubilee Road near Waverley Lodge and the Thelymitra Walking Trail.

Old Government House

This Victorian-style building was the official summer residence of South Australian governors during the 1860s. It was restored in the 1970s and opened its doors to visitors. There's a beautifully manicured garden on the property. *Open Sundays 1–4pm; weekday tours by appointment*

Bushwalking

There are five walking tracks throughout Belair, including the brief and brisk Playford Lake Walk and the longer walk from Playford Lake to the Upper Waterfall. All walks take in the native woodland, flora and fauna, such as western grey kangaroos, possums, koalas, lizards and falcons.

Recreation activities

There are lots of things to do in the park: there are four tennis courts for hire, as well as two large sporting ovals for a kick of the footy or a few overs of cricket. There are also playgrounds for the kids and loads of beautiful picnic and barbecue areas, and designated cycling and horseriding spots.

Kangaroo Creek

Around 10 kilometres north-east of Belair National Park is the spot where our three heroines cross the river shortly after they escape the Moore River settlement. Surrounded by lush green bushland, the creek (which runs off the Kangaroo Creek Reservoir) is a tributary of the River Torrens, one of the most significant water streams in all of South Australia. The water level of the creek was easily adjustable for the production, making it simple for the girls to physically cross the river by foot. *Located just east of the Black Hill Conservation Park*

WHERE TO STAY

Alessandro Maandini's Ryokan

For a taste of the Far East in South Australia, this special Japanese ryokan (guest house) in the Adelaide Hills has rooms with low-laying queen beds and traditional Japanese steam bath and spa. Go for the full experience by pre-ordering the 'oishii' (delicious) four-course traditional Japanese dinner. *16 Brightview Ave, Blackwood South; 0412 178 026; www.ryokan-maandini.com*

Nunyara Holiday Units

These affordable holiday units in Belair, just a short drive from the park, sleep up to six and have terrific views of the coastline and surrounding suburbs. *5 Burnell Dr, Belair; (08) 8278 1673; www.nunyara.com.au*

CARAVANS AND MOTORHOMES

Belair National Park Caravan Park

You don't even have to leave the park if you don't want to! For those who carry their homes on their back (or attached to their towbar), stay in the naturally sheltered surrounds of the park. Whether you need powered or unpowered sites, just want to roll out your swag at a camping site or check into cabin accommodation, it's up to you. The pristine wilderness is just a few feet from your camper. *Upper Sturt Rd, Belair; (08) 8278 3540; www.belaircaravanpark.com.au*

WHERE TO EAT

Caffe Primo

Located in Blackwood less than a couple of kilometres west of the park, Caffe Primo is total Italian yumminess with a mammoth selection of pasta, seafood, pizza and focaccias, including lunch and dinner specials that won't break the bank. Complimentary garlic bread is never a bad thing. *180 Main Rd, Blackwood; (08) 8278 3444; www.caffeprimo.com.au*

The Organic Market and Cafe

Travelling can be a great excuse to line your stomach with junk food. Yes, of course, it's cheap and quick and you have to get to that museum before it closes. Well give your innards some respite with organic goodness, including soups, salads and muffins. Also gluten-free beer on tap. You'll feel healthier just walking in. Located east of the park in the suburb of Stirling. *5 Druids Ave, Stirling; (08) 8339 7131; www.organicmarket.com.au*

NILPENA STATION
SOUTH AUSTRALIA

If you want to experience a real-life, fair-dinkum postcard of outback Australia, look no further than Nilpena Station. This working cattle station is 40 kilometres north-west of the town of Parachilna, right on the edge of Lake Torrens in the Flinders Ranges. It's Aussie outback at its most honest and was the perfect spot to recreate the harsh Western Australian desert. The shearers' quarters acted as the Evans homestead. Various areas around the station were utilised to shoot many of the wandering scenes along the fence. An assortment of landscape shots of the rocky plains were also filmed around the station. Nilpena Station is a private property, so public access is prohibited. Please don't go driving around unannounced. You can organise a tour of some of the film locations through the Prairie Hotel. Please book in advance; just ask for the friendly pub owners Jane and Ross Fargher.

Did you know?

Indigenous actor Rachel Maza was employed on the set as a drama coach and mentor for the film's three lead actors. Rachel's presence was invaluable in helping the young, inexperienced girls cope with the strangeness and rigours of their first film production.

This girl is clever. She wants to go home.

— *Moodoo*

Sand dunes and scrub at Nilpena Station

Prairie Hotel

Cnr High St and West Tce, Parachilna; (08) 8648 4844; www.prairiehotel.com.au

Angorichina Tourist Village

Parachilna Gorge, Parachilna; (08) 8648 4842; www.angorichinavillage.com.au

THINGS TO SEE AND DO

Shearers' quarters

The outback building in the middle of nowhere was used as the Evans homestead in the film for the scene when Aboriginal maid Mavis (Deborah Mailman) encounters the three young runaways and helps them to hide.

Around Nilpena Station

Just on the western edge of the Nilpena Station property is Lake Torrens, a 240-kilometre-long arid plain that has been dry for decades. Here they filmed the scene when the girls reached the end of the fence and began to walk around aimlessly with a hawk circling ominously above.

Gallipoli also used Lake Torrens as a location, also to recreate the WA desert (see the *Gallipoli* chapter for more info). Other scenes shot around Nilpena Station involved the girls treading along the fence on the sand dunes. Many of the rocky desert landscape shots (or 'second-unit shots') were also captured here.

North Moolooloo Station

The old shearers' quarters at North Moolooloo Station were dressed up to replicate the Jigalong Depot, the original home of Molly, Daisy and Gracie. Thus this was the shooting place for the harrowing scene of the girls being snatched away from their families without warning – an emotionally draining scene that took its toll on the entire crew, particularly the young actresses. The station is located north-east of Parachilna, a few kilometres east of Leigh Creek. It's a private property, so public access is prohibited.

Beltana Station

North of Parachilna, this abandoned station in the eerie ghost town of Beltana was the location for the scene when the three girls first find the rabbit-proof fence after escaping the Moore River settlement. Beltana was also a shooting location for *Gallipoli*.

WHERE TO STAY

Prairie Hotel

Historic and award-winning accommodation right in the heart of the Flinders Ranges. If you're feeling flush, stay in the hotel itself; if not, they have budget accommodation over the road in the Overflow. Fill up with a hearty breakfast to kick you off each morning and then go for the famous 'Flinders Feral Food' (aka bush food) at night, such as emu egg frittata or camel sirloin.

Feel free to ask Ross and Jane about the large number of films shot in the area – they have become somewhat expert on the matter. Kate Winslet and Harvey Keitel stayed at the hotel during the filming of *Holy Smoke!* (1999). *Cnr High St and West Tce, Parachilna; (08) 8648 4844; www.prairiehotel.com.au*

Parachilna Overflow

Straight over the road from the Prairie Hotel, the Overflow offers affordable ensuite cabins and basic dorm and twin rooms with shared amenities. Communal kitchen and recreation room with a pool table. *West Tce, Parachilna; (08) 8648 4814; www.prairiehotel.com.au/overflowframe.htm*

Blinman Hotel

This charming country hotel has historic town photos lining the walls and upstairs you'll find budget and heritage rooms, while out back, cottage units and camping and caravan spaces are available. Dump your bags and head for some cold beer and a warm meal at the pub. Blinman is around 33 kilometres east of Parachilna. *Mine Rd, Blinman; (08) 8648 4867; www.blinmanhotel.com.au*

CARAVANS AND MOTORHOMES

Angorichina Tourist Village

Take your pick according to your needs: caravan and camping sites, units, chalets or a sunset cottage. *Parachilna Gorge, The Ranges; (08) 8648 4842*

WHERE TO EAT

Wild Lime Cafe and Gallery

Country cafe with gourmet pies, quiches, soups and native bush foods (including quandong pies), not to mention espresso coffee and dev teas. Closed January and February (can open by arrangement). Gallery attached, art on sale ranges from textiles to watercolours and basketry to jewellery. *Old Schoolhouse, Mine Rd, Blinman; (08) 8648 4679; www.wildlimecafe.com.au*

TOURS

Nilpena Station 'Pinch of Salt' Lake Torrens Track

This four-hour, four-wheel-drive tour takes you through the remote and historic Nilpena Station all the way to the salt, flat plains of Lake Torrens. *Book at the Prairie Hotel, cnr High St and West Tce, Parachilna; (08) 8648 4844; www.prairiehotel.com.au*

OTHER LOCATIONS

CALLINGTON SOUTH AUSTRALIA

Located in between Murray Bridge and Mt Barker to the west of Adelaide, this small town was once a thriving copper mining town.

The town was used in one scene in the film, which takes place at the hen house shortly after the girls escape from the Moore River Native Settlement. The scene was shot at an actual farmhouse off Callington–Strathalbyn Road.

ST MARKS COLLEGE NORTH ADELAIDE, SOUTH AUSTRALIA

Not far north of the CBD is this residential development university in North Adelaide. The college was the location for the office of AO Neville as he tracks the progress of the search for the missing young girls. *46 Pennington Tce, North Adelaide; (08) 8334 5600; www.stmarkscollege.com.au*

Films shot in the Flinders Ranges

The Flinders Ranges is the second most prolific rural filming location in Australia (after Broken Hill). Its vast open spaces and desert landscapes are favourites for depicting the classic Australian outback on film. Following are some of the more famous productions shot in the area.

THE TRACKER (2002)

Rolf de Heer's brilliant story, set in 1922, traces an Aboriginal tracker (David Gulpilil) leading a group of men in the Australian outback as they hunt a killer. The film was predominantly shot in Arkaroola Wilderness Sanctuary, a 61 000-hectare privately owned area east of Leigh Creek, adjacent to Vulkathunha–Gammon Ranges National Park. Arkaroola is one of Australia's premier ecotourism destinations with four-wheel-drive Ridgetop and astronomy tours as well as spectacular scenic flights.

SUNDAY TOO FAR AWAY (1975)

'Friday night too tired; Saturday night too drunk; Sunday too far away' is the famous tagline from this classic from director Ken Hannam. The film stars Jack Thompson as a professional sheep shearer with an over-fondness for the grog as he and his fellow workers deal with the hardships of rural industry and the desolate loneliness of outback life.

Much of the film was shot on Carriewerloo Station, a working shearers' station around 50 kilometres west of Port Augusta, which was also used as a location. *Sunday Too Far Away* was the first feature film produced by the South Australian Film Corporation.

BEAUTIFUL KATE (2009)

The directorial-debut of Rachel Ward (actress and wife of Bryan Brown) tells the harrowing tale of a family torn apart. Through a series of flashbacks, we piece together the tragic tale of twins Ned (Ben Mendelsohn and Scott O'Donnell) and Kate (Sophie Lowe), two 16 year olds living in country Australia under the rough tutelage of father Bruce (Bryan Brown). The majority of the film was shot on a homestead in Wilpena Pound. The film also stars Rachel Griffiths and Maeve Dermody and was based on an American novel by Newton Thornburg. The story was originally set in Idaho.

HOLY SMOKE! (1999)

This erotically charged comedy/drama directed by Jane Campion stars Kate Winslet and Harvey Keitel as a mismatched couple stranded in the Australian outback. Early parts of the film are set in India and were shot in Delhi and Rajasthan. The scenes filmed in the desert were shot in the dusty red plains of the Flinders Ranges around the town of Hawker. Uncharacteristic heavy rains during production (Murphy's Law again!) caused headaches for the cast and crew. The film also stars Sophie Lee and '70s blaxploitation goddess Pam Grier.

BITTER SPRINGS (1950)

One of the first films shot on location in the Flinders Ranges, this movie stars Chips Rafferty as a stockman who moves his family to Bitter Springs, where they encounter trouble from the Indigenous locals. The film was shot in Quorn, Yarrah Vale and Warren Gorge and was directed by Ralph Smart.

LAST RIDE (2009)

Adapted from a novel by Denise Young, the film tells the story of a young boy who travels across Australia with his father (played by Hugo Weaving), who is wanted by the police. The film was shot in and around Quorn and Wilpena Pound. It was the first feature film from director Glendyn Ivin, who burst onto the scene in 2003 winning the Palme d'Or at Cannes for her short film *Cracker Bag*.

STEALTH (2005)

This blockbuster stars Jamie Foxx, Jessica Biel and Josh Lucas as US Navy pilots who must stop a rogue fighter jet that is run by a computer and which has developed its own mind. The film was shot on location in the Blue Mountains of New South Wales, but the scenes supposedly set on the Naval Air Test Range in Nevada were actually shot in the Flinders Ranges. With a large budget of around US$135 million, the film did dismally at the worldwide box office, making it one of the most financially unsuccessful films of the decade.

THE LIGHTHORSEMEN (1986)

Set in Palestine in 1917, this film revolves around a group of Australian Light Horse infantrymen fighting on the front lines during World War I. The film was directed by Simon Wincer, who also directed *Phar Lap* (1983), and stars Peter Phelps, Gary Sweet and Jon Blake. The film was shot in Hawker and the small town of Bandioota. It won two AFI Awards.

THE SHIRALEE (1988)

This acclaimed TV movie tells the story of a swagman by the name of Macauley (Bryan Brown) in the 1940s who gets lumped with taking care of his young daughter Buster (Rebecca Smart). The TV movie is adapted from a book by D'Arcy Niland, which had been made into a movie in 1957 starring Peter Finch. The production, which won two Logie Awards, was shot all over South Australia, including Quorn in the Flinders Ranges and Port Gawler, Wilmington and Adelaide. The TV movie became the highest rated program on Australian television to date when it aired on the Seven Network in June of 1988.

Romulus, My Father (2007)

Christina (Potente) outside Frogmore

Nothing's happening.

— *Raimond*

Just wait Raimond … they think it's the sun.

— *Romulus*

Director: Richard Roxburgh
Writer: Nick Drake
Producers: Robert Connolly, John Maynard
Cast includes: Eric Bana, Kodi Smit-McPhee, Franka Potente, Marton Csokas, Russell Dykstra, Jacek Koman

ABOUT THE FILM

Rural despair, impossible love and the ties that bind are the intrinsic themes of the autobiographical book and subsequent film, *Romulus, My Father*. The story begins in 1960 and plays out through the innocent eyes of young Raimond (Smit-McPhee), who lives with his somewhat volatile yet loving father Romulus (Bana) at Frogmore, a farm just outside Maryborough in Victoria's Goldfields region.

The story spans two harrowing years as the family undergoes hardships on both financial and emotional fronts. The latter is particularly prevalent with the coming and going of Christina (Potente), Raimond's fragile mother, who has a difficult time living in rural destitution while she struggles with her own inner demons. Although the film is fraught with tragedy, particularly the mental breakdowns of both Romulus and Christina right in front of Raimond's eyes, there are glimmers of hope for the fractured immigrant family that came to Australia for a better life.

It took actor-turned-director Richard Roxburgh almost seven years to develop the project. With the help of screenwriter and acclaimed playwright Nick Drake, Roxburgh does a superb job in adapting philosopher Raimond Gaita's autobiographical memoir, which was published in 1998 and won the Victorian Premier's Literary Award. The film gives a complex insight into the genuine

Raimond (Smit-McPhee) and Romulus (Bana) atop the Rock of Ages

hardships of post-war immigrant life in rural Australia in the early 1960s, as well as the layered relationship between father and son.

Roxburgh, a successful actor himself, does a marvellous job with his main players in his directorial debut. Bana and Potente are marvellous, as is Marton Csokas, who plays Romulus' empathetic friend Hora. But it's Smit-McPhee who steals the show, playing the role of Raimond with a maturity well beyond his years. The film was nominated for 15 AFI Awards (at the time tying the record), and took home four trophies, including Best Film and Best Actor for Eric Bana.

LOCATIONS

MALDON VICTORIA

Play a little Neil Young as you enter the township of Maldon, known as Victoria's 'Heart of Gold'. Maldon is one of Victoria's best-known gold towns and a hugely popular weekend getaway destination for Melburnians. In 1966, the National Trust declared Maldon as Australia's 'First Notable Town' and one truly worthy of preservation. This is something the town has prided itself on for decades; to this day it's still one of Australia's most preserved townships. In 2006 the National Trust awarded Maldon with the title 'Most Intact Historic Streetscape'.

Stroll down Main Street to see the beautiful old buildings and shopfronts – it's as though time

> Hey, listen to this. The time you enjoy wasting is not wasted time.
>
> — *Hora quoting Bertrnad Russell*

Raimond runs from Romulus on his motorcycle outside their home

has stood still. This made Maldon perfect for recreating 1960s Victoria for *Romulus, My Father*. Many locations in and around the town were used for filming. Maldon is located 138 kilometres north-west of Melbourne.

VISITOR INFO

Maldon Visitor Information Centre
93 High St; (03) 5475 2569; www.maldon.org.au

THINGS TO SEE AND DO

Maldon Station

This historic railway station was opened in June of 1884 and operated until its closure in January 1941. The station was re-opened in 1986 and is now operated as part of the Victorian Goldfields Railway (www.vgr.com.au), which runs restored steam trains between Maldon and Castlemaine.

The station was used for the scene in which Romulus says goodbye to Mitru before he boards the train back to Maryborough. Fire damaged the station in October 2009, but it was going to take more than fire to stop the trains from running on time. *Near cnr Reef and Ireland sts*

Roxburgh directs Smit-McPhee for the birthday party scene; in the background is cinematographer Geoffrey Simpson

Scotch Pie House

This former bakery on Main Street was used as the interior setting for the Maldon Cafe, where Romulus and Raimond enjoy a couple of milkshakes at the beginning of the film. The mouth-watering aromas of baked pies and scones are now a distant memory; the house is currently occupied by a local dairy business. *Cnr Main and Templeton sts*

Maldon Cemetery

Listed on the National Trust, this historic mid-19th century cemetery was used as the location for a funeral in the film. At Maldon's annual Easter Fair, the small graveyard is used as part of a cemetery walk. The Easter Fair is claimed to be the oldest in Australia and the fun range of activities includes the Great Aussie Scone Bake and the traditional Easter Parade. *80 Nuggety Rd*

Main Street in Maldon

Maldon Historic Reserve

Maldon is surrounded by this 2500-hectare reserve of grassy woodland and box-ironbark forest. Along the Nuggety Track to the north of the reserve is the Rock of Ages. This was the backdrop of the moving film's final scenes when Romulus takes Raimond to the top of the mountain cliff. *Rock of Ages Track can be accessed via Church St, which skirts Union Hill*

Maldon Gardens

Located on Fountain Street, this small garden area was used as the setting for the botanical gardens in the scene in which Hora meets with Mitru (Dykstra) to deliver groceries. *Fountain St*

Baringhup

Just 10 kilometres west of Maldon is the small town of Baringhup, which was a major location for the production. The Frogmore farm where Romulus and Raimond live was located here, on a private property just off Moolort Road. In a fabulous coup for authenticity, they rebuilt the Frogmore farmhouse only 50 metres from the original site where Romulus and Raimond Gaita actually lived in the 1960s. The house-set was pulled down shortly after filming concluded.

The Baringhup Community Hall on Alfred Street was used as the movie hall, while the Baringhup West State School on Baringhup West Road was the school that Raimond attends before he's sent to St Joseph's College. Watersons Road was another location, used for the scene at

the boulders where Raimond and his homeless friend share a meal of eggs boiled in urine. (Move over *MasterChef!*)

The Cairn Curran Reservoir was used in the scene when Hora gets all philosophical and quotes Bertrand Russell to Raimond in the boat.

WHERE TO STAY

Maldon Grainstore

This 140-year-old brick and corrugated iron building is another relic of a time gone by (though the accommodation has seen an upgrade, including air-con and heating). The building can be spotted in an exterior street shot when Romulus and Raimond motorcycle their way into town at the beginning of the film. The building began life as a general store, which eventually closed in 1986 after a very long innings. It has since been converted into two self-contained apartments with modern amenities. *6 Templeton St; (03) 5475 2902; www.maldonaccommodation.com.au/grainstore.html*

Palm House

Country-town B&B experiences don't get much better than the Palm House, a Victorian home set in an English-style cottage garden. Choose from the cream, red, blue or green rooms tastefully decorated with vintage pieces. *2–6 High St; (03) 5475 2532; www.palmhouse.com.au*

CARAVANS AND MOTORHOMES

Maldon Caravan Park

Situated at the foot of Mt Tarrengower, just a few minutes' walk to the centre of town, this park offers 40 powered sites, cabin and camping accommodation. Hike to the top of

Romulus wakes bees up with heat

Mt Tarrengower and climb the fire tower for views of the town and surrounding countryside. *Hospital St; (03) 5475 2344*

CAMPING

Butt's Reserve camping area

Camping area in Maldon Historic Reserve with few facilities – bring your own water. Enjoy some of the walking tracks and see old mining relics, but walk carefully to avoid falling down a long-disused mine shaft. Dog-friendly. *On Tarrengower Rd, access via Franklin St*

WHERE TO EAT

Penny School Gallery and Cafe

This former school, turned art gallery has a cute little cafe attached with seasonal lunch and dinner menus using fresh Maldon produce. Definitely won't dredge up any memories of school lunches! Open Wednesday to Sunday. *11 Church St; (03) 5475 1911; www.pennyschoolgallery.com.au*

Berryman's Cafe and Tea Rooms

The top spot in Maldon for a freshly made sandwich or focaccia, with speciality teas plus vegetarian and gluten-free menu options. Open seven days and for dinner on Monday nights. *30 Main St; (03) 5475 2904*

Maldon Hotel

No-fuss pub menu. If you're looking for a quality chicken parma or steak, you won't be disappointed. Maldon Blues Club has gigs here on Sunday afternoons every six weeks or so. *58 Main St; (03) 5475 2231*

Hora (Csokas), Romulus and Raimond marvel at the workings of their egg contraption

Did you know?

On the back of his performance in *Romulus, My Father*, actor Kodi Smit-McPhee was cast in two Hollywood blockbusters. One was *Wolverine*, the Marvel Comics adaptation starring Hugh Jackman, while the other was *The Road*, with Viggo Mortensen, based on the Pulitzer Prize–winning book by Cormac McCarthy. He chose the latter and for his role was nominated for Best Young Actor at the Broadcast Film Critics Association Awards.

Heritage post office in Castlemaine

Hey Raimond be careful. Those eggs sending you through boarding school.

— *Romulus*

Free tour guide

The township of Maldon offers free one-hour driving tours of the town. Local guides will show you around the town, including many sites used in the film. Don't be shy to ask your friendly Maldon experts about *Romulus, My Father* and what the town was like during production. *Tour guide bookings on 0427 005 940*

Walking tours

The town offers many self-guided walking tours. 'Walk 3' takes in the grainstore and Scotch Pie House. *www.kayecees.com/Maldon/maps*

CASTLEMAINE
VICTORIA

Around 18 kilometres south-east of Maldon is Castlemaine, another relic of Victoria's goldmining boom. The town is littered with old, Georgian-style buildings and expansive botanical gardens, which are stunning in the springtime. The area was the site of the largest alluvial gold rush the world had ever seen – by 1852 over 25 000 prospectors had flocked here to try their luck.

There is much to see and do in town, from the period Buda Historic Home and Garden to the Castlemaine Art Gallery and Old Castlemaine Gaol. Like Maldon, the township was chosen as a location for the film because of its older look. The film had its world premiere in Castlemaine at the Theatre Royal, heavily attended by some of the 200-plus locals who were cast as extras in the production.

VISITOR INFO

Castlemaine Visitor Information Centre
44 Mostyn St; (03) 5471 1795;
www.maldoncastlemaine.com

THINGS TO SEE AND DO

House on Templeton Street

This downtrodden property in the middle of Castlemaine was used as the boarding house in the film where Christina and Mitru first live with their newborn baby. A little bit of trickery took place with some of the scenes, though – the inside house shots were filmed at a property on Reef Street in Maldon. Templeton Street was also used for a couple of exterior street shots.

Hargraves Street

The north end of Hargraves Street was used to film the exterior of St Joseph's College, the boarding school Raimond attends. (The real St Joseph's College is located in Ballarat in Victoria's north-west.) The interior school scenes were shot at the Castlemaine and District Continuing Education building at 30 Templeton Street.

Castlemaine Enterprise Centre

This large community building was used for the interior and exterior shots of the psychiatric hospital that Romulus checks into after Christina's death. *1 Halford Rd*

Kennedy and Langslow streets

These streets were used for exterior scenes in the film.

Raimond has a birthday party

Buda Historic Home and Garden

Beautifully preserved house built in 1861, retaining many of its original furnishings, artwork and embroideries. Stunningly kept garden and gift shop open to purchase local handcrafts and other local goodies. *42 Hunter St; (03) 5472 1032; www.budacastlemaine.org*

Castlemaine Art Gallery

Specialises in Australian art, with a brilliant collection of landscape paintings from the late-1800s. Exhibitions throughout the year. *14 Lyttleton St; (03) 5472 2292; www.castlemainegallery.com*

WHERE TO STAY

The Midland

Stylish and affordable family-run private hotel on Templeton Street, close to a couple of *Romulus* filming sites. This grand hotel has been servicing the town since 1879 and has single and double rooms and one apartment. Fantastic old furnishings and paintings throughout. *2 Templeton St; (03) 5472 1085; www.themidland.com.au*

Tuckpoint Cottage

Bed and breakfast rooms in a charming National Trust home with a hep modern edge to its classical furnishings and decorations. *60 Kennedy St; 0439 035 382; www.tuckpointcottage.com*

The Empyre Boutique Hotel

The place to stay in Castlemaine, this award-winning luxurious hotel's rooms are furnished with French Provincial furniture. It's laden with armoires, chandeliers and gilt mirrors, but also a nod to the modern – contemporary amenities include an LCD TV in each room. Restaurant and cafe on site. Not cheap, but totally worth it. *68 Mostyn St; (03) 5472 5166; www.empyre.com.au*

Did you know?

While many book adaptations take liberties with the story, the film's finished product was very true to the memoir of Raimond Gaita's life. Almost everything seen on the screen actually occurred in his life in some shape or form.

CARAVANS AND MOTORHOMES

BIG4 Castlemaine Gardens Holiday Park

Drive-thru, powered and unpowered sites and cabin accommodation all served by barbecue sites and a camp kitchen. *1 Doran Ave; (03) 5472 1125; castlemaine-gardens-caravan-park.vic.big4.com.au*

Castlemaine Central Cabin and Van Park

Powered and unpowered sites, couples' cottages for lovers and family cabins, too. *101 Barker St; (03) 5472 2160; www.cabinscastlemaine.com*

CAMPING

Vaughan Springs

Eureka! Located in the Castlemaine Diggings National Heritage Park 10 kilometres south of the town. Great bushwalking on the Great Divided Trail, cycling and fishing in the Loddon River. Catch of the day could be trout, redfin, tench or blackfish (gold nuggets unlikely, but you never know). *Access via Vaughn Springs Rd*

Mt Alexander Regional Park

A no-frills campsite in Mt Alexander Regional Park near Harcourt, 10 kilometres north of Castlemaine. The park has numerous lookouts with great views. *Access via Mt Alexander Tourist Rd; www.parkweb.vic.gov.au*

WHERE TO EAT

The Good Table

Creative dining and drinking in a calm and inviting, uncluttered country ambience with a leaning towards organic and sustainable produce. Their seasonal menu may contain goat pie, yabby linguini or spatchcock, offset by an outstanding local and European wine and liqueur selection. Open lunch and dinner, Thursday to Sunday. *233 Barker St; (03) 5472 4400; www.thegoodtable.com.au*

Another conflict between Romulus and Christina in their kitchen at Frogmore

Tog's Place

Hugely popular breakfast and lunch spot serving sandwiches, salads, casseroles and curries, and showing local and Melbourne-based artwork. Eat outside for the town view. *58 Lyttleton St; (03) 5470 5090*

Railway Hotel

A local fave since 1875 offering a twist on classic pub grub – eggplant burgers and roast kangaroo loin might tickle your fancy, as may $12 value meals on Tuesdays and free pool on Sundays. *65 Gingell St; (03) 5472 1250; www.railwayhotel.com.au*

CINEMA

Theatre Royal

Built in 1852, this historic theatre screens new-release films and hosts live music performances by big-name Aussie musos. It's billed as the oldest continuously operating theatre on the Australian mainland. The official world premiere of *Romulus, My Father* was held here and was attended by the majority of the cast and crew.

A highlight is the unique backstage B&B accommodation – Valhalla for film lovers. The Art Deco style takes you back to the golden age of cinema, while one of the rooms is Harry Potter–themed. And the *pièce de résistance* – all movies in the theatre are free for guests! *30 Hargraves St; (03) 5472 1196; www.theatreroyal.info*

TOURS

Don't forget your iPod! Castlemaine offers podcast walking tours of major sites in town, downloadable from the Visit Victoria website. These take in some of the locations of the film on Templeton Street. Don't fret if you don't own an iPod, as the visitor information centre has tour MP3 players for hire. *www.visitvictoria.com*

Though there may be only one actor in the shot, behind the scenes the large crew is always buzzing around

The hard-working filmmakers early in the morning at Cairn Curran Reservoir.

Romulus, My Father movie slate

The camera crew tries to capture a shot as rain clouds gather

The crew prepares for a tricky shot on the water

MARYBOROUGH
VICTORIA

Maryborough is another thriving Goldfields township set on the northern slopes of the Great Dividing Range, approximately 25 kilometres west of Maldon. It's filled with grand buildings, historic cottages, charming cafes and – in springtime – bright golden wattle and wildflowers.

Maryborough was the third major location for the shooting of *Romulus, My Father*. Much like Maldon and Castlemaine, little set design was needed because the town is so well preserved. Locations such as the old flour mill and Maryborough Park were used for key scenes in the film.

> Excuse me, who was that singing?
>
> — *Raimond*

> Jerry Lee Lewis. They call him 'The Killer'.
>
> — *Girl on porch*

> Why?
>
> — *Raimond*

> Because he kills people I guess.
>
> — *Girl on porch*

VISITOR INFO

Maryborough Visitor Centre
Cnr Alma and Nola sts; (03) 5460 4511; www.visitmaryborough.com.au

THINGS TO SEE AND DO

Maryborough Park
This small park right near the Maryborough Railway Station was the location for the scene of Raimond out pushing his baby sister in a pram (moments before he discovers his mother getting to know a strange man – in the biblical sense). *Cnr Inkerman and Railway sts*

Maryborough Flour Mill
Spotting an old flour mill is the official sign that you're in the middle of a quaint and charming old country town. Just over the railway line at the north end of Maryborough Park is the mill, where Raimond finds his mother in the act of cheating with a strange man. The mill is open 11am to 5pm, Thursday to Sunday or by appointment. Inside the 120-year-old building is a fascinating extensive collection of antique sewing machines and other historic displays of local art and collectables. *Albert St (off Inkerman St); (03) 5461 1322; www.maryboroughflourmillgallery.com.au*

Loading dock on Alma Street
The loading dock at the back of the Lyal Eales camping store was used for the scene when Romulus and Raimond unload the metal furniture Romulus has made. Raimond returns

by himself later in the film when his father is in the psychiatric hospital. *The loading dock is located on Alma St at the back of the store; Lyal Eales Store is at 178 High St; (03) 5461 1911*

Hilton Street

One of the older, more ramshackle houses on the street was used for the scene when the girl dances her heart away on the porch to the rock'n'roll of 'The Killer', Jerry Lee Lewis.

McLandress Square

This is the town's civic centre. Its European-style buildings include a post office, town hall and courthouse. The clock tower can be seen in an aerial shot of the town. *Clarendon St*

Maryborough Railway Station

When American writer Mark Twain visited this impressive railway station – which has one of the longest platforms in the Southern Hemisphere – in 1895, he stated that Maryborough was 'a station with a town attached'. This functioning train station includes the Antique Emporium, Woodworkers Gallery and Twains Wood and Craft Gallery, plus a cafe and even a wine bar if you work up a thirst. Three times a year an antiques and collectables market attracts thousands of visitors. *Station St*

WHERE TO STAY

Junction Motel

Motel outside, but stylish hotel inside, the Junction Motel's 16 guest rooms have all been fully refurbished, from studios with queen beds to deluxe family rooms. Free wi-fi

Did you know?

Eric Bana has more in common with the story of *Romulus, My Father* than many realise. His birth name was Eric Banadinovic and his roots also stem from Eastern Europe – his father was born in Croatia (Romulus was born in Romania) and his mother was born in Germany (Christina was also German).

Maryborough Railway Station

(a rarity in Aussie country accommodation) and a swimming pool. *2 High St; (03) 5461 1744; www.maryboroughjunctionmotel.com.au*

Bristol Hill Motor Inn

Spacious and contemporary motel rooms with full amenities. Famous rib-eye steaks at Peppa's restaurant melt in the mouth. *1 High St; (03) 5461 3833; www.bristolhill.com.au*

CARAVANS AND MOTORHOMES

Maryborough Caravan Park

Set on the shores of Lake Victoria, this park has more than enough powered and unpowered sites, in addition to the deluxe cottages and cabins for that slightly more comfortable sleep. *7–9 Holyrood St; (03) 5460 4848; maryboroughcaravanpark.com.au*

Maryborough Golden Country Motel and Caravan Park

Plenty of ensuite caravan sites for use or take your pick of other comfortable digs, from motel rooms to villas and cabins. *134 Park Rd; (03) 5461 7700; www.goldencountry.com.au*

CAMPING

Paddy's Range State Park

Located 4 kilometres south-west of town, this is a superb place to discover old mining sites and go horseriding, or try to spot all 140 species of birds living here. Limited caravan spaces; bush camping with toilets, barbecues and rainwater tanks. *Access via Old Avoca Rd at the Karri Track*

WHERE TO EAT

Legenz Wine Bar and Cafe

Cold ales drunk alfresco and local wines are the ticket in this casual eatery. Great spot for a relaxing lunch or a good coffee. Chicken schnitzel night Thursdays; closed Sundays. *190 High St; (03) 5460 4033*

Romantic Vineyard Cafe

A taste of the world at this cosy cafe. Tuck into some jambalaya or Jamaican goat curry for dinner, a lighter soup of the day or an eggplant sandwich for lunch. As the name suggests, romantic four-course dinner for couples available by booking. *280 Lillicur Rd, Amherst; 0407 632 468; www.romanticvineyard.com*

TOURS

Guided bus tours of Maryborough can be arranged through the visitor centre. They'll show you many of the film's shooting locations, including Maryborough Park and the Maryborough Flour Mill. There are also self-guided walking tours available from the visitor centre or the website. *(03) 5460 4511; www.visitmaryborough.com.au*

The world premiere of the film at the Theatre Royal in Castlemaine

The AFI Awards – a brief history

On 6 December 2007, *Romulus, My Father* went into the 2007 AFI Awards holding the equal record of 15 AFI nominations. Let's look at Australian film's 'night of nights' and its proud 50 year history.

1958: A group of Carlton film enthusiasts set up the Australian Film Institute. The inaugural awards are held with 30 nominations across six different categories. The Best Film category includes non-features as well as documentaries and is split between two documentaries: *Conquest of the Rivers* and *Hard to Windward*. The awards are held during the Melbourne Film Festival.

1968: The Raymond Longford Award is first presented to director Ian Dunlop in honour of one of the great pioneers of the Australian film industry. The award is bestowed upon an individual who demonstrates a steadfast commitment to the craft of filmmaking, and its recipients have included directors, producers, actors and journalists. Other past awardees include Ken G. Hall, the McDonagh sisters, Russell Boyd, Peter Weir, Fred Schepisi, David Stratton, Jack Thompson, Jan Chapman and Geoffrey Rush. The award

is regarded as the highest accolade the AFI can bestow upon an individual.

1976: The awards are televised to a national audience on the Nine Network. This year the rules are changed and nominations for Best Film can only include narrative features. Fred Schepisi's semi-autobiographical feature *The Devil's Playground* takes out top honours and also wins Best Direction, Best Screenplay and Best Actor awards (which was a tie between Simon Burke and Nick Tate).

1980: *Breaker Morant* becomes the most successful film at the AFI Awards, taking home ten awards, including Best Film, Best Actor, Best Supporting Actor, Best Direction and Best Cinematography.

1984: AFI introduces the Bryon Kennedy Award, named in memory of the late and great producer. The award was created to recognise someone who demonstrates a 'quality of work that is marked by their relentless pursuit of excellence'. The inaugural award goes to sound mixer and editor Roger Savage. Other Bryon Kennedy Award recipients over the years have included Jane Campion, Baz Luhrmann, Rolf de Heer and Dion Beebe.

1986: Television categories are featured for the first time. *The Dunera Boys* wins for Best TV Miniseries while *The Perfectionist* wins Best Tele-featurette.

1989: Meryl Streep becomes the first big international star to win an acting award, which she wins for her portrayal of Lindy

Chamberlain in the Fred Schepisi-directed *Evil Angels* (aka *A Cry in the Dark* for its US release). Streep was also nominated for an Oscar for the role. In 1990, legendary Swedish actor Max Von Sydow followed in her footsteps, winning the AFI for Best Actor in the film *Father*.

1992: The first AFI Young Actor Award is presented to up-and-coming stars of film and television. Abbie Cornish, Emily Browning and Kodi Smit-McPhee are some of the past winners.

1993: Jane Campion becomes the first person to win an award in the same category at both the AFI Awards and the Oscars: Best Screenplay for *The Piano*. Geoffrey Rush replicated her feat a few years later when he won Best Actor AFI and Oscar awards for his role of David Helfgott in *Shine* in 1996.

1994: Despite being one of Australia's most successful films of all time, *The Adventures of Priscilla, Queen of the Desert* only wins two AFI Awards. It is pipped to the Best Picture post by *Muriel's Wedding*, and Toni Collette and Rachel Griffiths nab Best Actress and Best Supporting Actress respectively. Rolf de Heer wins Best Direction for *Bad Boy Bubby*, while actor Nicholas Hope takes home Best Actor for his role in the same film.

2001: Director George Miller becomes an AFI Patron and Cate Blanchett becomes an AFI Ambassador, which strengthens the Australian film industry's presence on a global scale.

2004: Cate Shortland's *Somersault* brakes all AFI Award records, taking home an astonishing 13 trophies from 15 nominations. It couldn't actually have won 15 trophies because the film had multiple nominations in the Best Supporting Actor and Best Supporting Actress categories.

2005: Russell Crowe hosts the awards. Geoffrey Rush took the reins in 2006 and 2007. AFI also introduces awards for performances by Australians overseas. The 2005 winners are Russell Crowe for *Cinderella Man*, Emily Browning for *Lemony Snicket's A Series of Unfortunate Events* and Roger Savage for his sound work on *The House of Flying Daggers*.

2007: *Romulus, My Father* ties with *Somersault* (2004), by attaining 15 AFI nominations. It scores four awards on the night, including Best Film and Best Actor for Eric Bana.

2010: *Animal Kingdom* rewrites the AFI record books, smashing the previous record and garnering 18 total nominations and winning 10. Orphaned at 17 by heroin, J goes to live with his grandmother, and armed robber and drug dealer uncles. With a sly nod to real events, the plot turns on the cold-blooded revenge killing of two young policemen. The film, which won the World Cinema Jury Prize at the 2010 Sundance Film Festival, was shot in a variety of locations in Melbourne. The film stars Ben Mendelsohn, Jackie Weaver (nominated for an Oscar for Best Supporting Actress for her role), Guy Pearce, Joel Egerton and Sullivan Stapleton.

Shine (1996)

> I know life is cruel, but ... but music ... music will always be your friend. Everything else will let you down in the end. Everything. Believe me ... everything.
>
> – *Peter*

David (Rush) and Gillian (Redgrave) get close

Director: Scott Hicks
Writers: Scott Hicks, Jan Sardi
Producer: Jane Scott
Cast includes: Geoffrey Rush, Noah Taylor, Armin Mueller-Stahl, Sonia Todd, Lynn Redgrave, Nicholas Bell

ABOUT THE FILM

It became blisteringly evident very early on in the piece that Scott Hicks' *Shine* was going to be something special. Upon its premiere at the Sundance Film Festival in 1996, a bidding war ensued between American distributors Miramax Films and New Line Features, with the latter winning out. When you watch the film, it's easy to see what all the fuss was about.

The enthralling story is a real-life account of genius pianist David Helfgott (Rush as an adult, Taylor as a youth). The film tracks Helfgott from his troubled years as a teenage prodigy under the strict rule of his father, Peter (Mueller-Stahl), to his nervous breakdown and subsequent return to a life of somewhat normalcy with his new beau Gillian (Redgrave).

Shine received local and international critical plaudits. The very sweet cherry on the cake came when relative unknown Geoffrey Rush beat big-name stars Tom Cruise, Ralph Fiennes and Billy Bob Thornton to win the Best Actor statuette at the 1997 Academy Awards.

There really aren't enough superlatives to describes Rush's performance in the film. Mueller-Stahl was also magnificent as David's overbearing father (the role earned him a Best Supporting Actor Oscar nomination), while Taylor is often forgotten, despite also shining (pardon the pun) as the young piano ingénue.

The film's journey wasn't without controversy, however, coming under fire after David Helfgott's sister Margaret claimed in a memoir she wrote that parts of the story and characters were exaggerated for dramatic effect. This is hardly new in the film industry; many true stories are slightly inflated to make a more entertaining product. Regardless, *Shine* is one of Australia's finest films, particularly for the fine performance from wonderful Mr Rush, thespian extraordinaire.

From the scene of David jumping on the trampoline

Adelaide South Australia

For some reason, Adelaide generally gets overlooked as a tourist destination. It's truly baffling – the 'City of Churches', as the state capital is fondly referred to, is a bustling blend of culture, heritage buildings and some of the best food and wine Australia has to offer. The city (the fifth largest in Australia) is situated on the south-east coast of the state, just north of the Fleurieu Peninsula.

It possesses the urbanity of Melbourne and Sydney, yet Adelaide also gives you room to breathe, with its beautiful ring of parklands, quiet suburban streetscapes and gorgeous beaches. There is plenty of touristy stuff to do in the CBD, from shopping in Rundle Mall to the Art Gallery of South Australia (and the museum next door) and viewing the giant pandas at Adelaide Zoo.

Adelaide was the main Australian location for the filming of *Shine*; numerous spots in the city and surrounding suburbs were used for locations. Parts of the film were also shot in the United Kingdom.

VISITOR INFO

South Australian Visitor and Travel Centre

18 King William St; (08) 8303 2220 or 1300 655 276; www.southaustralia.com

THINGS TO SEE AND DO

Botanic Gardens of Adelaide

This lush oasis on the outskirts of the Adelaide CBD is one of the city's stunning jewels. Strolling down the paths of the garden and taking in the exotic and native ornamental plants, towering palms and endangered cycads, you'll completely forget you're in a major metropolitan city.

The resplendent garden was used to film the scenes of David running through the park in his tan trench coat. The standout location was the leafy tunnel, where David passes a couple of Sunday joggers. There are actually two of these green tunnels parallel to each other, on either side of the Mediterranean Garden in the middle of the parkland. Also worth seeing in the gardens is the Palm House (one of the oldest glasshouses in Australia), the Bicentennial Conservatory (the largest indoor rainforest canopy in the Southern Hemisphere) and the Amazon Waterlily Pavilion. *Entrance to botanic gardens on North Terrace Rd, next to the Royal Adelaide Hospital. There are also entrances off Frome Rd and at the back of the gardens on Plane Tree Dr; (08) 8222 9311; www.botanicgardens.sa.gov.au*

Botanic Park

Between the north edge of the botanic gardens and east of the zoo is the 34-hectare Botanic Park, which was the backdrop for some of the exterior park shots involving David. The park has many uniquely shaped, century-old Moreton Bay fig trees providing shade for spring and summer picnics. At Speakers' Corner you might hear some lively debate and every March it metamorphoses into the WOMADelaide Music Festival, attracting over 20 000 people per day. *Entrance via Plane Tree Dr or Hackney Rd*

Adelaide Town Hall

This beautifully preserved heritage town hall was used as the location of the concert hall for David's moving climactic performance at the very end of the film. Life very much imitated art in 2009 when David Helfgott performed his first major recital in over a decade here, playing to a sold-out audience. He played Rachmaninov, sonatas by Beethoven and Mozart, and 'Flight of the Bumble Bee', which is the piece of music David (Rush) first plays in Moby's restaurant. Throughout the year the venue hosts numerous local and national orchestra performances and recitals. Guided tours of the building are available by appointment. *128 King William St; (08) 8203 7590; www.cityofadelaide.com.au/ attractions/adelaide-town-hall.html*

The pier at Henley Beach

Henley Beach

Perhaps it was better for Geoffrey Rush that his public profile was fairly low at the time of filming; it may have just saved him from the ignominy of the tabloids and gossip mags bombarding us with paparazzi snaps of his pale behind (not that he's been exactly bashful in his movie canon). Yep, this affluent seaside suburb, 10 kilometres west of the CBD, was the location for the memorable scene of David skinny dipping in the frozen waters right next to Henley Pier. The pier is located at Henley Square, a hugely popular spot in the spring and summer months bordered by restaurants and cafes.

In Henley Square you'll find Cibo Espresso, formerly Henley on the Sea Cafe, which was the location used as Moby's restaurant in the film. *Henley Square, The Esplanade (off Seaview Rd), Henley*

State Library of South Australia

Long a magnet for bookworms and lately also cheapskates in search of free internet, the state's largest library has a fascinating 'South Australiana' collection, which documents the history of the state from pre-European settlement to present day. A reading room at the library was used as the location for the scene when young David is introduced to Mrs Pritchard (Googie Withers) and where he has that flirty, slightly awkward conversation with the young woman. *Cnr North Tce and Kintore Ave; (08) 8207 7250; www.slsa.sa.gov.au*

Adelaide Town Hall

> Practical? No, of course not. Of course not. But then neither am I, Gillian. Neither am I. I'm not very practical at all.
> – David

Bonython Hall

For past and present students of the University of Adelaide, Bonython Hall might bring up some not-so-pleasant memories of sitting exams or happier ones of graduation. This hall on the South Australian Heritage Register was dressed as a synagogue and used for young David's bar mitzvah scenes. The hall has an unusual sloping floor, a design specificity requested by benefactor Langdon Bonython, who was a strict Methodist and didn't want the hall used for any dancing activities.

Inside the Art Gallery of South Australia

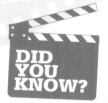

In 2009, Geoffrey Rush became the first Australian to secure the acting 'Triple Crown'. He won a Tony Award for his role in the broadway production *Exit the King* (opposite Susan Sarandon) to pop on the shelf next to his Oscar for *Shine* and his television Emmy Award for *The Life and Death of Peter Sellers*, won in 2004.

He is the only Australian on the list of only 20 other triple-crowners, which includes Ingrid Bergman, Vanessa Redgrave and Al Pacino. Rush also has an honorary Doctorate in Letters from the University of Queensland and a Lifetime Achievement Award from the Australian Film Institute.

Party pooper! *University of Adelaide, North Tce; (08) 8303 4455; www.adelaide.edu.au*

Glenside Hospital

This stunning old building was used as the mental institution where David laid his head during his breakdown. The interior and exteriors were used to shoot scenes in the film. The hospital, which started out as a 'lunatic asylum', has undergone an enormous multi-million-dollar redevelopment since filming took place in the mid '90s. *226 Fullarton Rd, Glenside; (08) 8303 1111*

Rosewater

This suburb was the location of the house in which David lived as a child and teenager in the film. The suburb is 10 kilometres north-west of the Adelaide CBD and borders Port Adelaide, a lively 'hood with heaps of cool cafes, galleries and antique shops.

West Terrace Cemetery

This large burial ground on the western edge of the Adelaide CBD was the location of the funeral scene towards the end of the film. *161 West Tce; (08) 8139 7400*

Gilberton

Just a couple of kilometres north of Adelaide CBD, this quiet residential suburb on the banks of the River Torrens was the location for the house of Ben Rosen (Bell), David's piano tutor. The house is located on Edwin Terrace.

North Haven

A house overlooking the water in North Haven was used as David and Gillian's house. North Haven is a pleasant suburb on a small spit of land 20 kilometres north-west of Adelaide CBD.

Rundle Mall

A short saunter from the botanic gardens and town hall, Rundle Mall is famous for being Australia's first ever pedestrian shopping mall. It's still the heart of Adelaide's CBD, with major department stores, souvenir and craft outlets, not to mention dozens of places for a bite in the food courts, restaurants, cafes and pubs. But you've just gotta have a Coopers or two, the local brew, at the Exeter. *At the end of Rundle St, between King William and Pulteney sts*

Art Gallery of South Australia

Get your culture fix at one of Australia's finest collections of Australian, European and Indigenous artworks. The gallery houses 38 000 pieces. The neighbouring South Australia Museum has six floors of fascinating displays delving into the history of this great state. You'll leave knowing more about South Australia than the premier. *North Terrace; (08) 8207 7000; www.artgallery.sa.gov.au*

Adelaide Zoo

Lions and tigers and panda bears ... oh my! Adelaide Zoo has been trusted with the responsibility of caring for (and hopefully mating!) the utterly adorable Wang Wang and Funi, two very intelligent and curious giant pandas, the only two giant pandas residing in the Southern Hemisphere. But wait, there's also 1800-plus other animals to swoon over. *Frome Rd; (08) 8267 3255; www.zoossa.com.au*

WHERE TO STAY

Adelaide Central YHA

People can't stop saying good things about the Adelaide Central YHA, rated one of the best hostels in Australia. With affable staff, clean and comfy shared and private rooms and all the amenities you could ask for, this is the one to choose if you're watching your budget. Free pancake day on Tuesdays and Fridays and a city walking tour every Saturday. Just a short stroll to all the major filming locations in the CBD. *135 Waymouth St; (08) 8414 3010; www.yha. com.au/hostels/sa/adelaide/adelaide-central*

Majestic Roof Garden Hotel

Only a five-minute walk from the botanic gardens, this hotel was rated the best value in the land by *The Australian* Travel and Tourism Awards in 2009. Deluxe, executive and superior spa suites with – yep, you guessed it – a lush rooftop garden. The hotel was used as the shooting location for another Scott Hicks vehicle, *The Boys Are Back* (2009), starring Clive Owen. *55 Frome St; (08) 8100 4400 or 1800 008 499; www.majestichotels.com.au/ mrgh_overview.htm*

Ambassadors Hotel

The heritage-listed site is one of the Adelaide's oldest buildings (and indeed hotels, operating since 1841), located diagonally opposite the Adelaide Town Hall. It has 30 rooms with comfy beds and reasonable tariffs. Dine in the Marble Bar and wine in the Ambar Lounge. *107 King William St; (08) 8231 4331; www.ambhotel.com.au*

Majestic Minima Hotel

Great things come in small packages. Located in North Adelaide, this ultra-modern boutique hotel offers rooms a tad smaller than standard hotels, but they still manage to fit each room with a king-size bed, flat-screen TV and hip decor. Inexpensive, as well as being the city's first 24-hour self-check-in hotel. *146 Melbourne St, North Adelaide; (08) 8334 7766 or 1800 779 554; www. majestichotels.com.au/minima_overview.htm*

CARAVANS AND MOTORHOMES

Discovery Holiday Parks Adelaide Beachfront

Only 10 kilometres from the city centre, this four-star park has powered ensuite sites, spa cabins and beach houses sleeping six. Close to vibrant Port Adelaide and the popular West Lakes shopping complex. *349 Military Rd, Semaphore Park; (08) 8449 7726; www.discoveryholidayparks.com. au/sa/adelaide/adelaide_beachfront*

BIG4 Adelaide Shores Caravan Park

A four-and-a-half-star park just a few kilometres south of Henley Beach and close to Adelaide Airport. There are powered ensuite sites, cabin accommodation and activities to keep the little ones (and the young at heart) happy in the skate and BMX park. *Military Rd, West Beach; (08) 8355 7320; www.adelaideshores.com.au*

WHERE TO EAT

Cibo Espresso

Cibo is a franchised Italian cafe with 11 stores throughout Adelaide (and growing). This Henley Square location played Moby's in the film, the restaurant that David aimlessly wanders into and ends up entertaining the astonished patrons with his luminous piano talent. At the time of filming it was called Henley on the Sea Cafe and before Cibo was a Croatian restaurant, Morska Vila.

Despair not! Although franchised, the quality at Cibo is outstanding – the coffee list is almost longer than a film script. The food is excellent; the warm calzones and paninis will make your stomach smile. They also have a diverse selection of sweets and gelati and walls of art on display as part of the Cibo Galleria Awards. *251 The Esplanade, Henley; (08) 8355 4079; www.ciboespresso.com.au*

Yakitori Takumi

Have you ever had a bad experience with meat or chicken on a stick? Didn't think so. This compact, truly authentic Japanese joint has a huge selection of mouth-watering yakitori (translation: skewered chicken, but they stab everything from king prawns to duck and veggie items) along with a primo selection of Japanese beer and sake. A short walk north of the botanic gardens, ideal for a cheap and tasty lunch. *55 Melbourne St, North Adelaide; (08) 8239 2111; www.yakitori-takumi.com*

Cocolat

Overindulgence never tasted so good! Gorge yourself in this land of chocolate (like Homer in that episode of *The Simpsons*), as you chomp through brownies, crepes, cakes, waffles and all-day breakfast pastries. It's also licensed and the Cocolat martini is an absolute (maybe with Absolut) must. Located on Rundle Street close to everything. *283 Rundle St; (08) 8232 6133; www.cocolat.com.au*

Botanic Garden Restaurant

Fine-dine in the middle of Adelaide's Garden of Eden. Rack of lamb and Wagyu tartare are just two of the highlights. For a quick and cheap meal or a cappuccino, try Cafe Fibonacci or Simpson Kiosk, also in the park. *Adelaide Botanic Garden; (08) 8223 3526; www.botanicgardenrestaurant.com.au*

FILM FESTIVALS

Adelaide Film Festival

This biennial festival (www.adelaidefilmfestival. org) is the city's most prestigious film festival and one of Australia's most important. The film bible *Variety* named the AFF in the world's top 50 film festivals in 2007. It screens in February and March every odd year at various cinemas around town.

CINEMAS

Nova Eastend Cinemas

Offers Q & A sessions with filmmakers all year and hosts the annual French Film Festival in March, the Spanish Film Festival in May, and the Greek and Italian film festivals in October. And it's fully licensed! *251 Rundle St; (08) 8232 3434; www.cinemanova.com.au/SA/default.htm*

Capri Theatre

A gorgeous curved Art Deco cinema located in Goodwood (south of the CBD) showing nostalgic films and hosting special screenings including live music shows. It has a stupendous organ (there's a DVD of its transport and restoration available if you're organ crazy). *141 Goodwood Rd, Goodwood; (08) 8272 1177; www.capri.org.au*

OTHER LOCATIONS

Port Gawler South Australia

A property on this coastal town (around 50 kilometres north-west of Adelaide) was used as the interior and exterior house of Mrs Pritchard. The house is located in the Buckland Park vicinity.

London United Kingdom

Good old London-town played a significant role in the middle part of the film when the young David heads to the UK to study piano at the Royal College of Music. The college itself (in south-west London) was used as a filming location. Royal Albert Hall, at the south end of Hyde Park, was also used.

In another London scene, the young David finds himself in Trafalgar Square one morning after a serious bender.

Cibo Espresso, which acted as Moby's restaurant in the film

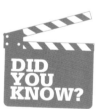

DID YOU KNOW? Geoffrey Rush played the piano until he was 14 years old. He resumed lessons for the film and was so adept at playing that he acted as his own 'stunt hands' in the close-up shots of David tickling the ivories.

Aussies at the Oscars, part 2

For such a tiny country, Australia has produced an extraordinary number of Academy Award winners. Here we list individual Australian actors and filmmakers who have taken home that shiny golden man.

ROBERT KRASKER (1913–1981)

Best Cinematographer for *The Third Man* (released in 1949, won Oscar the following year). The legendary Perth-born director of photography (DOP) worked on close to 30 films in the '50s and '60s, none greater than *The Third Man*, an adaptation of a Graham Greene novel about a writer investigating the mysterious death of a friend.

ORRY-KELLY (1897–1964)

Best Costume Design for *An American in Paris* (1951), *Les Girls* (1957) and *Some Like it Hot* (1959). Kelly was a Hollywood legend when it came to costume design, winning multiple Oscars and working on films such as *42nd Street* (1933), *The Maltese Falcon* (1941), *Casablanca* (1942), *Arsenic and Old Lace* (1944) and *Harvey* (1950). When Kelly passed away in 1964 the pallbearers at his funeral included Cary Grant, Tony Curtis and Billy Wilder.

JOHN FARROW (1904–1963)

Best Adapted Screenplay (with James Poe and S.J. Perelman) for *Around the World in Eighty Days* (1956). Farrow was a former sailor turned writer and later director, who worked on over 80 Hollywood productions. He was also nominated for a Best Directing Oscar in 1942 for *Wake Island*.

JOHN TRUSCOTT (1936–1993)

Best Art Direction and Best Costume Design for *Camelot* (1967). Amazingly, Truscott only worked behind the scenes on two feature films. He also dabbled in acting, having roles in a few TV shows, as well as playing a navy crewman in the Bond film *The Spy Who Loved Me* (1977).

KEN MUGGLESTON (1930–)

Best Art Direction (with John Box, Terence Marsh and Vernon Dixon) for *Oliver!* (1968). The talented art director also worked on *Lawrence of Arabia* (1962), *Doctor Zhivago* (1965) and *The Taming of the Shrew* (1967).

PETER FINCH (1916–1977)

Best Actor for his turn as a maniacal television anchorman in *Network* (1976). Finch is one of only two Australians to posthumously receive an Academy Award (the other being Heath Ledger in 2008 for *The Dark Knight*). The film also won him a Golden Globe and his fifth BAFTA.

PETER ALLEN (1944–1992)

Best Song (with Burt Bacharach, Carole Bayer Sager and Christopher Cross) for *Arthur* (1981). The boy from Oz could do it all, including Oscar-winning songwriting. In actual fact, Allen only contributed one line to the song ('When you get caught between the moon and New York City'), which was from an earlier song he co-wrote with Bayer Sager.

DEAN SEMLER (1943–)

Best Cinematography for *Dances with Wolves* (1990). Semler is an enormously successful cinematographer who has worked on such Australian classic as *Mad Max 2: The Road Warrior*, *The Lighthorsemen* (1987) and *Dead Calm* (1989). He's currently working in Hollywood and his recent films include *2012* (2009), *Date Night* (2010) and *Secretariat* (2010).

LUCIANA ARRIGHI (1940–)

Best Art Direction (with Ian Whittaker) for *Howard's End* (1992). Arrighi was responsible for the design of the beautiful glass church in *Oscar and Lucinda*. Her other impressive credits include *Sunday Bloody Sunday* (1971), *My Brilliant Career* (1979), *The Remains of the Day* (1993) and *Sense and Sensibility* (1995).

PAUL PATTISON

Best Achievement in Makeup (with Peter Frampton and Lois Burwell) for the striking long hair and blue battle faces in *Braveheart* (1995). Pattison has also done make-up for films including *The Man From Snowy River II* (1988), *Mission: Impossible II* (2000), *Scooby Doo* (2002) and *The Waiting City* (2009).

BRUCE DAVEY

Best Picture (with Mel Gibson and Alan Ladd Jr) for *Braveheart* (1995). Davey is to date the only Australian to win the Best Picture Oscar. With Mel Gibson he founded Icon Productions in 1989. They have gone on to produce *Payback* (1999), *What Women Want* (2000) and *The Passion of the Christ* (2004). Davey started out as Gibson's accountant and business manager.

GEOFFREY RUSH (1951–)

Best Actor for *Shine* (1996). This was something of a surprise win for Rush. Many people didn't know much about this small Australian film, even though it received seven nominations. Rush won the award over a very hot field in the Best Actor category, including Tom Cruise for *Jerry Maguire*, Ralph Fiennes for *The English Patient*, Billy Bob Thornton for *Sling Blade* and Woody Harrelson for *The People vs Larry Flynt*.

JOHN SEALE (1942–)

Best Cinematography for *The English Patient* (1996). In 1997 this movie swept the Oscars, taking home nine awards. Seale's career has spanned almost 40 years and includes credits such as *BMX Bandits* (1983), *Witness* (1985), *Rain Man* (1988) and *Dead Poets Society* (1989).

DAVID LEE (1958–)

Best Sound (with John Reitz, Gregg Rudloff and David Campbell) for *The Matrix* (1999). Lee has worked as a sound mixer and a recordist for three decades on a long list of local and international films. His latest film was the Stuart Beattie–directed Aussie film *Tomorrow, When the War Began* (2010) based on the John Marsden novel.

STEVE COURTLEY

Best Visual Effects (with John Gaeta, Janek Sirrs and Jon Thum) for *The Matrix* (1999). It would have been utterly ridiculous if the team responsible for the effects in *The Matrix* weren't recognised. Courtley has worked effects on some classic Aussie films, including *Gallipoli* and *Mad Max 2: The Road Warrior*.

RUSSELL CROWE (1964–)

Best Actor for *Gladiator* (2000). While he may have been born a Kiwi, we like to claim him as our own (he lived in Australia from the ages of four to 14 and has a home base here now). No-one can forget his portrayal of uber-hero Maximus, fighting off lions and fierce warriors in the Colosseum. It was the polar opposite of his role in *The Insider* (1999) a year earlier, when he played an aged and overweight corporate whistle-blower for which he also earned an Oscar nomination.

ANDREW LESNIE (1956–)

Best Cinematography for *The Lord of the Rings: The Fellowship of the Ring* (2001). The Rings franchise brought in a small army of little gold men, including one for DOP Lesnie. Lesnie was responsible for shooting both Babe movies and his recent Hollywood exploits include *King Kong* (2005), *I Am Legend* (2007) and *The Lovely Bones* (2009).

NICOLE KIDMAN (1967–)

Best Actress for *The Hours* (2002). Although she only had 28 minutes of screen time, such was the power of Kidman's performance as Virginia Woolf that the Academy voters just couldn't ignore her. Kidman was nominated for Best Actress for *Moulin Rouge!* in 2001 and *Rabbit Hole* in 2010.

RUSSELL BOYD (1944–)

Best Cinematography for *Master and Commander: The Far Side of the World* (2003). This legend of Australian film received his dues for his stunning work behind the camera in Peter Weir's story about a British ship during the Napoleonic Wars.

CATE BLANCHETT (1969–)

Best Supporting Actress for *The Aviator* (2004). She had been extremely unlucky to miss out on the Best Actress Oscar for her role in *Elizabeth* (1998), but Blanchett did take home the statue six years later thanks to her remarkable depiction of actress Katharine Hepburn. She has since earned three more nominations for *Notes on a Scandal* (2006), *I'm Not There* (2007) and *Elizabeth: The Golden Age* (2007).

DION BEEBE (1968–)

Best Cinematography for *Memoirs of a Geisha* (2005). Beebe continued the tradition of Australian cinematographers dominating the Oscars when he won for Rob Marshall's adaptation of the hugely popular book. Beebe was the fifth Australian DOP to win the award in the last 15 years. His latest film is the comic book adaptation, *Green Lantern* (2011).

GEORGE MILLER (1945–)

Best Animated Feature for *Happy Feet* (2006). Miller's charming story about dancing emperor penguins earned him his first Oscar. While most know he was nominated as a producer for *Babe*, many don't realise he was also nominated for Best Original Screenplay with Nick Enright for *Lorenzo's Oil* back in 1993 (*The Crying Game* won the award).

EVA ORNER (1969–)

The Melbourne producer won Best Documentary (with Alex Gibney) for *Taxi to the Dark Side* (2007), a harrowing documentary about US torture practices in Iraq, Afghanistan and Guantanamo Bay.

HEATH LEDGER (1979–2008)

Best Supporting Actor for *The Dark Knight* (2008). Ledger's sensational turn as the malevolent Joker stands as one of film history's all-time greatest acting performances. Ledger's untimely and tragic death in January 2008 was an premature end to what had already shaped up as a legendary career in film.

See pages 46–7 for more Oscar winners.

Ten Canoes (2006)

Director Rolf de Heer and actor Richard Birrinbirrin on set

> I'm going to tell you a story from long ago and I want you to listen very carefully.
>
> — *Minygululu*

Director: Rolf de Heer (with Peter Djigirr as co-director)
Writer: Rolf de Heer
Producers: Rolf de Heer, Julie Ryan
Cast includes: Crusoe Kurddal, Jamie Dayindi Gulpilil, Richard Birrinbirrin, Frances Djulibing, David Gulpilil, Peter Minygululu

ABOUT THE FILM

The beautiful, aerial opening shot of *Ten Canoes* has our wise narrator David Gulpilil revealing to the audience that he's going to tell us 'a story like you've never seen before'. Truer words have never been spoken. *Ten Canoes* is actually a story within a story. It centres on the ancient Ramingining tribe, inhabitants of the Arafura wetlands of central Arnhem Land since centuries before European settlement.

As they glide down the crocodile-infested waters in their canoes hunting for goose eggs, Minygululu (Minygululu), one of the tribe elders, tells a tale to his younger brother Dayindi (Dayindi Gulpilil, son of legendary actor David Gulpilil).

He tells a story of forbidden love, sorcery and kidnapping, an engaging adventure infused from start to finish with unexpected humour, tension and the ethereal beauty of the natural surrounds.

The film's origin stemmed from photographs taken by anthropologist Dr Donald Thomson, who studied and documented the Indigenous people of central Arnhem Land in the 1930s.

Ten Canoes is the first Australian feature film shot entirely in an Aboriginal language, which adds to the experience of having an unfiltered and authentic glimpse of Indigenous culture, something director Rolf de Heer pulls off masterfully. The entire cast is made up of

Dayindi (Jamie Gulpilil) strikes a pose in one of the canoes

Ramingining people and they all do a superb job, especially Kurddal as Ridjimiraril and Birrinbirrin as the grandfather of the tribe – the jovial one with a penchant for honey.

Ten Canoes is astonishing. And it is one of the most daring and groundbreaking Australian films to date. The film received international acclaim, winning the Special Jury Prize at the 2006 Cannes Film Festival and six AFI Awards, including Best Film. Plus it cemented Rolf de Heer as one of this country's greatest directors.

LOCATIONS

ARNHEM LAND
NORTHERN TERRITORY

Arnhem Land is one of Australia's true untouched beauties. Bounded by Kakadu National Park, the Arafura Sea and the Gulf of Carpentaria, this 97 000-square-kilometre paradise is made up of rugged coastlines, dense flourishing rainforests, ancient rock formations and savannah woodlands.

The Cobourg Peninsula to the west is trimmed with glorious sandy beaches, while to the far east the Gove Peninsula has pristine wetlands and some of the best adventure fishing in the world. Throughout the vast space there's a plethora of native wildlife, including crocodiles, nestling turtles and migratory birds. The entire film was shot in and around the Arafura Swamp, a large floodplain just east of the town of Ramingining.

The seed for *Ten Canoes* was planted when actor David Gulpilil brought Rolf de Heer a photograph of ten Indigenous canoeists in

This land began in the beginning. Yurlunggur, that great water goanna, he travelled here. Yurlunggur made all this land, all this water, and he made this swamp that stretches long and gives us life.

– *The Storyteller*

Nowalingu (Djulibing) by the waterfront

the middle of a swamp (as mentioned, above, this photo was taken by anthropologist Dr Donald Thomson). Thomson lived with the Yolngu people in Arnhem Land for months, documenting their traditional lifestyle through still and moving images. He left a legacy of thousands of images; many of these photos were inspiration for specific shots that de Heer tried to recapture in the film.

Some of the Thomson photos and cultural artefacts can be viewed at Museum Victoria in Melbourne. Unfortunately, thousands of feet of Thomson's film was destroyed in a Melbourne warehouse fire.

In 1931 Arnhem Land was declared an Aboriginal Reserve. Today it's controlled by Indigenous people through the Northern Lands Council. You need to obtain permission to enter – and are only allowed in certain parts – so it's indeed quite untouched (and dry: note the alcohol restrictions).

VISITOR INFO

Vibrant Mt Borradaile and Cooper Creek

Ramingining Shire Office

(08) 8979 7906; www. ramingining.net

Walkabout Lodge

12 Westal St, Nhulunbuy; (08) 8939 2000; www. walkaboutlodge. com.au

Tourism Top End

(08) 8936 2450 or 1300 138 886; www.tourismtopend.com.au

East Arnhem Tourism

www.ealta.org

Northern Territory Road Service

Due to the tropical climate, many roads are closed in the wet season because of flooding. The Northern Territory Government has a 24-hour recorded message service with up-to-date information on the condition of all government-controlled roads in the NT as well as information about road closures, restrictions and impassable river crossings. Check this service before venturing out in any vehicle in the territory. *1800 246 199; www.ntlis.nt.gov.au/roadreport*

Aboriginal children in Mikinj Valley

THINGS TO SEE AND DO

Arafura Swamp

The 700-square-kilometre freshwater basin on the northern coast of Arnhem Land was the setting for *Ten Canoes*. The entire film was shot in and around the wooded swamp – which was a major challenge for both the cast and the

Did you know?

Ten Canoes is the only Australian film to win the Special Jury Prize (*Un Certain Regard*) in the history of the prestigious Cannes Film Festival. The only other two Australian films to win a major award at Cannes are Shirley Barrett's *Love Serenade* (1996) and Warwick Thornton's *Samson and Delilah* (2009), both of which won the Camera d'Or for best first feature.

crew. Not only did they have to contend with an overabundance of annoying mosquitoes and leeches, but the swamp also has one of the world's largest biomasses of crocodiles. So serious was the danger for Rolf and his crew that there were 11 croc spotters on set at all times, just in case things got a little hairy ... or should we say snappy. You'd be hard pressed to find another director willing to go to such lengths to get the right shots!

For their downtime, the cast and crew set up base camp at Murwangi, an old cattle station at the western edge of the swamp. The Arafura Swamp is a relatively unknown territory and can be dangerous, so solo exploring is not advised. Trek with a local who knows the terrain or with a tour group. *Located east of Ramingining*

Ramingining

Ramingining is a remote Aboriginal community of about 650 people in the northern part of central Arnhem Land, right on the edge of the Arafura Swamp. The town was created in the early 1970s when the Mission of Millingimby became overcrowded. It is made up of several Aboriginal tribes.

The people of Ramingining were essential to the production – making up the entire cast as well as assisting the crew to navigate

Birrinbirrin and Ridjimiraril

the harsh and unpredictable terrain of the Arafura Swamp.

Rolf visited Ramingining on numerous occasions in the lead-up to the film, getting to know the community, which was crucial to the success of the production. Language was somewhat of a barrier, though, with many of the Yolngu residents speaking multiple Indigenous dialects, and English being maybe a fifth or sixth language. Luckily, Peter Djigirr, Rolf's co-director, as well as Richard Birrinbirrin and Frances Djulibing, spoke English quite well and helped bridge the divide between cast and crew.

The film continues to have an impact on the community here; a variety of 'Canoe' projects run, allowing community members to learn a range of multimedia skills, from video recording to website design.

Ramingining is open to visitors, but is a traditional Aboriginal land so a permit is required to enter. Permits can be obtained from the Northern Land Council (08) 8920 5100; www.nlc.org.au

The best way to access Ramingining, and other smaller communities in Arnhem Land, is by charter plane. Katherine Aviation and Airnorth fly to the area and other aviation services offer charter flights. Contact the Ramingining shire office for more details.

Katherine Aviation (08) 8971 1277; www.katherineaviation.com.au; Airnorth (08) 8920 4001 or 1800 627 474; www.airnorth.com.au

Garig Gunak Barlu National Park

This national park is the only one in the Northern Territory to have land and marine features. It encompasses the entire Cobourg Peninsula and spreads to Van Diemen Gulf and the Arafura Sea. The park is brimming with tropical mangrove forests, corals reefs, magnificent sand dunes and a vast array of marine life.

Come well prepared with sufficient food, water and fuel (if using a vehicle), and a decent first-aid kit. The park can be accessed by four-wheel drive (vehicle fees apply), air charter or sea. You need a permit to camp overnight.

A wide variety of fish cruise the coastal waters of the park, including mackerel, queenfish, trevally and snapper. Don't even think about swimming in the area; sharks, box jellyfish, blue-ringed octopus and yes, crocs, inhabit the briny waters. *Park ranger (08) 8979 0244; www.nt.gov.au/nreta/parks/find/gariggunak.html*

Fishing around Garig Gunak Barlu National Park

Black Point Cultural Centre

Learn about Aboriginal culture, Macassan traders (from Indonesian islands) and European settlers through artefacts and traditional nosh (bush tucker). Located at the Black Point Ranger Station. *Via Smith Point Rd, Garig Gunak Barlu National Park; (08) 8979 0244*

Nhulunbuy

Located at the north-eastern tip of Arnhem Land on the Gove Peninsula, this relaxed hideaway, owned by Rio Tinto and used for mining, is a

Watch out for crocs in designated areas

haven for anglers, four-wheel-drive adventurers, bushwalkers and birdwatchers. Nhulunbuy is the base camp for anyone who wants to explore the fascinating eastern section of Arnhem Land.

The Gayngaru Wetland Interpretive Walk surrounds a stunning lagoon bursting with local birdlife, flora, fauna and bush medicine. If you're visiting in August, partake in the annual Garma Festival, a massive celebration of Indigenous arts and culture.

If that isn't enough for you, head 18 kilometres south-east of Nhulunbuy to the small community of Yirrkala, home to the Buku-Larrnggay Mulka Centre, a community-based Aboriginal art museum. Built on the site of an old hospital and clinic, the centre showcases some award-winning Indigenous art, from paintings on bark, didgeridoos (yidaki), memorial poles (larrakitj) and wood sculptures (dharpa).

Further south-east of Yirrkala and about 38 kilometres from Nhulunbuy is the fascinating Macassan Beach. You can go on an interpretive walk of the Yolngu stone arrangement recording the history of the Macassan traders who frequented the shores centuries earlier.

There are other fascinating areas and communities around Nhulunbuy and the eastern area of Arnhem Land that are worth exploring. See the 'Tours' section below for further suggestions.

Nhulunbuy is best accessed via air; Qantas Link has daily services from Darwin and Cairns. It can also be accessed via four-wheel drive; it's around 440 km east of Ramingining via Central Arnhem Rd. Permits are not needed to enter Nhulunbuy, however, they are required if you want to explore the surrounding areas. Permits are obtained through Dhimurru Land Management (08) 8987 3992; www.dhimurru.com.au

WHERE TO STAY

Ramingining Visitors Centre

Being only a small Aboriginal community with less than 700 people, the visitors centre is the only accommodation option in Ramingining. It offers eight clean, air-conditioned rooms with shared kitchen and bathroom facilities. *Ramingining; (08) 8979 7906; www.ramingining.net*

Arnhemland Barra Fishing Lodge

This award-winning lodge has four deluxe ensuite cabins on the edge of the Tomkinson River Valley escarpment. There are also more modest tented cabins for travellers on a budget. As its name suggests, the area is perfect for fishing, as well as for birdwatchers and nature lovers. It's near Maningrida, which is over 90 kilometres west of Ramingining. Road access is limited in the wet season; at this time guests are flown in and out via a regional carrier. *Djinkarr, near Maningrida; (08) 8983 1544; www.barralodge.com.au*

Walkabout Lodge

Laze on your balcony or patio imbibing Arafura Sea views. Book your spacious room or select one of 12 fully serviced camper-trailer sites if exploring the area by four-wheel drive. Poolside restaurant and bar on site. *12 Westal St, Nhulunbuy; (08) 8939 2000; www.walkaboutlodge.com.au*

Dugong Beach Resort

A classy eco-resort with luxurious bungalow and suite accommodation (and even some fancy tents). The resort operates a cultural centre displaying local arts and as a venue for Indigenous performances. There's a Li'tya day spa onsite offering rock massages, body wraps and the like. Located on Groote Eylandt off the south-east coast of Arnhem Land. *1 Bougainvillea Dr, Alyangula; (08) 8987 7077 or 1800 877 077; www.dugongbeachresort.com.au*

Banu Banu Wilderness Retreat

Who would've thought staying in a tent could be so comfortable? This eco-retreat offers

I refuse to walk at the end. Someone ahead keeps farting

— Canoeist

Not me. Not me.

— The group

It's you again. You're always so silent. Silent but deadly. Admit it.

— Canoeist

Rolf de Heer risks life and limb to get the shot

five twin-share guest tents with comfortable mattresses and bed linen.

Owners Helen and Trevor cook up some delicious homemade Top End meals for guests, including bacon and eggs for brekkie and just-caught fish for dinner.

Tours are available through the retreat, which is located on the northern tip of Bremer Island just north of Nhulunbuy. *Bremer Island; (08) 8987 8085; ecotoursonbanubanu.com.au*

CAMPING

Garig Gunak Barlu National Park

There are two unpowered camping sites within the park, with barbecue facilities and limited amounts of bore water. Permits required. *Park ranger (08) 8979 0244; www.nt.gov.au/nreta/parks; for camping permits contact the Cobourg Peninsula Sanctuary and Marine Park Board (08) 8999 4814*

East Arnhem Land

There are many campsites scattered around the east Arnhem Land area, including one at Macassans Beach. *For information on campsites and required permits, contact Dhimurru Land Management (08) 8987 3992; www.dhimurru.com.au*

WHERE TO EAT

The Waterfront Kitchen

Ask any local about the best place to eat in town and most will tell you to get down to The Waterfront. Located at the Gove Country Club, this bistro offers up anything your heart desires, from filling salads to all things meat and seafood, served with sensational balcony views of the town wetlands. Open Wednesday to Sunday for lunch and dinner and brunch on Sundays. *East Woody Rd, Nhulunbuy; (08) 8987 8388; www.govecountrygolfclub.com.au*

Macassans Restaurant

Serene views of the Gulf of Carpentaria just 50 metres from the beach – perhaps you'll spot a dugong or a dolphin. Situated in the vibrant Arnhem Club (an RSL with pokies, pool, happy hour, the works) there's a strong emphasis on steak and seafood. *1 Franklyn St, Nhulunbuy; (08) 8987 0601*

Seagrass Restaurant

Part of the Dugong Beach Resort, take your pick from an eclectic mix of modern Australian and Asian cuisine and settle in for the sunset, you're less than 20 metres from the sea. *1 Bougainvillea Dr, Alyangula; (08) 8987 7077; www.dugongbeachresort.com.au*

Gove Yacht Club

A family-friendly eatery at the Gove Yacht Club, perched on the edge of the brilliant-blue Melville Bay. Affordable lunch and dinner meals available Friday to Sunday (with take-away choices on request). Located 12 kilometres out of Nhulunbuy. *Drimmie Head Rd, Melville Bay (12km from Nhulunbuy); (08) 8987 3077*

TOURS

Ten Canoes Cultural Odyssey

Venture North offers the eight-day 'Ten Canoes Cultural Odyssey', a tour of Arnhem Land taking in the Arafura Swamp, Ramingining and Murwangi Station. You'll be able to visit some of the exact spots where the film was shot and have an opportunity to meet local cast members. *Venture North (08) 8927 5500; www.northernaustralia.com*

Ridjimiralil rests in his hut

Arnhem Land Aboriginal Culture Tours

Authentic Indigenous tours including bush tucker, rock art and traditional hunting. Two-, three- or four-day packages led by traditional land owners. *(08) 8983 2167; www.arnhemlodge.com.au*

Bawaka Cultural Experiences

Embrace the Yolngu way of life with this memorable two-day cultural awareness tour. You will immerse yourself in Indigenous culture and learn about Yolngu law, music, communication, black magic and even try a spot of spear fishing. Departs from Nhulunbuy. *(08) 8987 3433 or 0447 087 091; www.bawaka.com.au*

Rripangu Yidaki Didgeridoo Masterclass

Being able to make a didgeridoo from scratch is a pretty impressive skill to add to your resume. Join Djalu Gurruwiwi, one of the finest didgeridoo makers in Arnhem Land, as he gives a masterclass in the art of yidaki making. Located in the friendly community of Gikal, north-west of Nhulunbuy, the masterclass encompasses a five-day stay, which also includes bush tucker and other Indigenous cultural experiences. *(08) 8987 8333 or 0447 087 091; www.rripanguyidaki.com*

Arnhem Weavers

Workshops offered to people with an interest in Yolngu handicraft and textile culture. Guests learn from community elders such skills as pandanus weaving, string making and how to harvest a variety of foods. Located in the community of Mapuru, around a ten-minute flight south of Elcho Island to the west of Nhulunbuy. Featured in the 2006 documentary *Going Bush* with Cathy Freeman and Deborah Mailman. *(08) 8946 6983 or john.greatorex@cdu.edu.au (email preferred method of contact); www.arnhemweavers.com.au*

Gove Sports Fishing and Diving

Choose from a variety of excellent fishing expeditions from half-day to week-long packages around the Nhulunbuy area. *(08) 8987 3445; www.govefish.com.au*

Orion Expedition Cruises

This luxury eight-day cruise departs from Darwin, takes in glorious Arnhem Land and terminates in Cairns. It's great, but you'll need deep pockets to afford this one. *(02) 9033 8700; 1300 361 012; www.orionexpeditions.com*

Did you know?

The majority of the Ramingining cast had never acted in a film before *Ten Canoes*. As well as learning new skills associated with screen acting, they also had to re-learn old skills, such as poling a bark canoe through thick reeds without falling off.

The Yolngu people of Ramingining were also responsible for making all the props for the film – each canoe was handmade from the bark of trees found in the Arafura Swamp and they also made all the spears, stone axes and other implements.

Q & A Rolf de Heer, director of *Ten Canoes*

Netherlands-born and Adelaide-based director Rolf de Heer is the man behind such movies as *Dingo* (1991), *Bad Boy Bubby* (1993), *Alexandra's Project* (2003), *The Old Man Who Read Love Stories* (2001) and *The Tracker* (2002). He is the winner of an armload of awards, including multiple AFIs and the prestigious Special Jury Prize at the Cannes Film Festival for *Ten Canoes*.

Q: *How long was the shoot for* Ten Canoes?

A: It was a touch under two months.

Q: *Prior to shooting* Ten Canoes, *had you spent much time in the Arafura Swamp region of Arnhem Land?*

A: I'd spent a week up there with David (Gulpilil) prior to doing *The Tracker* (2002). In the 18 months leading up to the shoot, I'd go up about once a month for a week or so. By the time we actually started shooting, I was quite familiar with the conditions.

Q: *What were the major challenges of shooting in the Arafura Swamp?*

A: I remember when I first came to grips with the swamp. I was walking across it by myself. Apart from the fact that it was difficult, all of a sudden I realised that these paths … well they weren't paths so much as room in the reeds. And **these weren't people paths, but crocodile paths. Once I understood that, I scooted back as quickly as I could!**

I went out again with 'Mango', the camera operator Greg Gilbert, armed with the advice that you take a 'snout stick' with you. **Ninety-five per cent of the time, if you bash a croc on the snout, it'll just go away.**

I remember struggling waist deep in the swamp because I wanted to get across to some trees where I thought the tree platforms could be built. It was very difficult, extremely hard going and quite scary.

The physical difficulty, just to find places to shoot, was enormous. [Peter] Djiggir, who ended up being my co-director, would find good places to shoot.

Q: *Directing the film waist-deep in a crocodile-infested swamp – was that a distraction for you at any point?*

A: Not a major distraction. You have to watch yourself, but **we had lookouts and we had a crocodile shooter. I must say that the second half of shooting, when we were on dry land, was a lot easier.**

But that also presented difficulties. We were able to shoot much faster and it was much less physically debilitating and much less time-consuming than I'd expected.

There were days [shooting in the swamp] when you could only get two shots done. They were two fantastic shots, but geez they took some setting up.

Q: *Is this a shoot you would do again if you had the chance?*

A: If I had the chance, I would avoid it [laughs]. But that was my attitude at the beginning.

Previous pages: The men make themselves a platform to sleep out of reach of the crocs

After *The Tracker*, David was nagging me to make a film up there. Having been up there, I thought, 'Absolutely no way. Forget it. It's far too difficult.' And then **in the end I did it because I couldn't get it out of my head.**

There was no earthly way of doing it without the local Ramingining people [as cast and crew]. Don't even begin, don't even try.

Q: *Have you been back since the film shoot?*

A: I've been up a lot since. We finished shooting five years ago; I guess I've been up a dozen times since. There's an ongoing relationship with that community, or as best as I can keep it up. **Sometimes it's just important to go for no reason other than keeping up the ties with the community.**

AND ANOTHER THING ...

SPOTLIGHT ON DAVID GULPILIL

Australia's most successful Aboriginal actor is undoubtedly David Gulpilil (full name: David Gulpilil Ridjimiraril Dalaithngu). In his early life, David was an accomplished hunter, tracker and ceremonial dancer. In fact, it was his ceremonial dancing that caught the eye of British director Nicholas Roeg, who had come to Maningrida in Arnhem Land to scout the location for his film *Walkabout* (1971). He ended up casting David in one of the lead roles.

Since then, David has had a tremendous career, acting in more than 15 feature films, including *Storm Boy* (1976), *Crocodile Dundee* (1986), *Dark Age* (1987), *The Proposition* (2005) and *Australia* (2008). He has also starred in a couple of international films, including the Wim Wenders–directed *Until the End of the World* (1991) and *The Right Stuff* (1983).

In 2002, he won the AFI Best Actor Award, as well as the IF Award, Critics Circle of Australia Award and the Cinemanila International Film Festival Award for his role in *The Tracker* (2002). David has also appeared in numerous TV series. In 1987 he was awarded an AM (Member of the Order of Australia) for services to the arts through interpretation of Aboriginal culture.

Important Indigenous films

From Australia's first film shot in colour to gaining worldwide attention via accolades at Cannes, films about Indigenous Australians tend to make a significant impact.

JEDDA (1955)

One of the earliest Aboriginal films is historic on two levels – it was the first film to star Aboriginal actors in the lead roles and it was the first Australian production to be shot entirely in colour. The story centres on Jedda (Ngarla Kunoth), a teenage Aboriginal girl raised by a white mother, who is abducted by an Aboriginal man Marbuck (Robert Tudawali), who takes her back to his tribe. The film was shot on location in the Northern Territory and was one of the more influential films in early Australian cinema.

WALKABOUT (1971)

Based on a brief 14-page script by playwright Edward Bond, *Walkabout* tells the story of two young city kids stranded in the Australian outback who enlist the help of an Aboriginal boy (David Gulpilil) to find their way back to civilisation. Directed by Englishman Nicholas Roeg, the film was shot in various parts of the Northern Territory, including Arnhem Land and Alice Springs, as well as Lake Eyre in South Australia. While the film did poorly at the box office, it stands today as one of our industry's most culturally important films.

STORM BOY (1976)

Based on the children's book by Colin Thiele, this beloved tale tells the story of an illiterate young boy who befriends a pelican named Mr Percival, as well as the Aboriginal loner trying to protect it. The film earned David Gulpilil the first of his three AFI nominations to date. (He won Best Actor for his role in Rolf de Heer's 2002 film *The Tracker*.) Since its release, the film has been a popular teaching film in classes around Australia and was also one of the first Aussie films to be distributed in Japan. The film was shot in a few spots around South Australia, including The Coorong and Goolwa. It won the AFI Best Film award in 1977.

THE CHANT OF JIMMIE BLACKSMITH (1978)

Based on the book by Thomas Keneally, this is one of the truly defining films in the history of Australian cinema. Jimmie Blacksmith (Tommy Lewis) is a young half-caste Aboriginal man raised and educated by Methodists. He sets out into the world with the simple ambitions of finding work and starting a family. Directed by Fred Schepisi, the film was nominated for the Palme d'Or at the 1979 Cannes Film Festival and garnered 12 AFI nominations and three awards. The film was shot in numerous spots around the north coast of New South Wales, including Scone, Armidale, Mudgee and Dorrigo National Park.

DEAD HEART (1996)

Starring Bryan Brown and Ernie Dingo, this 'westernish' tale follows a lawman out for justice when an Aboriginal man is murdered in the tiny village of Wala Wala. The screenplay was based on a stage play by Nick Parsons, who also directed the film. It was shot on location in Jay Creek in the MacDonnell Ranges, not far west of Alice Springs. The film won the Film Critics Circle of Australia Award for Best Adapted Screenplay and was nominated for three AFI Awards.

YOLNGU BOY (2001)

A contemporary look at what happens when ancient Aboriginal culture clashes with the modern world, this film follows three Aboriginal teenagers and the different paths they take, from football and girls to jail. The film was shot entirely in the Northern Territory, including Arnhem Land, Darwin and Kakadu National Park. The film was nominated for four AFI Awards.

AUSTRALIAN RULES (2002)

Set in a remote fishing village in South Australia, the film examines the clash of white and Aboriginal culture, with the local Australian Rules Football team the only bridge between the two groups. Played out through the eyes of best friends Gary (Nathan Phillips) and Dumby (Luke Carroll), the story deals with the modern racial landscape in current Indigenous communities, as well as the strong bonds of friendship. The fictional township of Prospect Bay was made up of a variety of locations, from Port Wakefield to Thompsons Beach and Middle Beach in the north of Adelaide. It was nominated for six AFI Awards, though it only won one. The film created some controversy for dramatising a real-life event.

SAMSON & DELILAH (2009)

A love story about two Aboriginal youths living in a small community just outside of Alice Springs. From first-time director Warwick Thornton, this harrowing drama was a critical darling upon release. The film received an astonishing 12 AFI nominations, winning seven awards, including Best Film and Best Director. It premiered at the 2009 Cannes Film Festival and took home the Camera d'Or – the Golden Camera Award for best first feature.

BRAN NUE DAE (2010)

This one's a vast departure from most Aussie films with Indigenous main characters. A colourful musical set in 1969, the story follows shy schoolboy Willie (Rocky McKenzie), who escapes from boarding school and heads back home to Broome to attempt to win back the love of his life, Rosie (Jessica Mauboy). The film was shot on location in Perth, Fremantle, Broome and Kununurra. It also stars Ernie Dingo, Geoffrey Rush and musician Missy Higgins as an extroverted hippie.

Two Hands (1999)

Jimmy (Ledger) and Alex (Byrne)

Director: Gregor Jordan
Writer: Gregor Jordan
Producer: Marian Macgowan
Cast includes: Heath Ledger, Rose Byrne, Bryan Brown, Tom Long, David Field, Susie Porter, Kiri Paramore

> You loaded your gun with old f--king bullets you put through the f--king wash?
> — *Pando*

ABOUT THE FILM

Before movies like *Chopper* (2000), *Dirty Deeds* (2002) and *Gettin' Square* (2003), the Australian criminal underworld was a seedy realm that had seldom been explored on the big screen. But Gregor Jordan changed all that with *Two Hands*. Set on the grimy streets of Kings Cross in Sydney, the film tells the story of hapless young Jimmy (Ledger), who falls prey to a criminal world he thinks he belongs to.

Jimmy is sent to work by crime kingpin Pando (Brown), given a simple job to start with. But when he stuffs it up, the tides are turned and Jimmy is pursued by Pando and his bogan henchmen Acko (Field) and Wally (Long). Along the way Jimmy manages to fall in love with Alex (Byrne), a sweet country gal and aspiring photographer. What ensues is an unpredictable series of events, culminating in one of the most memorable endings in Aussie cinema, played out to the sound of legendary Aussie band Powderfinger.

In an interview about the film (check the DVD's special features), Heath Ledger said, 'It's something that we haven't really seen before in Australia … the gangster side of Sydney. You know, we see it on *The Godfather*, we see them driving around in their Rolls-Royces, but we don't see the Australian godfathers in their stubby shorts and singlets drinking VBs.'

Released only a month after *Ten Things I Hate About You*, the modern American retelling of *The Taming of the Shrew* that stars Ledger as the bad-boy male lead, *Two Hands* cemented Ledger's status as a bona fide star on the rise. It also marked the big-screen debut of Rose Byrne.

With a great script, a stellar cast and a talented first-time director, *Two Hands* is proudly not only one of Australia's best crime films, but one of the finest films this country has ever produced.

Jimmy tries to put his two hands to good use

Kings Cross Sydney, New South Wales

An inner-city suburb a 2-kilometre slippery slide east of Sydney's CBD, the notorious Kings Cross is very much Jekyll and Hyde. By day, The Cross is a flourishing, vibrant locale with a whimsical air, charming cafes and tree-lined streets that used to be inhabited by bohemian writers and artists.

When darkness falls, however, neon transforms it into a seedy and edgier nightscape packed with bars, strip clubs, adult book stores and working girls (and boys who look like girls) prowling the streets in their 6-inch stilettos. The Cross's association with crime in the fair city of Sydney started with an illegal casino in the '60s; heroin brought drug-related misdeeds in the '70s and the crime bosses kept doing their crime thang under the greedy eyes of corrupt police in the '90s. The latter was depicted in the 2010 TV series *Underbelly: The Golden Mile*.

In light of the suburb's notorious history, not shooting *Two Hands* in Kings Cross would have been a crime in itself.

VISITOR INFO

Sydney Visitors Centre

Cnr Argyle and Playfair sts, The Rocks or 33 Wheat Rd, Darling Harbour; (02) 9240 8788 or 1800 067 676; www.sydney.com

THINGS TO SEE AND DO

The Love Machine

Kings Cross, lap dances and stripper body glitter really do go hand in hand. The Love Machine has long been an exotic dance club stalwart in The Cross and so it was rightly used as the location for the famous slo-mo scene of Jimmy leaving Pando's crime lair towards the end of the film, magnificently overscored by Powderfinger's 'These Days', a song specifically written for the film. Probably not a place you want to take the kids, and asking a dancer, 'Do you take Visa?' is generally met with disdain. *60 Darlinghurst Rd (opposite Kings Cross Station); (02) 9357 4794*

Jimmy works the strip club

Diagonally opposite the Love Machine on the other side of Darlinghurst Road is the area where Jimmy and his sleazy colleague Les (Paramore) loiter, trying to lure patrons into the exotic dance venue that employs them. This is where we first meet Pando and also where Jimmy is first introduced to Alex. The facade of the strip club was actually purpose-built for the film. It was situated a couple of doors down from the famous *Showgirls* strip club, whose bright flashing sign can be seen in the background of these scenes. *Darlinghurst Rd*

Fitzroy Gardens

Feathery palm trees and hard-luck park benches dominate this quiet garden huddled in the heart of Kings Cross. The area was the location for the scene when the two street youths (who nick Jimmy's wad of dirty cash) converse with another group of street kids. The scene takes place in front of the spherical El Alamein Fountain, Sydney's most photographed fountain. Grab a lazy lunch and a pew on a sunny spring day and watch the passing parade or come on a Sunday for the market. *Macleay St*

Orwell Street

A mere 100 metres west of Fitzroy Gardens is a large, well-kept, open courtyard on Orwell Street. This courtyard was used as location for the scene of Jimmy and Alex having their first, slightly awkward conversation. What's most notable about this scene is the slow-motion shot of the beautiful Rose Byrne staring directly into the camera. All the action here takes place in front of the Jolly Swagman Backpackers hostel. *27 Orwell St*

WHERE TO STAY

Funkhouse Backpackers Hostel

Popular budget accommodation with dorm and private rooms and a funky rooftop terrace where the libations and the travel tales flow long into the night (not to mention a cross-cultural flirtation or two). The exterior of the hostel appeared in the scene where Alex stands outside the one-hour photo shop waiting for her film to be developed. *23 Darlinghurst Rd; (02) 9358 6455; www.funkhouse.com.au*

Jolly Swagman Backpackers

You can't help but notice the large yellow exterior of this hostel in the scene when Jimmy and Alex strike up a conversation in the courtyard. The four-star-rated hostel offers shared dorms, twin and double rooms and boasts of its reputation for 'the friendliest staff, the cleanest beds and the best rates'. Put them to the test! *27 Orwell St; (02) 9358 6400; www.jollyswagman.com.au*

Lido Suites

Affordable boutique hotel accommodation right in the heart of The Cross boasting outstanding 360-degree views of the city from the rooftop. *2 Roslyn St; (02) 8354 0956; www.lidohotelkingscross.com*

Pando (Brown) checks in on Jimmy on Darlinghurst Road

Something that's good can still have a little bit of bad in it, and something that's bad still has a little bit of good.
– *The Man*

WHERE TO EAT

Bay Bua Vietnamese Restaurant

A hugely popular restaurant serving traditional South-East Asian fare, you can't go wrong ordering the banquet but it's also worth trying the spicy soft-shell crab or five-spice steamed pork belly. Though, if you go the whole hog, you might pay for it next morning. Easy to find; it's in the courtyard right near Jolly Swagman Backpackers (the big yellow one). *2 Springfield Ave; (02) 9358 3234; www.baybua.com.au*

Kings Cross skyline

Jimmy in a world of trouble with Pando and his men

The Bourbon

A stylish bistro and bar serving up sophisticated pub meals (including $10 steaks all day, every day), with both comfy indoor and alfresco dining. It's a stone's throw from Funkhouse Backpackers and the Love Machine and the bar stays open till 6am. *24 Darlinghurst Rd; (02) 9358 1144; www.thebourbon.com.au*

Tharen's

Lavish costumes and quality food is the ticket at Tharen's, one of the best theatre restaurants in Australia. Be entertained by in-house drag queen Prada Clutch as you enjoy a delicious three-course menu. *13–15 Kellett Way; (02) 9326 9510; www.tharens.com.au*

NIGHTSPOTS

Empire Hotel

The ultimate after-hours venue in The Cross, with live music Friday nights and theme nights throughout the week. For 30 years Les Girls, the massively popular drag queen stage show, starring Carlotta, brought cross-dressing shenanigans to a mainstream audience from this building – until they took the show on the road. *32 Darlinghurst Rd; (02) 9360 7531; www.empirehotel.net*

> The trick is to think very hard before you take the high road or the low road. Because the wrong choice can really f––k you up.
> – *The Man*

Melt Bar

Dimly lit with retro furnishings, it feels very much like an art gallery after closing time. Well, it kind of is an art gallery – the walls are littered with kooky paintings. Occasional live music and some funky alcoholic concoctions. *Upstairs, 12 Kellett St; (02) 9380 6060; www.meltbar.com.au*

Bondi Beach Sydney, New South Wales

There isn't a more famous stretch of golden sand in Australia than Bondi Beach, located 7 kilometres east of Sydney's CBD. The beach and surrounding 200 acres used to be privately owned. In 1882 the government officially opened the beach to the public. Today, the kilometre-long strip of sand attracts hundreds of thousands of visitors each year, from sunbathers to casual doggie paddlers and serious surfer dudes. The beach stretches from the rockpools at the north (actual swimming pools generally used for swimming) to the Icebergs sea bath at the southern side, an end generally reserved for surfboard riding.

Bondi Beach was the setting for one of the pivotal scenes in the film: Jimmy, while waiting to deliver a hefty sum of cash to one of Pando's associates, foolishly decides to go for a swim and buries the cash in the sand. Upon returning from his dip, Jimmy realises the money has been found and nicked. Not exactly a great first day on the job!

During September, Bondi hosts the annual Festival of the Winds, in which hundreds of kites of all shapes and sizes take to the sky. There are food stalls, rides and kite-making workshops.

VISITOR INFO

www.bondivillage.com

WHAT TO DO

Swimming

Follow in Jimmy's footsteps – drop your dacks and take a dip in the refreshing Bondi waters. Though *Two Hands* is fictitious, it's probably not the best idea to bury a cache of cash under your clothes. The beach is patrolled by surf lifesavers and there are two sets of flags designating where it's safest to swim (generally in the centre and towards the northern end).

The large pavilion seen in the movie has changing rooms where you can make sure your budgie smugglers aren't riding up to too high. Bondi Icebergs to the south is a popular rockpool swimming area, which also has a very swish restaurant and bar facilities. A small fee applies to swim at Icebergs.

Surfing

This is probably not what eager skegheads want to hear, but Bondi Beach is known for its fairly inconsistent swells. One day can produce very large, surfable waves for the Mick Fanning wannabes of the world, while others days can be fairly tame. Let's Go Surfing runs beginner classes for those new to the game (advisable). *(02) 9365 1800; www.letsgosurfing.com.au*

Walking

The Bondi to Coogee Coastal walk is a stunning 6-kilometre trek giving you some breathtaking coastal vistas. The walk typically takes two hours to complete and starts at the southern end of Bondi Beach and finishes at Coogee Beach. During November, the Bondi to Tamarama section is alive with Sculpture by the Sea, a free exhibition of over 100 kooky modern sculptures that use the coast as their inspirational backdrop. Don't forget to slip, slop and slap.

DID YOU KNOW?

Acko's purple XB Falcon, which he reluctantly lends to Jimmy in the film, belonged to director Gregor Jordan at the time of filming.

Bondi Beach

WHERE TO STAY

Swiss-Grand Resort Bondi Beach

It's rather grand and surprisingly affordable, this four-and-a-half-star luxury resort overlooks the beach. Kiss goodbye to those aches and pains with a Balinese massage at the day spa. *Cnr Beach Rd and Campbell Pde; (02) 9365 5666; www.swissgrand.com.au*

Hotel Bondi

Look out for the pink place with the clock tower. A range of rooms for those on a budget (if it's really tight you can forego air-con): single rooms to the State suite and family rooms. Star Fish Cafe on site. *178 Campbell Pde; (02) 9130 3271; www.hotelbondi.com.au*

WHERE TO EAT

Flying Squirrel Tapas Parlour

So-cool Euro-style tapas bar with nods to Spanish, Asian and Italian cuisines. Some faves include the chorizo and minted peas, spicy edamame and delightful zucchini flowers.

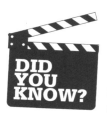

DID YOU KNOW?

***Two Hands* wasn't the first collaboration between Gregor Jordan and Bryan Brown.** Jordan directed Brown in an episode of *Twisted Tales* (an Aussie *Tales of the Unexpected* or *Twilight Zone*), a TV series created and produced by Brown. In the episode, titled 'The Confident Man', a robbery at a bottle shop goes wrong.

No squirrels were harmed in the making of the menu. *249 Bondi Rd; (02) 9130 1033; www.flyingsquirreltapasparlour.com.au*

Brown Sugar Cafe

Enjoy Moroccan eggs for a relaxed breakfast by day and a more formal bistro setting for dinner at night. Open seven days. Leave room for a hazelnut chocolate fondant with espresso maple ice-cream after dinner or you'll never forgive yourself. *106 Curlewis St; (02) 9130 1566; www.brownsugarbondi.com.au*

FILM FESTIVALS

FLiCKERFEST

This Academy-accredited short film competition takes place on the Bondi beachfront every January, showcasing some of this country's most cutting-edge short films and then touring 30-odd venues around Australia. *www.flickerfest.com.au*

CINEMA

Event Cinemas Bondi Junction

Eleven cinemas, including Gold Class and Vmax, screening the latest new releases. *Levels 7 and 8, Westfield Shopping Town, 500 Oxford St, Bondi Junction; (02) 9300 1555; www.eventcinemas.com.au*

Haymarket Sydney, New South Wales

Haymarket is home to Sydney's Chinatown, the epicentre of noodles and tea houses, dumpling joints and quirky gift shops. It's the largest Chinatown in Australia and actually the third location for Chinatown in the history of Sydney. The previous locations were at The Rocks in the late 19th century and then Darling Harbour, both nearby. Chinatown lies between Dixon Street and George Street, bordered by Hay Street and Goulburn Street, with the smaller Spanish quarter also sharing this area. Haymarket was used as a production location for the scenes of Jimmy and Alex's first date and their romantic monorail ride.

THINGS TO SEE AND DO

Sydney Monorail

Hop on the monorail at Chinatown or Paddy's Market stations and ride through the city just like Jimmy and Alex (minus a gun-toting crime lord on your tail). The film saw Jimmy and Alex get on at the station in Chinatown and disembark at the Galleries Victoria Station on Pitt Street. The monorail loop winds its way above Chinatown and George Street, then past the historic Queen Victoria Building and to the entertainment and dining hub of striking Darling Harbour. *(02) 8584 5288; www.metrotransport. com.au/index.php/monorail-home*

Star Hotel

This former pub was the location of Jimmy and Alex's first date. The hotel has been transformed into a dimly lit pokies venue. Stick to just getting a digital snap of yourself posing outside. *Cnr Sussex and Goulburn sts; (02) 9281 8343*

Paddy's Market

There's no shortage of stuffed toy koalas and thong fly swatters at Sydney's first and most famous market. This shopping mecca, open 9am to 5pm, Wednesday to Sunday and public holidays, specialises in fresh fruit, vegies and produce, and bargains in clothing, kitschy Aussie souvenirs, toys and gifts. There's also a Paddy's Market in Flemington in Sydney's west, near Homebush, a major site of the Olympic Games in 2000. *Cnr Hay and Thomas sts; www.paddysmarkets.com.au*

Sydney's Chinatown – Haymarket

Jimmy and Alex have their first conversation

I guess I just wanted to do something with my hands, you know? Not like fighting, I don't want to be a fighter or anything. But um, fixing things, making things, that sort of stuff.
– *Jimmy*

Jimmy and Alex in Chinatown on their first date

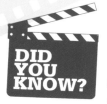
DID YOU KNOW?

Before his breakout roles in *Two Hands* **and** *Ten Things I Hate About You*, **Heath Ledger honed his craft on the small screen. He featured in the TV series** *Sweat* **and the American show** *Roar*, **as well as a few episodes on the Aussie soapie stalwart** *Home and Away.*

Home and Away **has been the launching pad for many careers. Naomi Watts, Guy Pearce, Simon Baker, Isla Fisher, Melissa George and Julian McMahon – all household names in the US – have all done their time on the show.**

Capitol Theatre

Australia's most famous theatre stages lavish musical productions and live music acts. Fingers crossed that they'll one day make a *Two Hands* stage musical with Todd McKenney as a more flamboyant and toe-tapping version of Pando! *13 Campbell St; (02) 9320 5000; www.capitoltheatre.com.au*

WHERE TO STAY

Pensione Hotel Sydney

While there's not a lot of room to move (much like Chinatown at times), the Pensione offers clean, modern and affordable premium and deluxe single, double and family rooms surrounding a fabulous Federation staircase. On the doorstep of Chinatown and the Star Hotel, it's terrific value for money. *631–635 George St; (02) 9265 8888; www.pensione.com.au*

Oaks Harmony

A popular Chinatown hotel boasting well-appointed and affordable studio, one- and two-bedroom suites, all fitted with kitchenette and laundry facilities. Indoor pool, gym and games room on site, only a stone's throw from Darling Harbour. *121 Quay St; (02) 9211 9303 or 1300 652 440; www.oakshotelsresorts.com/Site.aspx?pid=74*

Sydney Central YHA

One of the city centre's best hostels with clean, comfortable shared dorms and private rooms. Pizza nights are always a riot and a great opportunity to meet your new Dutch or Swedish BFF. *11 Rawson Pl; (02) 9218 9000; www.yha.com.au/hostels/nsw/sydney-surrounds/sydney-central*

WHERE TO EAT

Din Tai Fung

Have you ever been to dumpling heaven? Well, after you visit Din Tai Fung, you can emphatically scream 'YES' at the top of your lungs. This worldwide phenomenon is packed to the rafters for lunch and dinner (queue patiently, you'll be eating dumplings before you know it). Try the speciality soup dumplings. Or anything else. Anything! *Level 1, World Square Shopping Centre, 644 George St; (02) 9264 6010*

Passionflower

A speciality dessert eatery that will simply blow your mind. Asian exotic ice-cream concoctions named Pandora's Box, Final Fantasy ... and one simply titled 'Awesomeness'. Enough said. *730–732 George St; (02) 9281 8322; www.passionflower.com.au*

OTHER LOCATIONS

Ingleside Sydney, New South Wales

This semi-rural suburb 30 kilometres north of Sydney CBD was the spot where Pando and his offsiders take Jimmy in attempt to 'punish' him for losing their money. The spot is to the left off Lane Cove Road, heading east just over Ingleside Road. Once filled with trees and bushland, the location has since had property developed on the site.

Balmain Sydney, New South Wales

This peninsula suburb 5 kilometres north-west of the Sydney CBD was used for Pando's crime lair, as well as Jimmy's apartment. A set was built for both interiors in a small studio in Roberts Street. The corridor outside Jimmy's apartment was actually shot at the Hollywood Hotel in Surry Hills.

The Rocks Sydney, New South Wales

The purple-walled apartment where Alex stays while she is in town was shot at a run-down building in Hickson Street. The building used to be the headquarters of the Seaman's Union, but it has since been demolished. The Rocks is on the western side of Circular Quay just north of the CBD.

Revesby Sydney, New South Wales

Just south of Bankstown (around 20 kilometres west of Sydney), this suburb was used for the scenes in which Jimmy and his mates rob the Australia Mutual Bank. The bank building was a great find for the *Two Hands* production crew, as it had been closed down for a while, but was a piece of cake to dress up as a bank for filming.

Waterloo Sydney, New South Wales

This suburb a stone's throw south of Sydney's CBD was used for shooting the scene in which Acko and Wally hit a young kid with their XB Falcon and callously flee the scene.

Greenacre Sydney, New South Wales

A house in this south-west suburb was used for the scenes involving Deirdre (Porter) and Jimmy. This is where Jimmy hides out when Pando goes after him and where he and his bank-robber buddies head back to after the hold-up.

Q & A **Malcolm McCulloch, cinematographer of** *Two Hands*

Malcolm McCulloch has been working as a director of photography (DOP) for the last 20 years. In addition to feature films, which include *Two Hands* and *Kiss or Kill* (1997), he has also shot a number of TV commercials.

Q: How did you first get involved in the project?

A: I had worked a lot with the associate producer, Mark Turnbull, and he recommended me to Gregor. So Gregor gave me a call and asked me to read his script. I read it and rang him up and said I'd love to do it. **I still think it's one of the best scripts I've ever read.**

Q: As a cinematographer, how much input do you have in location scouting?

A: What happens is this: the director briefs the location manager and he'll have an image in mind of how he sees it. Then we'll generally go out and look at maybe two or three locations that are suitable for each scene. Then we'll talk about the pros and cons of each one, with the whole look of the film in mind, and which is the most film-friendly. **On an Aussie film for $5 million you've got to be able to get in and out of there quick. So logistics come into play as well.** The look of the film is determined by the director, so we talk about the look and we check out the locations. Then we work out which is going to be best for the look and for logistics.

A whole lot of things affect locations as well, depending on your schedule. If you need to fit in two locations in a day, you might not necessarily choose the best location, but maybe one that's closer to the other one so you can shoot in the morning in one location, move to the second location and be able to complete a day of shooting within the time that you've got.

On a small budget you have all these considerations, because you're shooting at twice the speed (compared to a bigger-budget film). You have to make it all work within the time that you have.

Q: What were the major challenges of shooting in such busy areas like Kings Cross and Haymarket?

A: Kings Cross was no problem because we had the strip club bouncers on side. But **shooting in Sydney is a nightmare**. Sydney is expensive – location costs are high so we're losing a lot of work to Melbourne. Sydneysiders are less receptive to crews shooting on the streets. **People will barge through your shot and swear at you.**

Q: Did you have any difficulties with the shoot?

A: It was a very well-run shoot. The only problem we had was weather – we had a lot of rain! We had to light our way around that and constantly reschedule around bad weather. It was particularly wet at the time we were shooting. Locations would drop out all the time. **It was an ongoing thing, in a five-day week of shooting our locations kept changing and shifting around because of weather.**

Q: Do you have any shots or scenes that you're particularly proud of?

A: There are shots that are memorable for me. The shot of Rose Byrne, when she meets the character or Jimmy, is a slow motion shot of her looking into camera and we just track in on her. That was memorable because **it was one of**

the first times we had shot Rose and we instantly realised what sort of screen charisma she has. It was very memorable, I was looking through the eye piece of the camera and going, 'Wow, this is really someone!' That also happened quite a lot with Heath as well. **That's the joy of being a cameraman, you see that screen charisma first!**

Q: What was it like working with Heath and Rose, two relatively unknown actors at the time?

A: They were fantastic, both fantastic. Heath worked incredibly hard, he was so interested in the whole process. **He would hang around to watch what was being done in the scenes that he wasn't in, just to gain the knowledge.** I had absolutely no problems with Heath at all, he was a charming young man. It's very sad that he is no longer with us.

Q: The movie you shot before *Two Hands*, *Kiss or Kill*, **was predominantly shot in rural towns. For you, what are the major differences shooting a film in country Australia versus shooting in the city?**

A: I don't know really if there is much difference. It's all about the script. You analyse the script for the directors – they have a vision.

With good directors like Bill Bennett [*Kiss or Kill* director] and Gregor, they have a very strong vision. They'll often give you references from other films that they've seen. You look at those with them, you go on location recces and do your pre-production and you talk about the film and work it out shot by shot.

To be honest, whether the location is city or country, you're still working to the script. When I was a young cameraman I asked Russell Boyd what's the secret to cinematography. He said, 'Tell the f--king story, son.' It's a very interesting thing to think about, when you're looking at

shots and designing the shots – **if you're not telling the story it's not working. You have to keep going back to the script and make sure everything you do is about forwarding that story** – whether it's outdoors or indoors or city or country, it doesn't make a difference. Each scene and each location has to have a reason to be there.

One of the locations Phillip Roope scouted for *Two Hands*

Films made in the noughties

NED KELLY (2003)

Directed by Gregor Jordan, this is a biopic about our most famous bushman and outlaw. Jordan once again teamed up with Heath Ledger, who played Ned alongside other A-list talent, including Orlando Bloom, Naomi Watts and Geoffrey Rush. With a hefty $30-million budget, the production based itself in Victoria for the entirety of the shoot, using locations such as Hepburn Springs, Ballarat, Clunes and Little River. The world premiere of the film was screened at the Regent Theatre in Melbourne – only a couple of blocks away from the Old Melbourne Gaol where Ned was ultimately hanged for his sins in 1880.

THE DISH (2000)

The follow-up film from the makers of *The Castle* brings us this mostly fictitious story of the tiny NSW town of Parkes and its gigantic satellite dish, which played a pivotal part in the broadcast of the first moon walk in 1969. While the interior shots of the dish were filmed on a set, the exterior shots were filmed on location in Parkes, with the large hunk of metal being shut down for three weeks to accommodate the production. The town scenes supposedly shot in Parkes were actually filmed in the neighbouring town of Forbes, which had more of an old-school feel and more easily mimicked 1960s Australia. *The Dish* is the eighth highest grossing Australian film of all time.

THE PROPOSITION (2005)

Legendary Aussie muso and part-time screenwriter Nick Cave penned the script for *The Proposition* in a mere three weeks. He was initially approached to work on the soundtrack, but director John Hillcoat ended up asking him to actually write the whole movie script. This Australian western, set in the harsh 19th-century outback, was predominantly shot in the small central Queensland town of Winton. The film stars Guy Pearce and British actor Ray Winstone, and won four AFI Awards, including Best Cinematography and Best Costume Design.

MOULIN ROUGE! (2001)

It was almost nine years between drinks (of Tooheys New) for Baz Luhrmann, with *Moulin Rouge!* the first film he shot on Australian soil since *Strictly Ballroom*. The tale of an English poet who falls in love with a terminally ill showgirl was set in Paris, but the filming was done at Fox Studios in Sydney. The production actually ran over schedule, which was a problem as *Star Wars Episode II: Attack of the Clones* needed the studio space. Baz took the cast and crew to Madrid to finish the shoot. The film, which stars Nicole Kidman, Richard Roxburgh and Ewan McGregor (ironically, also in the *Star*

Wars prequels), was nominated for eight Academy Awards – the most-nominated Australian film in history. It was the first musical to be nominated for Best Film since *All That Jazz* in 1980.

MAO'S LAST DANCER (2009)

Based on the worldwide best-selling autobiography by Li Cunxin, this film delves into the life of a Chinese ballet dancer, from his poverty-stricken childhood to international acclaim as a performer for the Houston Ballet and the Australian Ballet Company. Directed by Bruce Beresford, with a screenplay by *Shine* scribe Jan Sardi, the film was predominantly shot in Sydney, including the suburbs of Newtown, Vaucluse, The Rocks, Kensington and Redfern. Parts of the film were also shot in China, as well as Houston and Washington D.C. in the US. The movie is the twelfth highest grossing Australian film of all time.

LOOK BOTH WAYS (2005)

Sarah Watt's fantastic directorial feature debut centres on a group of people dealing with a tragic train accident during a hot summer in Adelaide. The film, which won four AFI Awards, including Best Film and Best Director, was shot in a variety of locations around Adelaide, including the Art Gallery of South Australia, National Rail Museum, Norwood Swimming Pool and Adelaide Festival Theatre. The film stars William McInnes (husband of Watt) and Justine Clarke. Watt's follow-up feature

My Year Without Sex (2009), starring Sacha Horler and Matt Day, was shot in suburban Melbourne.

TOMORROW, WHEN THE WAR BEGAN (2010)

This film, based on John Marsden's 1993 youth fiction book about a band of high school teens who defend their home town of Wirrawee when it's invaded by a foreign power, blitzed the Australian box office in 2010. It was the highest grossing domestic film of the year, taking in just over $13 million, although it didn't clear the $27 million it cost to actually shoot the film. The movie was shot in the Hunter region of New South Wales, with Raymond Terrace a major shooting location.

Wolf Creek (2005)

> I was doing people a service really, by shooting them. There's kangaroos all over the place ... like tourists.
> – Mick

Liz (Magrath) wakes on the beach and ponders a dip

Director: Greg McLean
Writer: Greg McLean
Producers: Greg McLean, David Lightfoot
Cast includes: Nathan Phillips, Kestie Morassi, Cassandra Magrath, John Jarratt

ABOUT THE FILM

Wolf Creek might just top the list of Aussie films that people have actually walked out on (or turned off mid-viewing). This is not because the movie is lousy. On the contrary – it's so gut-wrenchingly sickening and distressing to watch (in a good way, of course) that those with faint hearts just couldn't bear another minute of it. Isn't that what a kick-arse horror movie is meant to do?

Influenced by real events, the film is set in Western Australia in 1999 and follows three life-loving backpackers Ben (Phillips), Kristy (Morassi) and Liz (Magrath) as they make their way from Broome to the Wolfe Creek Meteorite Crater in a beaten-up red station wagon (the Aussie road trip vehicle of choice). After a day at the crater, they meet the maniacal Mick Taylor (Jarratt), who promises to fix their broken-down ride. Instead he treats them to an assortment of torturous deeds that truly can't be done justice in print.

Wolf Creek premiered at the Sundance Film Festival in 2005 and was screened at the Cannes Film Festival later that year. It was released in the US to moderate success; its graphic scenes of violence and torture polarised many critics. Well-known US film critic Roger Ebert said in his review, 'When the killer severs the spine of one of his victims and calls her "a head on a stick" I wanted to walk out of the theatre and keep on walking.'

While *Wolf Creek* may not be everyone's cup of tea, there is no doubting it's a scary-as-hell thrill ride that hits all the notes that a good slasher film should.

The film is loosely based on the true events of the Backpacker Murders (seven travellers killed in 1989–92), while the disappearance of English

A bloodied and battered Kristy (Morassi) crawls along the Quorn–Hawker Road

The road trip continues

Kristy (Morassi) outside a roadhouse

tourist Peter Falconio in the Northern Territory in 2001 has also been cited as an influence. The character of Mick Taylor is based on the infamous killer Ivan Milat. To get into character, Jarratt didn't shower for six weeks prior to the shoot, a piece of method acting prep I'm sure his fellow cast members truly appreciated.

In late 2010, a Wolf Creek sequel was announced, with McLean to direct and Jarratt to reprise his role as Mick.

LOCATIONS

Hawker South Australia

Located over 380 kilometres north of Adelaide and with a population of only 300, the tiny town of Hawker in the Flinders Ranges used to be much more populous; the famous *Ghan* railway once ran through the town, bringing with it a mess of tourists each year. In 1956, however, the train line was upgraded and moved further west. Yet this setback hasn't stopped the stubborn little town from attracting tourists with its well-preserved historic buildings and gorgeous panoramic lookouts. It's also a great base to explore the vast and wonderful Flinders Ranges, which is the Australian outback at its most unfiltered and stunningly breathtaking. The

town and surrounding areas were major players as locations for the filming of *Wolf Creek*. Hawker has also featured in other films, including the TV miniseries *Alice to Nowhere* (1986), *The Lighthorsemen* (1987) and *Holy Smoke* (1999).

VISITOR INFO

Hawker Motors (information centre)
Cnr Wilpena Rd and Craddock Rd; (08) 8648 4014; www.hawkersa.info

THINGS TO SEE AND DO

Quorn–Hawker Road
Around 20 kilometres south of Hawker, on the way to Quorn, a spot on the side of the desolate Quorn–Hawker Road was used in the scene when the terrified Kristy runs through the thistle trying to escape the tyrannical clutches of Mick. This scene culminates in the 'poster shot', the striking image of a bloodied Kristy lying on the road in utter terror (see page 271). The subsequent car chase involving Mick and Kristy also took place on the Quorn–Hawker Rd. There is an air of spookiness as you motor along this quiet stretch of road; you'll be fine as long as you keep reciting the words, 'It's just a movie'. And don't stop for any filthy looking guys wearing Akubra hats.

I think it'd be cool; you get to go from place to place saying things like 'that's not a knife – this is a knife'.
– Ben

Partacoona Station

The private rural property of Partacoona Station is around 60 kilometres south-west of Hawker. The 76 000-plus-hectare station is usually home to many peacefully grazing cows and sheep, but had its 'moment in the sun' when it was immortalised as a *Wolf Creek* filming location. Sun is probably not appropriate, with heavy rains throwing the location and general schedule into mayhem (Rule #461 in moviemaking: film crews always bring rain. Plan appropriately.) In fact, it was quite a remarkable feat for McLean and his crew to even finish the film; of the 25 days they had to shoot, it rained for at least part of 21 of those days. Some of the scenes involving Ben, Liz and Kristy supposedly at the Wolfe Creek Meteorite Crater were shot on parts of the station.

When the weather got too bad, the cast and crew had to improvise, finding a tourist lookout nearby where they shot the scene of Ben and Liz's first kiss.

Partacoona Station is a private property so access is prohibited without permission. *Via sealed road off the Quorn–Hawker Rd*

Heritage walk

There's a self-guided walk taking in all the interesting historical buildings and sights the town has to offer. Highlights include Fred Teague's Museum and the former Hawker railway station, which is now the Old Ghan Restaurant and Gallery. The walk begins at the Pioneer Memorial next to the Hawker District Council Offices on Craddock Road. A walk booklet is available from Hawker Motors (the info centre) for a small fee.

Port Augusta

This thriving tourist city is known as 'the Crossroads of Australia', and is the busiest and most populated settlement in the Flinders Ranges. Situated just over 100 kilometres south-west of Hawker, the port township has some must-see attractions, from the award-winning Wadlata Outback Centre to the Australian Arid Lands Botanic Gardens.

Port Augusta Airport was used as a location in the scene of a mangled Ben returning back to civilisation, post-crucifixion, thanks to the Royal Flying Doctor Service. *Port Augusta Visitor Centre, Wadlata Outback Centre, 41 Flinders Tce, Port Augusta; (08) 8641 9193; www.wadlata.sa.gov.au*

Port Germein

This chilled seaside town nestled in the foothills of the Flinders Ranges doubled as the location for Broome at the beginning of the film. They fooled us again – all the exterior road shots of palm trees and the town jetty were not, in fact, shot in the popular WA holiday town! Port Germein is 70 kilometres south of Port Augusta and is the crabbing capital of South Australia, nip nip! *www.portgermein.com*

WHERE TO STAY

Hawker Hotel Motel

A century-old Aussie pub with fully equipped motel units with air-conditioning (a must in the outback most of the year) and a fridge in every room (vital for keeping your beer cold). Counter meals available in the pub. *80 Elder Tce, Hawker; (08) 8648 4102*

> What was it your mate said again? Oh, yeah, that's not a knife – THIS is a knife!
>
> – *Mick*

Outback Chapmanton Motel

There are 14 rooms with en-suite bathrooms and ten units. Attached outback-style restaurant perfect for some home-style Aussie brekkie. *1 Wilpena Rd, Hawker; (08) 8648 4100*

Majestic Oasis Apartments

Stylish and beautifully kept serviced apartments ideal for unwinding in comfort, overlooking the waters of the Upper Spencer Gulf. *Marryatt St, Port Augusta, (08) 8648 9000; www.majestichotels.com.au/oasis_overview.htm*

CARAVANS AND MOTORHOMES

Hawker BIG4 Caravan Park

Powered sites and a range of self-contained cabins. Shady picnic areas and a short walk to the town's main attractions. *Cnr Wilpena Rd and Chaceview Tce, Hawker; (08) 8648 4006; www.hawkerbig4holidaypark.com.au*

Flinders Ranges Caravan Park

A four-and-a-half-star-rated caravan park with powered sites, camping, cabins and lodges. They offer unique four-wheel-drive tours of the Arkaba Sheep Station in the Elder Ranges. *Leigh Creek Rd, Hawker; (08) 8648 4266; www.flindersrangescaravanpark.com.au*

Port Augusta BIG4 Caravan Park

Powered ensuite sites, camping, cabin and spa units; there's a playground and games room for the kiddies and cable television in each cabin for all. *Cnr Highway 1 and Stokes Tce, Port Augusta; (08) 8642 2974; www.aspenparks.com.au*

Port Germein Caravan Park

A quiet and relaxed park on the waterfront with powered sites and cabins. Internet access available. *The Esplanade, Port Germein; (08) 8634 5266; www.portgermein.com*

CAMPING

Willow Waters Ruins

Fully self-sufficient bush camping 20 kilometres east of Hawker. The campground's located on a private property and caravan and vehicle access are allowed. *Access via Orroroo–Hawker Rd*

The Dutchmans Stern Conservation Park

Located 10 kilometres west of Quorn, this park offers magnificent views of the ranges and Spencer Gulf. Bush camping with self-guided walking trails. Camping permits required. No designated camping areas, only backpack camping allowed in the west of the park. *Permit accessed through National Parks and Wildlife South Australia, (08) 8634 7068; www.environment.sa.gov.au/parks*

WHERE TO EAT

Old Ghan Restaurant and Gallery

Dine on the old train platform while enjoying the famous Ghan Burger. Kangaroo dishes are also a speciality here; dine on our official mascot in 'country-sized' portions! Cast and crew ate here while shooting in the area. Open Thursday to Saturday; local artwork also on display. *Barndioota Rd, Hawker; (08) 8648 4176; www.hawkersa.info/biz/ghan.htm*

Sightseer's Curiosity Cafe

There's no better place in town for a relaxed lunch or quick meal on the go: freshly made sandwiches, wraps, pies, burgers and all-day breakfast. Souvenirs can be purchased in the gallery. Closed Mondays. *66 Elder Tce, Hawker; (08) 8648 4475; www.hawkersa.info/sightseers/ menu.htm*

Old Ghan Restaurant and Gallery

The Outback Tuckerbox

Enjoy a relaxed alfresco eating experience from sizzling and well-sized steaks to tasty baguettes and sandwiches; located in the Wadlata Outback Centre. *41 Flinders Tce, Port Augusta; (08) 8641 9196; www.wadlata.sa.gov.au*

TOURS

Derek's 4WD Tours

Half- and full-day tours of the central Flinders Ranges departing from Hawker. The popular Gorges Tour takes in the Bunyeroo and Brachina gorges. *0417 475 770; www.dereks4wdtours.com*

Ben (Phillips) desperately waves for help after his escape

Aldinga South Australia

This small coastal town is part of the greater Fleurieu Peninsula and just 45 kilometres south of Adelaide. Aldinga Beach is certainly the treasure of the township, a long curve of smooth, white sand facing the Gulf of St Vincent. Summer brings out the bronzed Aussies and their budgie smugglers. This beach is one of the very few in Australia where vehicles are permitted on the sand (in certain sections).

Tourists also flock to the town to dive at the Aldinga Drop-off, an underwater cliff with some of the most extraordinary marine life you'll ever see. The town was used as a location for some of the scenes at the beginning of the film. Nearby Maslin Beach and Myponga to the south were also used as locations for filming.

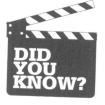

DID YOU KNOW? **The October 2005 release of *Wolf Creek* in the Northern Territory was delayed by a court order.** **The Director of Public Prosecutions in the Northern Territory requested that the film's distributors delay the release until after the trial of Bradley John Murdoch, the man accused of killing British backpacker Peter Falconio. Although the film was in essence fiction, the prosecutors felt the movie might prejudice the jury. Murdoch was subsequently found guilty of the murder.**

Aldinga Beach

Nothing like rainwater from the Top End.
– *Mick*

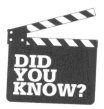

The scenes filmed on Maslin Beach were pretty difficult for Cassandra Magrath – the water was so freezing that when she emerged she said she was so cold she couldn't even remember her own name.

VISITOR INFO

McLaren Vale and Fleurieu Visitor Centre

Main Rd, McLaren Vale; (08) 8323 9944; www.mclarenvale.info

THINGS TO SEE AND DO

Aldinga Beach

This area was used early in the film, just before our ill-fated trio begin their road trip. The scene when Ben purchases the used station wagon from the lot was shot in town, as was the scene where the group eats at the outdoor cafe (Lake Coolangatta Cafe, closed in 2006). The themed Gnome Cave is a great attraction for kids, while the beach has terrific reef fishing. Plus a cooling dip in the ocean is never a bad idea.

Maslin Beach

A few kilometres north of Aldinga is this famous 3-kilometre stretch of sand. In 1975, the southern part of the beach was officially declared Australia's first-ever nude beach, much to the joyful fervour of local teenage boys. A section of the beach (actually not the nude part) was the backdrop for the scene of Liz going for an early morning swim. Liz doesn't quite nude up, but she does remove her top before she dives into the water. Every year around Australia Day the beach holds a 'Nude Olympics', which includes three-legged races (get your mind out of the gutter) and the 'best bum' competition. It was cancelled in 2010 due to lack of volunteers (previous competitors couldn't get the sand out of their nooks and crannies for weeks afterward). *Access via Oleander Rd*

Myponga

This tiny speck of a town around 17 kilometres south of Aldinga is the centre of rich grazing and dairy country in the Fleurieu Peninsula. Myponga was used for one scene in the film when Ben gets his car checked by the mechanic at the garage. The town is worth a stopover, especially on the weekends, when they have a craft and produce market. Pick up a local brew at the Lovely Valley Beverage Factory – 'tis a lovely drop indeed.

WHERE TO STAY

Aldinga Beach Reef Retreat

Retro '50s Aussie beach shack that is so daggy it's actually cool. Bright, colourfully painted rooms with vintage decor (check out their fridge covered in old vinyl LPs) coupled with modern amenities for added comfort and a fab location directly on the beach. *4 Gordon St, Aldinga Beach; 0434 404 860; aldingareefretreat.com*

Sliver Sands Bed and Breakfast

Stylish apartment with stunning views of the ocean from every room. Complimentary fruit and chocolates and the option of a generous country breakfast. *277 The Esplanade, Aldinga Beach; (08) 8557 4002; www.silversandsbnb.com.au*

Heysens Rest

Cosy private cabins right in the middle of the bush. You may see a hopping roo or two on the property and if you're lucky they'll be in the designated area where you can feed the adorable marsupials. *10 Nunn Rd, Myponga; (08) 8558 6397*

CARAVANS AND MOTORHOMES

Beach Woods Eco Tourist Park

A quiet woodland park near Maslin Beach with powered sites, camping, various cabins and spa units. Tennis and beach volleyball for the actively inclined. *2–4 Tuit Rd, Aldinga; (08) 8556 6113; www.beachwoods.com.au*

Aldinga Beach Holiday Park

Powered and unpowered sites in addition to a variety of cabin and cottage accommodation. Heated pool, barbecue facilities and basketball and beach volleyball activities. *Lot 339 Cox Rd, Aldinga Beach; (08) 8556 3444; www.aldingaholiday.com.au*

WHERE TO EAT

Aldinga Bay Cafe

Perfect stop at any time of the day – brekkie with the lot in the AM and curries and lasagne a treat in the PM. Friday nights are themed Mexican nights (yes, that means burritos) while Saturday night it's Indian. *162 The Esplanade, Aldinga Beach; (08) 8556 5547; www.aldingabaycafe.com*

The Hundred Eaves

Cafe and restaurant in a charming old church. Local and organic products make up an exciting breakfast and lunch carte du jour. *The Old Church, Sellicks Beach; (08) 8557 4255; www.thehundredeaves.com.au*

CINEMA

Noarlunga Cinema Centre

South of Aldinga with five cinemas showing new releases. *38–42 David Witton Dr, Noarlunga; (08) 8326 1313; www.wallis.com.au/cinema.php?cinema_id=5*

Barossa Valley and the Mid-north South Australia

Known far and wide as Australia's pre-eminent and most-visited wine region, the Barossa Valley offers up a wino's and gourmand's paradise with stunning landscapes of vine-stitched hills and historic buildings. Only an hour's drive from Adelaide, The Barossa has too many wineries and cellar doors to name, not to mention fabulous restaurants as well as shopping, nature activities, golf courses and a host of annual events. The eastern part of the region was used for a few locations in the film, particularly Sandy Creek, which is a few kilometres east of the historic town of Gawler. Further west on the coast are other locations used in the film, including Port Gawler, Middle Beach and Thompson Beach. The Barossa Valley is around 70 kilometres north-east of Adelaide.

VISITOR INFO

Barossa Visitor Information Centre

66–8 Murray St, Tanunda; (08) 8563 0600; www.barossa.com

THINGS TO SEE AND DO

Sandy Creek

This tiny town is at the gateway to the Barossa Valley. A private quarry in town was the location for Mick's 'playground' – the torture shed where the depraved killer takes his victims. Much of the set on the quarry had to be built from scratch. A clever touch from the production designers was the sign outside of the quarry, which read 'Navitalim Mining Co.' – Ivan Milat spelled backwards.

While in town, you must visit the Sandy Creek Hotel, which has been operating for over 120 years. It was popular with US soldiers during World War II, as their camp was not far away. *Via Barossa Valley Hwy*

Port Gawler Off-road Hire Park

This former extreme-sports park in Port Gawler was the location used for the roadhouse where

Ben, Kristy and Liz stop to fuel up their car. The interior was used for the scene where Ben has words with the beer-swilling, tattooed truckie. The park was once a hugely popular spot for motocross, flat-track motorcycling and quad-bike riding, but it closed its gates for good in 2006. *Port Gawler Beach Rd, Port Gawler*

Middle Beach

This small beach town off Port Wakefield Road is renowned for its swampland fishing. The Middle Beach Caravan Park was the location for the scene when our backpacking travellers camp out in tents under the vast Australian night sky. *Off Port Wakefield Rd*

Thompson Beach

Near the small farmland town of Dublin is Thompson Beach, which doubled as the location of the Wolfe Creek Meteorite Crater car park. Nearby Port Parham was also used for numerous car travelling sequences.

WHERE TO STAY

Barossa Valley Farmhouse YHA

A renovated farmhouse deep in Sandy Creek Conservation Park, this unique lodging has cooking amenities, a dining area and panoramic views of the bush. Take in the fresh country air as you take a relaxed stroll on the nature trail. *Pimpala Rd, Sandy Creek Conservation Park; (08) 8414 3000; www.yha.com.au*

Eagle Foundry B&B

This quaint little bed and breakfast in the town of Gawler is surrounded by striking gardens and offers heritage and luxury accommodation. *23 King St, Gawler; (08) 8522 3808; www.eaglefoundry.com.au*

Two Wells Motel

Sited a few kilometres east of Middle Beach, this stock-standard motel has ten rooms with ensuites. *Old Port Wakefield Rd, Two Wells; (08) 8520 2210*

CARAVANS AND MOTORHOMES

Middle Beach Caravan Park

This caravan park was used as a location in the film. Powered and unpowered sites with camping under the stars and cabin accommodation. For long-term stays only, call the park for details before booking. *5 Recreation Reserve, Middle Beach; (08) 8520 2374*

Gawler Caravan Park

Offers powered and unpowered sites, units and deluxe ensuite cabins. *Main North Rd, Gawler; (08) 8522 3805; www.barossavalleyaccommodation.com.au*

CAMPING

Port Parham

A popular camping area on the council reserve. Port Parham is a great spot for crabbing. *Access via Port Wakefield Rd*

WHERE TO EAT

Sandy Creek Hotel

Historic hotel with traditional pub meals, proud holder of the unauthorised South Australian record of serving the most beer in a week at the end of World War II. No better time to party. *Barossa Valley Hwy, Sandy Creek; (08) 8524 4188*

Empire Pizza Cafe

Pizza joint with great atmosphere and prices. Try the ice-cream pizza for dessert – it certainly is an adventure! *108 Old Wakefield Rd, Two Wells; (08) 8520 2800*

La Dolce Vita

Live the sweet life at this relaxed restaurant specialising in Italian, European and Mediterranean cuisines. *111 Murray Rd, Gawler; (08) 8522 1009; www.restaurantgawler. websyte.com.au*

CINEMA

Gawler Village Twin Cinemas

Two cinemas screening new releases. *11 Murray St, Gawler; (08) 8523 1633*

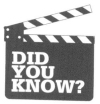

DID YOU KNOW? **Although John Jarratt has been quoted as saying that Greg McLean is the best director he has worked with since Peter Weir, that doesn't mean it was all smooth sailing on set. So much into the character of Mick was Jarratt that he would often yell at McLean when he was unhappy between takes. Jarratt later apologised to McLean, blaming the outbursts on Mick.**

Winery cellar doors abound in the Barossa Valley

CELLAR DOOR SALES
OPEN 7 DAYS
10.30 AM - 4.30 PM

Arial shot of the Wolfe Creek Meteorite Crater

Glen Osmond
South Australia

This suburb just a few kilometres south-east of the Adelaide CBD was used for two locations. The first was an exterior shot of the youth hostel pool party at the beginning of the film. This took place at a hotel on Glen Osmond Road. The other location was the Glen Osmond Mines, a series of old, individual mines that were once used for silver ore production. They also shot here the gruesome scene of Ben literally being crucified. The City of Burnside runs tours of the mine; bookings essential. *Mine tours: City of Burnside; (08) 8366 4222*

Wolfe Creek Meteorite Crater Western Australia

The actual Wolfe Creek Meteorite Crater is located in Western Australia as part of the larger Wolfe Creek Meteorite Crater National Park. Aerial shots of the real crater were used in the film. The crater is said to be just less than 300 000 years old and has a diameter of 875 metres. *145 km south of Halls Creek via Tanami Rd*

Semaphore Beach
South Australia

This beach location was used as the setting for a shot early in the film when Kristy and Liz sunbake on the beach. The suburb of Semaphore in Adelaide's north-west has some beautiful heritage buildings and trendy sea-view cafes. The Semaphore Waterslide Complex is a great treat for small kids and big kids.

Port Adelaide
South Australia

This suburb to the north of Adelaide's CBD was used as the location for the final shot of the film, when Ben is led to court in police custody. Port Adelaide is steeped in rich maritime history and has many attractions, including weekend wharf markets, galleries and antique shops.

Australia's most evil film villian?
The maniacal Mick (Jarratt)

Q & A **Kestie Morassi, who played Kristy in** *Wolf Creek*

Although she's only been acting for ten years, Kestie Morassi has accumulated a seriously impressive resume. Including her dark and bloody turn in *Wolf Creek*, Kestie has also appeared in the Aussie flicks *Dirty Deeds*, *Thunderstruck*, *Strange Bedfellows* and *The Illustrated Family Doctor*. She also starred in the critically acclaimed and award-winning TV series *Satisfaction* and played Zarah Garde-Wilson in *Underbelly*.

Q: How did you land the role of Kristy in *Wolf Creek***?**

A: I just went along for the audition like I do with all my auditions. I went and was really happy with it and then I didn't hear anything for three or four weeks. I thought it was strange that I didn't get a call back at least, just because I felt quite connected to the role. Then they called me back.

Cassandra Magrath had already been cast; she's a friend of mine so that was nice and helped me relax. I went in and Will Gibson, the cinematographer, had a hand-held camera. Cassandra and I acted out the scenes. I had a really good rapport with Greg, we were chatting about the films that we loved. So I felt a great connection there and I was given the role a few days later.

Q: From a viewer's perspective it seemed like quite a difficult shoot – both physically and mentally. When you read the script, did you have any idea how tough it would be?

A: While reading the script, I looked at it very positively and saw all the emotional intensity of the role that I'd be playing. I noticed all the locations work, which would be fantastic – you know, a road trip movie is always fun to shoot. So I looked at it in a very positive light.

I'm always ready for hard work when it comes to a film. It's always a hard slog, especially on a lower budget, when a lot of the niceties and the comforts aren't there. But the low-budget situation and battling the elements really helped me to get into the part. When you're out there in the cold, it's easy to act uncomfortable and terrified. And the sets that they built as well – the horrible shed scene – it helps you get into it. When I was in the shed, tied up, with blood all over my face and it's cold, it's dingy ... it's easy to imagine that you're really there.

Q: Were there any scenes that were particularly physically hard?

A: I never saw them as difficult. Running through the thistles was very uncomfortable. It was early morning and we only had a certain amount of time to shoot me running barefoot through the field. They wanted it when the sun was coming up. But, you know, when the sun's coming up its absolutely freezing! My feet were numb and I didn't realise that I was running through all these thistles until we had finished the scene, the sun came up and my feet thawed out. I realised there were a million and one prickles in my feet! I had to sit in the make-up bus for an hour while they picked all these prickles out of my feet, it was agonising. But we got the shot, that's the most important thing!

Hanging off the cliff in a harness was a bit confronting for me. I'm not afraid of heights, but I don't enjoy them. But once I got down there on the ropes and knew that I was safe, it was fun. Again, it enhances the performance when there's an element of fear.

Q: It hadn't rained in ten years on one of the locations and the second you got there it started to bucket down.

A: It was amazing! Mother Nature doesn't know that you're shooting a film. But these things contributed in a positive way to the final cut. The scene when the three of us were driving to the crater, it was scripted as being a nice, bright sunny day. Because it was raining, we had to change the script and it really worked in the end because it added to that sense of dread, that they were driving into something unpleasant.

Q: Was there much other improvisation on the movie?

A: We stuck pretty closely to the script. We'd add a few words here and there to make it our own. We would continue on with the scenes – we would act out the scene and then continue it with some improvisation. But most of that was cut out, most of that was for us to sort of get into the characters and create our back story.

Q: I read that Greg [the director] at one point actually stormed into the shed as he thought your cries for help were really genuine and John may have gone too far. Was it a mentally taxing process for you to shoot those torture scenes?

A: I found it a really cathartic experience, as I do with any emotional roles that I have. It's not like you ever really feel in danger for your life, it's a controlled environment. I wasn't emotionally distraught after it or anything, I was more interested in finding the truth in the moment and hoping that we got the shot.

Q: As an actor, does your process differ when you're shooting on location and moving around a lot?

A: For me, shooting on location is more about battling the elements and allowing that to colour your performance. Being on location is always fun. It's like a bit of a holiday. You inevitably become very close to the rest of the cast and crew because you're living with them in close quarters and working 12- to 14-hour days, and then socialising with them as well. It's quite sad when you have to say goodbye to them. That's a hard part of my job, creating a family with the people you work with and then all of a sudden just going, 'Right then, see ya'.

Q: The film was so successful – from screenings at Cannes and Sundance film festivals to your AFI Award nomination. What was the most rewarding part for you?

A: So many things. Travelling around the world promoting it ... seeing people love it and enjoy it, it was such an amazing experience. I learnt a lot about myself, my creative process, I suppose, having a chance to act in a way where I'm not really acting and just *behaving* in front of the camera, which was a really new experience for me.

Every day that we were filming was rewarding. We'd come back and just know that we had something special. We'd see the rushes at the end of the day and they just looked fantastic. Shooting out on location, using that sort of natural light and the countryside, it's hard to get a bad shot. It just gelled from day one, it was like a well-oiled wheel. It was great.

Q: Did it open many more acting doors for you?

A: It did. People always remember *Wolf Creek* – the people that saw it, anyway, the people that were brave enough to see it. People still talk about it. If I go for auditions, sometimes the director or the producer will say, 'I loved you in that film.' People remember me in it, which is always a great thing. Being nominated for an AFI is a great honour and a great thing to have on your CV.

Q: Do you have any dream locations around Australia where you would love to shoot a movie one day?

A: I missed out on *Rogue* (also directed by Greg McLean), which was shot in the Kimberley. I've always been fascinated with the Kimberley. I think it would be such a magical place. The Australian landscape is honestly some of the most diverse and incredible scenery in all the world. There are lots of places ... the Daintree would be nice, the Nullarbor would be cool, too.

Q: So did John Jarratt smell really bad? Apparently he didn't shower for weeks leading up to the role.

A: I didn't notice that! I didn't notice that at all, maybe I smelled really bad, too [laughs]. I think he sort of avoided us for a lot of the time. He said he needed to view us as pieces of meat to help him get into the horrendous character of Mick Taylor.

AND ANOTHER THING ...

THE WILHELM SCREAM

Film geeks will know all about this little moviemaking secret. In 1951, Warner Bros. produced a western titled *Distant Drums* starring Gary Cooper. For the production of this film, six different types of screams were recorded and later used in certain parts of the movie. The screams were archived and later re-used in a number of Warner Bros. productions during the '50s, '60s and '70s.

The scream took on a new life when sound designer and general sound effects nerd Ben Burrt found the original recording and used one of the screams in a scene of *Star Wars IV: A New Hope* (1977). The particular scene was when Luke shoots a stormtrooper right before he and Princess Leia swing from platform to platform; as the stormtrooper falls into the empty abyss he lets out a 'Wilhelm scream'.

The term 'Wilhelm scream', bestowed upon the sound effect by Burrt, was actually named after the character Private Wilhelm in the 1953 film *The Charge at Feather River*. Poor ol' Wilhelm lets out the girlish shriek as he is shot by an arrow. This film was the first to use the reproduced scream.

Burrt used the Wilhelm scream as his own sound signature and featured it in all Star Wars sequels and prequels, as well as the Indiana Jones movies.

Since then, the Wilhelm scream has become a favourite among sound editors, a kind of in-joke in the industry. The yell has been featured in dozens of movies (and TV shows) over the last few decades, including *Reservoir Dogs* (1992), *Toy Story* (1995), *The Lord of the Rings: The Two Towers* (2002) and *Transformers* (2007).

It's yet to be confirmed whether the Wilhelm scream has featured in an Australian film. The closest contender may have been in the movie *Knowing* (2009), the Nick Cage action flick shot in Melbourne. The scream can be heard during the subway crash scene.

The ultimate Aussie soundtrack playlist

Wind down your windows and turn up the volume as you enjoy a playlist from great Aussie film soundtracks.

THESE DAYS – POWDERFINGER

Two Hands (1999)
When: Jimmy leaves Pando's crime lair after paying back his debt.

ON THE ROAD AGAIN – WILLIE NELSON

Japanese Story (2003)
When: A jubilant Sandy and Hiromitsu sing in the car shortly after unbogging their car.

WATERLOO – ABBA

Muriel's Wedding (1994)
When: Muriel and Rhonda perform the memorable dance scene to win the Hibiscus Island Talent Show.

OVER THE RAINBOW – JUDY GARLAND

Australia (2008)
When: Lady Ashley sings to Nullah shortly after his mother dies.

TAKIN' CARE OF BUSINESS – BACHMAN-TURNER OVERDRIVE

Kenny (2006)
When: Kenny unloads the contents of his truck into the arrogant suit's car.

FLIGHT OF THE BUMBLE BEE – RACHMANINOV

Shine (1996)
When: David first astounds Moby's restaurant patrons with his ivory-tickling skills.

SHAKE YOUR GROOVE THING – PEACHES & HERB

The Adventures of Priscilla, Queen of the Desert (1994)
When: When Mitzy, Felicia and Bernadette put on a drag show for the locals outside Coober Pedy.

EAGLE ROCK – DADDY COOL

Wolf Creek (2005)
When: Ben, Liz and Kristy drive through Western Australia at the start of the film and their ill-fated road trip.

REAL WILD CHILD – JERRY LEE LEWIS

Romulus, My Father (2007)
When: Raimond approaches the girl in the white dress on the porch who is dancing to the song.

LIVE IT UP – MENTAL AS ANYTHING

Crocodile Dundee (1986)
When: Mick and Sue attend the party in New York.

Acknowledgements

The publisher would like to acknowledge the following individuals and organisations:

Publications manager
Astrid Browne

Project manager
Melissa Krafchek

Editor
Jo Tayler

Design
David Thomas

Layout
Megan Ellis

Illustrations
Emily Maffei

Cartography
Emily Maffei

Pre-press
PageSet Digital Print & Pre-press

Photography credits
Main cover image: Empty road in the Northern Territory (© photolibrary. All rights reserved.)

Front cover film stills (left to right): Ten Canoes (James Geurts); *Kenny* (Thunderbox Films); *The Adventures of Priscilla, Queen of the Desert* (Latent Image Productions Pty Ltd); *Japanese Story* (Megan Lewis and Gecko Films); *Muriel's Wedding* (House and Moorhouse Films Pty Ltd); *The Man from Snowy River* (Snowy River Productions)

Film stills and posters (supplied for each film):

The Adventures of Priscilla, Queen of the Desert: Latent Image Productions Pty Ltd; CINETEXT Bildarchiv and Big Australia (bus image only)

Australia: 20th Century Fox/CINETEXT and Big Australia

Babe: CINETEXT and Big Australia

Breaker Morant: South Australia Film Corporation

Crocodile Dundee: Rimfire Films Pty Ltd

Gallipoli: Alain Dejean and Associated R & R Films Pty Ltd

Japanese Story: Megan Lewis and Gecko Films

Jindabyne: AAP/Mary Evans © 2006 AAP

Kenny: Thunderbox Films

Mad Max 2: The Road Warrior: CINETEXT and Big Australia

The Man from Snowy River: Snowy River Productions

Muriel's Wedding: House and Moorhouse Films Pty Ltd

Oscar and Lucinda: CINETEXT and Big Australia

Picnic at Hanging Rock: Picnic Productions Pty Ltd

Rabbit-proof Fence: Arsenal/CINETEXT and Big Australia

Romulus, My Father: Image stills courtesy of Arena Films. On location images courtesy of Cameron Wood and Reel Locations

Shine: CINETEXT and Big Australia

Ten Canoes: Photos by James Geurts

Two Hands: Macgowan Films

Wolf Creek: Will Gibson (pp. 270, 272 and 280) and Daniel Guerra (pp. 271 and 275), Emu Creek Pictures and Kestie Morassi (p. 281)

Other internal page images (left to right, clockwise from top to bottom, where multiple images appear on a page):

Page vii Steve Baccon (Jack Thompson photo); viii Judy Roberts (author photo); 4 Hamilton Lund/TNSW; 9 (a) Reg Morrison/AUS (b) Attila Bicskos/AUS; 12 & 14 TNT; 16 AR; 23 & 24 AG; 27–30 AR; 33 TNT; 34, 40–5 & 51–5 AR; 65 & 66 TNT; 68 TQ; 70 © photolibrary. All rights reserved.; 77 SATC/Ken Stepnell; 78 SATC; 80 & 81 AG; 82 AR; 90 Nick Rains/AG; 92 & 93 AG; 95 Steven David Miller/AUS; 96 Suzanne Long/AUS; 104 Sally Mayman/TNSW; 107 (a) Don Fuchs/TNSW (b) Tourism Snowy Mountains; 108 Don Fuchs/TNSW; 110 TNSW; 111 & 112 Paul Sinclair/TNSW; 118 TVIC; 124 AR; 131 Hamilton Lund/TNSW; 132 Broken Hill Tourism/TNSW; 139–44 TVIC; 155 AR; 157 TQ; 158 & 161 AR; 162 Hamilton Lund/TNSW; 168–73 AR; 175 Hamilton Lund/TNSW; 176 Ross Barnett/TNSW; 177 Adam Taylor/TNSW; 183 & 186–90 AR; 192 FPT/Adam Bruzzone; 201 Fleurieu Peninsula Tourism/SATC; 203 SATC; 206 AG; 213, 216 & 223 TVIC; 231 AR; 232 SATC; 235 AR; 243 & 245–6 TNT; 260 Tony Yeates/TNSW; 261 AR; 263 North Sullivan/TNSW; 267 AR; 275 AG; 276 & 279 SATC

Abbreviations
AG Australian Geographic
AR Anthony Roberts
AUS Auscape International
EAP Explore Australia Publishing
SATC South Australian Tourism Commission
TNSW Tourism New South Wales
TNT Tourism NT
TQ Tourism Queensland
TVIC Tourism Victoria